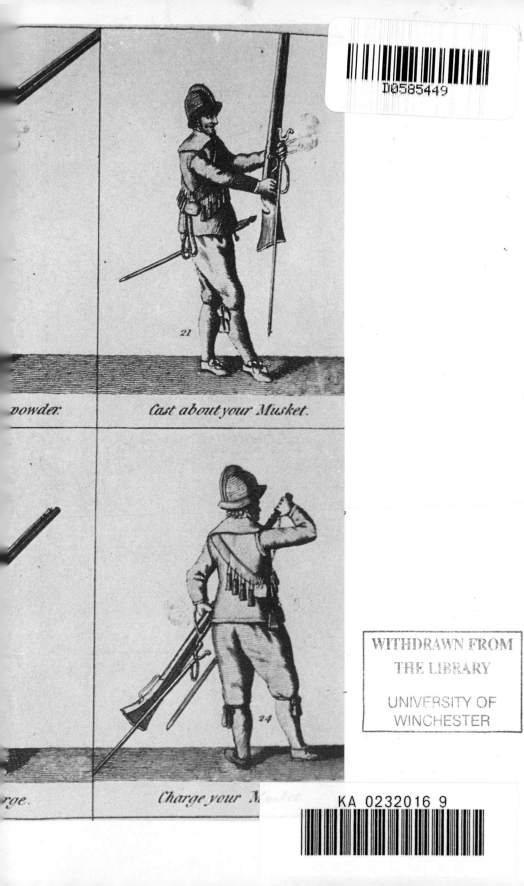

*vowder.*     *Cast about your Musket.*

*rge.*     *Charge your M̶̶̶̶̶̶*

# THE
# CIVIL WARS
# OF ENGLAND

# THE
# CIVIL WARS
# OF ENGLAND

## John Kenyon

WEIDENFELD AND NICOLSON · LONDON

Copyright © 1988 by John Kenyon

First published in Great Britain by
George Weidenfeld & Nicolson Limited
91 Clapham High Street
London sw4 7ta

isbn 0 297 79351 9

Printed and bound in Great Britain by
Butler & Tanner Ltd, Frome and London

# CONTENTS

List of Illustrations                                    vii
List of Maps                                              ix
Preface                                                   xv

1  Introduction                                           1
2  The Gathering Crisis                                   5
3  The Descent to War                                    23
4  The Opening Campaign                                  48
5  The War for the Centre: 1643                          63
6  Deadlock: 1644                                        89
7  The Last Campaign                                    123
8  Peace or No Peace                                    158
9  The Second Civil War                                 176
10 The Bitter End                                       200
11 Epilogue                                             222
12 A Nation Disarmed                                    236

Bibliographical Essay                                   247
Dramatis Personae                                       252
Index                                                   263

# ILLUSTRATIONS

John Pym (by kind permission of the Trustees of the Chequers Estate)

Thomas Wentworth, 1st Earl of Strafford (by kind permission of the Trustees of the Rt Hon. Olive, Countess Fitzwilliam's Chattels Settlement, and the Lady Juliet de Chair.)

Royalist battle standards (British Library)

Prince Rupert (National Portrait Gallery, London; by kind permission of the Earl of Dartmouth)

William Cavendish, 1st Earl, Marquess, later Duke of Newcastle (by kind permission of the Earl Spencer, Althorp, Northampton)

George, Lord Goring (The National Trust Photographic Library, London; photo A. C. Cooper)

Sir Marmaduke Langdale (National Portrait Gallery, London)

Sir Ralph Hopton (National Portrait Gallery, London)

James Butler, Earl, Marquess, later Duke of Ormonde (National Portrait Gallery, London)

Sir Edward Hyde, later Earl of Clarendon (National Portrait Gallery, London)

Contemporary armies and warfare (Weidenfeld & Nicolson archive)

Musketeer (British Library)

Steel 'pot, breast and back' (National Army Museum, London)

Infantryman's buff coat (National Army Museum, London)

Archibald Campbell, 8th Earl and 1st Marquess of Argyll (Scottish National Portrait Gallery)

Robert Devereux, Earl of Essex (Ashmolean Museum, Oxford)

Sir Thomas Fairfax (the Cromwell Museum, Huntingdon)

Sir William Waller (from Goodwood House, by courtesy of the Trustees)

Edward Montagu, 2nd Earl of Manchester (Kimbolton School, Cambridgeshire)

Plan of London's Lines of Communication (British Library)

The Queen's Sconce, outside Newark (The Royal Commission on the Historical Monuments of England)

The siege of Basing House (by kind permission of Professor John Adair)

Heavy artillery (Weidenfeld and Nicolson archive)

St Mary's Church, Putney (Guildhall Library, City of London)

Fairfax and the Council of the Army (Weidenfeld and Nicolson archive)

Charles I at his trial (by gracious permission of Her Majesty Queen Elizabeth the Queen Mother)

The execution of Charles I (The Museum of London)

Oliver Cromwell (in the collection of the Duke of Buccleuch and Queensbury KT)

Bridget Ireton (by kind permission of the Trustees of the Chequers Estate)

Henry Ireton (Fitzwilliam Museum, Cambridge)

The battle of Dunbar (Ashmolean Museum, Oxford)

John Lambert (National Portrait Gallery, London)

George Monck (by gracious permission of Her Majesty the Queen)

Charter of Oliver Cromwell (The Council of the City of Chester)

Charles II (by courtesy of the Board of Trustees of the Victoria and Albert Museum, London)

*Endpapers:* Musketeer's drill, from Francis Grose's *Military Antiquities* (National Army Museum, London)

# MAPS

England                                    x–xi
Scotland                                    xii
Ireland                                     xiii
The campaign of Edgehill                    50
The battle of Edgehill                      58
The battle of Roundway Down                 72
The first battle of Newbury                 83
Marston Moor: the armies deployed        106–7
The second battle of of Newbury            120
The battle of Naseby                       144
The Preston campaign                       190

The battle and campaign maps are reproduced (with slight amendments) from
*The English Civil Wars*, by Peter Young and Richard Holmes (Eyre Methuen,
1974).

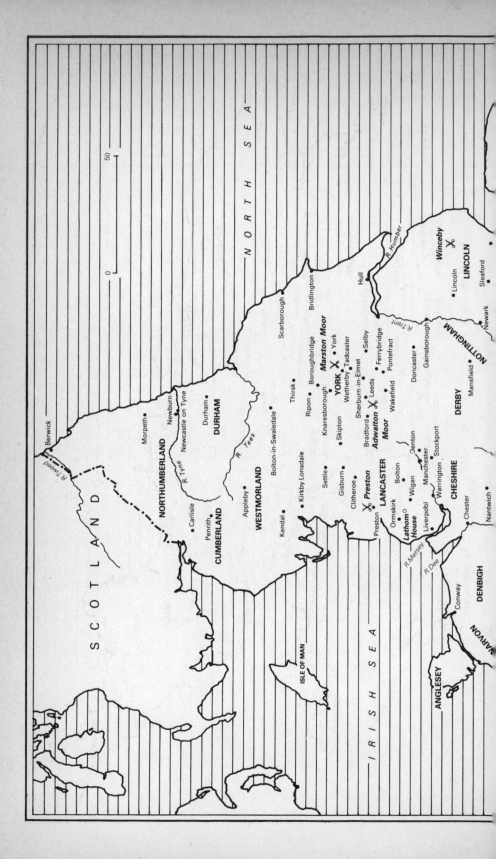

SCOTLAND

NORTH SEA

IRISH SEA

ISLE OF MAN

R. Tweed

Berwick

Morpeth

Newburn

Newcastle on Tyne

R. Tyne

DURHAM

Durham

NORTHUMBERLAND

Carlisle

Penrith

CUMBERLAND

Appleby

WESTMORLAND

Kendal

R. Tees

Bolton-in-Swaledale

Kirkby Lonsdale

Settle

Gisburn

Clitheroe

*Preston*

Preston

LANCASTER

Ormskirk

Bolton

*Lathom House*

Liverpool

Wigan

Manchester

Denton

Warrington · Stockport

CHESHIRE

Chester

Nantwich

R. Mersey

R. Dee

Conway

DENBIGH

CARNARVON

ANGLESEY

Thirsk

Ripon

Boroughbridge

Knaresborough

Skipton

*Marston Moor*

YORK

Wetherby · Tadcaster

· York

Sherburn-in-Elmet

Bradford

Leeds

*Adwalton Moor*

Wakefield

Selby

Ferrybridge

Pontefract

Doncaster

Gainsborough

Mansfield

DERBY

NOTTINGHAM

R. Trent

Scarborough

Bridlington

Hull

R. Humber

*Winceby*

LINCOLN

Lincoln

Sleaford

Newark

50

0

ENGLAND

SCOTLAND

IRELAND

# PREFACE

The greater part of this book was researched and written during my tenure of an Andrew Mellon Senior Research Fellowship at the Henry E. Huntington Library in 1985. Anyone who has ever worked at the Huntington will appreciate the advantages I enjoyed. I am also grateful to Paul and Gracia Hardacre for many kindnesses.

Professor Geoffrey Parker kindly allowed me to read the text of his Lees Knowles lectures on 'The Military Revolution of Early Modern Europe', and gave me the benefit of his advice on a wide variety of matters. Similarly, Professor Joyce Lee Malcolm showed me a draft of her forthcoming study of 'The Right to Bear Arms', which was particularly valuable when I came to write Chapter 12.

I must also acknowledge Professor Austin Woolrych's generosity in allowing me to use an unpublished paper which encapsulated the revisionist conclusions reached in his book *Soldiers and Statesmen*, then unpublished. He also fielded a great many queries fired at him in letters and by 'phone, as did Dr John Morrill. Major David Baxter of Earlshall placed at my disposal his extensive knowledge of seventeenth-century weaponry. I am also grateful to the many scholars who allowed me to use information derived from their unpublished research dissertations, which are set out in the Bibliographical Essay at the end of the book.

J.P.K.

# 1

# INTRODUCTION

Historians have usually approached the Civil Wars from one of two angles. Some treat them simply as a piece of military history, analysing the campaigns and the conduct of the generals who directed them with no more than an occasional nod at the political or religious issues involved. Others have treated them as a crucial episode in English constitutional history, to which the actual fighting is a mere backdrop. Not since Samuel Rawson Gardiner's *History of the Great Civil War*, first published in the 1880s, has there been a convincing attempt to combine the two.

So, in recent years we have had several military histories of the wars and detailed studies of individual battles, many of them written by distinguished retired army officers. There have also been many biographies of individual commanders, particularly of Oliver Cromwell, whose fame in later life has in fact been projected much too far back into the 1640s, at the risk of distorting the historical record. On the other hand there have been many studies, beginning in 1941 with J. H. Hexter's *Reign of King Pym*, of the political, constitutional and religious intrigues which formed much of the history of the Long Parliament, studies in which we usually catch only a faint echo of the war proceeding in the distance. The fact that most political historians' ignorance of military history is only matched by military historians' ignorance of politics serves to accentuate this polarisation.

Moreover, there are certain basic questions which no one seems to be asking, let alone answering. The key question is this: how did a small, poor, underpopulated nation, which had no regular army and no evident military tradition later than the fifteenth century, whose manufacturing industry was minuscule, whose parliaments prior to 1640 had insisted time and again on the poverty of the taxpaying classes – how did this nation raise, equip, pay and sustain very sub-stantial armies, reaching by 1644 a level of well over 30,000 men on each side, fight two civil wars with considerable skill and sophistication, and emerge in the 1650s as a formidable military power, to be reckoned with in the councils of Europe? (The same applies to Scotland; if anything more so.)

Of course, it is becoming clear that both sides were heavily dependent, in training and organisation as well as action, on the experience which many Englishmen and Scotsmen had gained in the European theatre of war in the 1620s and 1630s, and to some extent on that of foreign soldiers of fortune, but the extent of this contribution has never been properly assessed. Similarly, research undertaken over the past twenty years or so has added considerably to our knowledge of the way in which the 'war effort' was organised, but it is slanted usually towards the royalist side, and for the recruitment and supply of Parliament's armies we are still dependent to a large extent on Sir Charles Firth's *Cromwell's Army*, published in 1901.* The civilian 'back-up' has been the subject of one unpublished doctoral thesis, but otherwise historians seem indifferent to a question which bears directly on our assessment of the capacity and efficiency of British industry at this time. The finances of the King and Parliament have been the subject of one short article each, despite the obvious importance of this issue. The King's financial records, in the nature of things, are scattered and woefully deficient; on the other hand, the 300-odd volumes of the misnamed 'Commonwealth Exchequer Papers' in the Public Record Office (SP 28) are by their very bulk a disincentive to research.

Yet everywhere we turn we are faced by problems of supply, though they do not seem to have worried contemporaries overmuch. For instance, we know next to nothing about the small-arms industry of the time; indeed, the history of weaponry is still the preserve of the

* For the details of recent research see my Bibliographical Essay, p.247 below.

antique dealer and the specialist collector. Yet the wastage rate in small arms was very high; in September 1643 Sir Ralph Hopton wrote to Prince Rupert, 'It is inconceivable what these fellows are always doing with their arms; they appear to be expended as fast as their ammunition'; and an industry which could produce two hundred muskets and thirty pairs of pistols a week from one factory, or 15,000 muskets and 5,000 pikes a year from another, obviously deserves our attention. Even such humdrum items as shoes pose a similar problem (see p. 128 below); we really have no idea how they were supplied to the troops and how often.

Taking a broader view, why did so many medieval castles, supposedly vulnerable to seventeenth-century artillery, hold out for such long periods? I have suggested that this is because it was difficult in wartime to transport heavy guns to the scene (p. 86 below), but this does not explain how Pontefract Castle defied its besiegers from September 1648 to April 1649, when it was the only remaining pocket of royalist resistance to the might of Parliament. Nor is it clear how the armies found their way through the crazy patchwork of the English road system when the only maps available were on a small scale and showed no roads at all.* Yet when Wilmot, for instance, was ordered to march from Oxford to Devizes in 1643, Fairfax from Oxford to Taunton in 1645, Cromwell from London to Pembroke in 1648 – to take a few examples at random – they set off without hesitation and reached their destination in record time. The armies all had 'scoutmasters', about whom we know very little, but how did the scoutmasters navigate? We do not know.

Clearly, where the basic research is yet to be done a historian like myself, attempting nothing more than a brief general survey, can only pose such questions, not answer them. On the other hand, it will no longer do to treat the Civil War armies as if they sprang from the ground like dragons' teeth, their equipment and their mounts magicked like Cinderella's from pumpkins and white mice. Behind the romantic and exciting clash of Cavalier and Roundhead lay the hard reality of

---

* These were Christopher Saxton's famous county maps, redrawn by Wenceslas Hollar on a scale of about five miles to the inch, and reissued in pocket form in 1644: *The Kingdom of England ... exactly described ... in six maps, portable for every man's pocket. ... Useful for all commanders for quartering of soldiers and all sorts of persons that would be informed, where the Armies be.* This was presumably the 'book of maps' used by Monck on his way south in 1660; there was no other. Roads were added to the 1674 edition, under a different title. (I am grateful to Professor Paul Hardacre for this information.)

logistics, and my narrative tries to reflect this, however inadequately. As Sir Charles Firth once wrote: 'A civil war is not only the conflict of opposing principles, but the shock of material forces.'

# 2

# THE GATHERING CRISIS

The Great Rebellion which erupted in the autumn of 1642 was one of the most traumatic events in English history, and it had repercussions just as grave in Scotland and Ireland, but its causes are still in dispute.

In a sense English government simply collapsed in 1641 and 1642, which in itself produced a dangerously unstable situation; in the words of the republican James Harrington, 'The dissolution of this government caused the war, not the war the dissolution of this government.' To some extent this can be seen as the culmination of certain long-term trends, particularly in the sphere of government finance. The staggering inflation which swept Europe from about 1540 to about 1650 reduced the 'real' income of the Crown to a dangerous level, and James I's and Charles I's attempts to supplement this income by imposing taxes and levies on the strength of their prerogative alone raised grave constitutional and legal problems, and from time to time led to abrasive disputes with Parliament. A difficult situation was exacerbated by the severe economic depression of 1618–23 in Europe, which undermined England's staple trade in wool and woollen cloth, and in the succeeding years, 1624–9, Charles I, like all his fellow monarchs, found that the cost of war had risen alarmingly even in this generation.

In fact, viewed in perspective, England's troubles were just part of a

European-wide phenomenon which some historians call 'The General Crisis of the Seventeenth Century'. In an age of galloping inflation even the most powerful rulers were finding it difficult to finance their armies and the ever-expanding bureaucracy which went with them, and at the same time maintain the lavish lifestyle now considered necessary for a Renaissance monarch, without imposing taxation at a level calculated to provoke a reaction, or without quarrelling stormily with their nobility. In the 1650s the powerful and successful French monarchy overcame with difficulty two successive rebellions known as the 'Frondes'. In the 1640s Catalonia, Portugal and Sicily all rose in revolt against Spain, which incidentally illustrated the difficulty of holding down ethnic minorities in formerly independent kingdoms – a problem Charles I was to experience in an acute form in Scotland and Ireland. Even the Dutch Republic, engaged in a war for survival against Spain, was riven by periodic disputes; a confrontation between the Stadholder Maurice of Nassau and the Grand Pensionary John Oldenbarneveldt ended in the latter's execution in 1619; and an attempted coup by William II of Orange in 1650 was averted only by his premature death. All this, plus the Scots, Irish and English rebellions, plus the savage and debilitating war which racked Germany from 1618 to 1648 ('The Thirty Years' War'), led many serious-minded men – not necessarily religious fanatics – to fear that the end of the world was at hand.

Moreover, the English kings had problems all their own. England was almost unique in Europe in that her medieval 'estates', or parliament, had survived into the modern era with its powers and rights not only intact but even increasing. True, parliaments were not a regular working part of the constitution, their meetings were infrequent, and they could be dispensed with altogether for long periods; but, together with the monarch, they were seen as the ultimate authority in law, and they had retained a jealously guarded right to approve taxation. The Tudors had never challenged Parliament's position, nor had they built up a provincial bureaucracy or a regular army which would have given them the leverage to do so. Seventeenth-century England was still to a large degree governed and administered by the landed classes, functioning as justices of the peace, deputy lieutenants, tax commissioners, commissioners for sewers, and much more, while up to 1640 the only armed forces which stood between the Stuart kings and riot or rebellion were the picturesque Yeomen of the Guard stationed at the Tower of London, and the Band of Gentlemen Pensioners, an elite group of courtiers numbering about forty. In fact, though the kings were respected and even venerated as the Lord's anointed, and their theoretical powers were vast and ill-defined, their practical day-to-day rule depended on a high degree of mutual trust and co-operation between them and the upper classes.

The Stuarts, arriving from Scotland in 1603 – just as much foreigners as if they came from Portugal – and succeeding one of the most charismatic monarchs in English history, Elizabeth I, never found this easy. But James I, a much underrated ruler, survived happily enough. He talked a great deal of his absolute powers, and he even published two treatises on the Divine Right of Kings, but he was careful not to introduce any innovations for which he did not have legal warrant. (In any case, the powers he claimed were no more than the Church of England had claimed on behalf of the Crown since the Reformation.) His reign was punctuated by minor disputes with Parliament, which used to be seen as portents of disaster, but in fact they were not destabilising. The most serious was over the new import duties, or 'impositions', which he introduced in 1607 after the High Court had declared in his favour. But even this had died down by the 1620s, and his last parliament, in 1624, was an exercise in mutual amiability.

The real trouble began in 1625, with the accession of his son Charles I. Even the contemporary historian Clarendon, who was one of Charles's strongest supporters in the Civil War, admitted this.

Charles I had many initial advantages. At the age of twenty-five he was handsome and distinguished, if rather short in stature; his chasteness and his austere self-discipline contrasted markedly with his father's slovenliness, drunkenness and barely concealed homosexuality. But for all his faults James had been expansive, loquacious, straightforward and essentially benevolent, and he had a shrewd political brain. He was not altogether a good judge of men, but he was adept at face-to-face negotiation, and even enjoyed it. In contrast his son was cold, proud and reserved; he suffered from a slight stammer which inhibited him in private conversation as well as public speaking, but in any case his temperament made him a poor communicator. His early life was spent in the shadow of his splendid elder brother Henry, who died of typhoid in 1612, aged eighteen, and King James never troubled to disguise the fact that he regarded 'baby Charles' as second best. Father and son were never close, and indeed Charles found it impossible to warm to any man outside a small circle of friends and favourites, usually ill-chosen. As king he found it difficult to win over people whose support he needed, and he was too apt to resort instead to petulant bullying, and ultimately to the use of force. He was a man for cutting Gordian knots, only to find in the end that these very knots were holding together the structure of his own rule. Moreover, very early in his reign he acquired a reputation for dissimulation and dishonesty which stayed with him, and which in fact was not undeserved.

He began with another handicap, his close friendship with George Villiers, Duke of Buckingham. Handsome, flamboyant and macho, young Villiers had come to court in 1616, caught the eye of James I and soared into his favour, rising effortlessly through the ranks of the nobility; baron, earl, marquess and, in 1623, duke. He was not without ability, but in high policy he was a rash and unlucky gambler. The strong element of homosexuality in his relations with James I, whether physical or not, and the effrontery with which he monopolised royal patronage and dominated royal decision-making, had alienated the ruling classes in Lords and Commons and thrown a shadow over the old King's closing years. Strangely enough, he also engaged the affections of the chaste, prudish Charles, over whom his authority was all but absolute.

This would not have mattered so much had England not been at war, and if much of the responsibility of waging that war had not fallen on the Duke, as Lord High Admiral and virtual Commander-in-Chief.

England had almost been sucked into the Thirty Years' War in Germany at the very beginning. In 1618 the Bohemian nobility, about to elect a new king, rejected the Habsburg candidate Archduke Ferdinand of Styria, the spearhead of the Catholic Counter-Reformation in South Germany; instead their choice fell on the leader of the German Calvinist princes, Frederick Elector Palatine, who five years before had married James I's attractive and popular daughter Elizabeth. Much against his father-in-law's advice Frederick accepted, but in 1619 Ferdinand of Styria was elected Holy Roman Emperor, and at once engaged the Catholic Duke Maximilian of Bavaria to drive Frederick out of Bohemia; in return he was promised a slice of Frederick's dominions and eventually his electoral title. Maximilian duly defeated the 'Winter King' in 1620 at the battle of the White Mountain, near Prague, saw Ferdinand installed in his place, and occupied the Lower Palatinate. In 1621 the Spanish Army of Flanders under its great Genoese commander Ambrogio Spinola invaded the upper Palatinate. Frederick and Elizabeth took refuge at The Hague.

English public opinion was thoroughly roused by these events, so ominous for German Protestantism as well as for the much loved Elizabeth, 'Queen of Hearts', and naturally there was strong pressure on James to intervene. But without an army, and in the midst of a severe economic depression, a full-scale military expedition to central Europe was out of the question, even if Parliament would finance it. In 1620 he recalled the veteran Sir Horace Vere from the Dutch army and sent him to the Upper Palatinate with 2,000 volunteers; he held out against Spinola for two years in the fortresses of Mannheim, Frankenthal and Heidelberg, but this was a mere temporary obstruction.

James himself preferred the diplomatic approach. He hoped to marry Prince Charles to the Infanta Maria, sister to Philip IV of Spain – a project which had been in the air for nearly ten years – then use Philip to bring pressure to bear on his Habsburg cousin and ally Ferdinand II. This was by no means a visionary idea, but Parliament peremptorily rejected it in 1621 without offering any plausible alternative. After another year of frustrating diplomatic manoeuvre Charles rashly left for Madrid early in 1623 to press his suit in person, accompanied by the ubiquitous Buckingham. The result was a humiliating fiasco; the lady herself was manifestly unwilling, and the King her brother imposed impossible conditions. It was rumoured that these included Charles's own conversion to Catholicism, and that, egged on by Buckingham, he had given undertakings to this effect. The result was a public confrontation between Buckingham and the English Ambassador to Madrid, the Earl of Bristol, which was prolonged into 1626 and seriously damaged Charles's reputation as a man of honour. Moreover, news now arrived from Vienna that the Emperor had duly stripped Frederick of his electoral title and assigned it to Maximilian of Bavaria.

Charles and Buckingham returned with their tails between their legs, and childishly determined on war against Spain. Where James's pacific diplomacy had failed, naval and military pressure might succeed. A new parliament summoned in 1624 heartily endorsed this new war policy, but voted quite inadequate sums of money to sustain it, and these earmarked principally for the Navy, and for aid to the Dutch, whose eighty-year war of liberation against Spain had been resumed in 1621 and was going badly. In April 1625, in the midst of furious war preparations and hectic public excitement, the old King died.

At once things went badly wrong. Not content with mounting an amphibious expedition against the great Spanish port of Cadiz, which his first parliament, that summer, naturally approved, Charles recruited a heterogeneous force of conscripts under the German mercenary general Count Mansfeld to intervene directly in the Palatinate, and pledged financial help, plus a small force of English volunteers, to Christian IV of Denmark, who had emerged as the new Protestant champion in North Germany. Unfortunately Mansfeld's sorry army dissolved in desertion and disease soon after it disembarked in the Netherlands, wasting money which Charles could ill afford, and indeed which it is doubtful if he had. Worse still, the Cadiz expedition that autumn was a complete failure, distinguished by every kind of military incompetence, including cowardice and drunkenness. As for Christian IV, he was decisively defeated by the new Imperial general Wallenstein at Lutter in 1626, and the following year he was driven right off the mainland and onto the Danish islands. He took no further part in the German war, though the last English contingent did not trickle home until 1629. Over and above all this, having escaped the arms of one popish princess (providentially, it seemed), Charles had promptly married another, Henrietta Maria of France, who was so loyal to her faith that she refused to attend his coronation.

Parliament, of course, had deluded itself if it believed that Spain could be coerced by short-term raids on her coast, however successful. But Charles had deluded himself too, if he thought that he could extend England's war into Europe without parliamentary approval or financial backing; and now Parliament was free to argue that if the Cadiz expedition, representing its own preferred policy, had been fully backed, or if it had been organised by anybody else but Buckingham, it might well have succeeded. In fact, it was not surprising that in 1626 it launched an intemperate attack on the Lord Admiral, refusing to vote further taxation unless he were dismissed. Charles refused and dissolved Parliament, but the unwisdom of backing his accident-prone favourite was demonstrated almost immediately, when his heavy-handed diplomacy pushed England into war with France – supposedly her principal ally against Spain. The war against Spain was now virtually abandoned, and all Buckingham's efforts were focused on the relief of the Huguenot stronghold of La Rochelle, closely besieged by the French army under the personal command of Louis XIII's chief minister, Cardinal Richelieu. Not a despicable objective for a Protestant state in the early seventeenth century, but low on England's list of priorities compared with the relief of the Palatinate. Moreover, Parliament having refused to vote new taxes, Charles had to levy forced loans on the nobility and gentry, imprisoning without trial those who refused. Under these conditions the money came in, and he might have succeeded had

Buckingham succeeded, but the Duke let him down again. When his assault on the Île de Rhé, guarding the entrance to La Rochelle, was beaten off, Charles had no alternative but to summon another parliament for February 1628.

Parliament's first priority was to push through the Petition of Right, which forbade imprisonment without due process of law and the levy of any taxes not authorised by them, but in return they had to endorse Buckingham's lunatic war policy, which seemed more irrelevant to the main concerns of European Protestantism with every month that passed. The great Dutch general Maurice of Nassau had died in 1625 during the siege of the key fortress of Breda, which then fell to the Spaniards; Maurice's brother and successor Frederick Henry was barely holding his own. By the spring of 1628 the Emperor's armies under Tilly and Wallenstein had reached the Baltic coast, and only the Swedes held out in Stralsund under the Scots field marshal Alexander Leslie. There was a real danger that Protestantism would be extirpated in the Netherlands and the whole of Germany in this generation, and Charles's war policy since his accession had done nothing to halt the process or even hinder it. The Earl of Bristol voiced his frustration in the Lords in June 1628:

> In all our enterprises lately we have been as he that shoots against marble, whose arrow rebounds back upon himself. The Lord has not gone forth with our armies. We have been like the broken staff of Egypt to all that have relied upon us. How lives the Lady Elizabeth and her children? How stands it with the King of Denmark? The distress of our friends lies before us, the power and malice of our enemies.

But did this apparent incompetence conceal something more sinister? Some thought that it did, and the drift of Charles's Church policy confirmed their fears.

For in the first year or two of his reign the King had come down off the fence on which his father had found a comfortable perch and thrown himself wholeheartedly behind the right wing of the English Church, led by the abrasive and aggressive William Laud, Bishop of London, who by 1628 enjoyed a complete monopoly of key ecclesiastical appointments. Laud called a halt to further Church reform, including that creeping reform sponsored by the Puritans, who looked forward to the gradual withering away of episcopacy (like the state in Marxist theory) and the gradual amendment of the Prayer Book, a hope encouraged by King James's lax and tolerant attitude. Now Laud declared that the Church of England was perfect as it then stood, subject to some discreet 'purification', chiefly of Puritan error, and insisted on strict and universal compliance with its tenets. The attempt by him and his fellow bishops, firmly supported by the King, to enforce this compliance in the years that followed was never entirely successful but was certainly deeply divisive. Rightly or wrongly he was also accused of Arminianism, that Protestant 'heresy' which had split the world of international Calvinism in the previous generation, and against which James I had set his face. Certainly some of his measures of 'purification' – notably that the wooden communion table used in most parish churches be removed from the nave to the east end of the chancel, railed in and ideally replaced by a stone altar – could be regarded as popish, or tending towards popery. Worse still, in recent years many Laudian clergy had taken to delivering indiscreet sermons extolling the Divine Right of Kings and declaring it a sin to resist royal demands for money, with or without parliamentary approval. For this one of them, Roger Manwaring, was impeached by Parliament in 1628.

Time was to show that Laud's conception of the English Church enjoyed much more grass-roots support than his opponents supposed, but in the conditions of acute international religious tension which obtained in the 1620s and 1630s it was distinctly rash for Charles to give his support to this reactionary movement with its undertones of popery and arbitrary power (two concepts which always went together in the popular mind). As it was, the tension was momentarily relieved by Buckingham's assassination in August 1628 by an unbalanced ex-officer. This opened the way to a reconciliation between Charles and some of his leading opponents, notably Sir Thomas Wentworth, one of the architects of the Petition of Right, who was given a viscountcy in December 1628 and appointed Lord President of the Council of the North, moving on to Dublin in 1634 as Lord Deputy in Ireland. But when it reassembled early in 1629 the House of Commons was unrepentant, and it was soon locked in a violent dispute with the King over his religious policy and over his continued collection of customs duties, a technical infraction of the Petition of Right. On 3 March some MPs even tried to prolong the session by barring the door to Black Rod and holding the Speaker down in his chair. Charles dissolved them in a fury, publicly announcing that he would not call another parliament until there were evident prospects of reaching an accommodation with them.

In fact, the eleven-year period of 'Personal Rule' began well. The irresponsible conduct of the Commons in 1629, unsupported by the Lords, led to a revulsion of feeling in the King's favour. The fall of La Rochelle, though it was another dire blow to the cause of European Protestantism, at least enabled him to wind up the war; peace was signed with France and Spain in 1629 and 1630. He was still carrying a considerable burden of debt from the war years, but his regular income steadily increased, and by 1635 his finances were on a sound footing. He could even afford to pay Rubens to paint the wonderful ceiling of the Whitehall Banqueting House, built for his father by Inigo Jones in 1619. This was mainly due to increased income from the customs in a period of booming mercantile prosperity, but he further added to it by unpopular devices such as distraint of knighthood (fining gentlemen qualified for knighthood who had not assumed that honour at his coronation) and the enforcement of the medieval limits of the Royal Forests (fining landowners who had encroached upon them). But these were mere pinpricks, and there is no evidence of widespread opposition to the regime prior to 1639, though some historians have simply assumed it; certainly there was no public agitation for another parliament. In retrospect his most controversial device – certainly the most celebrated – was the levy of 'ship money', an annual charge for the refitting and improvement of the Navy, first imposed on the coastal counties in 1634 and extended to the inland counties the following year. However, the Navy, in contrast to the army, was never regarded as an instrument of political repression, and the need to protect English shipping from the privateers of the warring powers, France, Holland and Spain, and to guard the western coasts against raids by Algerine corsairs, was obvious. Thus right up to 1638 and beyond this tax showed an unprecedented yield of 90–95 per cent, and John Hampden's celebrated challenge to its legality, which was in fact repulsed by the High Court early in 1638, seems to have made little difference. That autumn only £69,000 was requested, as against nearly £200,000 in previous years, and £55,000 was duly collected. Resentment against ship money, which was certainly evident in 1640 and 1641, seems to have been provoked as much as anything by the unwonted efficiency of its administration, though its opponents chose to present their motives as more elevated and public-spirited.

However, no amount of new ships could strengthen England's overall position in Europe, and in fact they were singularly ineffective in their stated function of keeping down piracy. In marked contrast was the heroic policy of Gustavus Adolphus of Sweden, the 'Lion of the North', who landed at Stralsund in 1630 with the announced intention of rescuing German Protestantism. He routed the Imperialists at Breitenfeld in 1631 and drove on, deep into the German heartland; the Emperor even talked of retreating to Italy. Here was the new Protestant hero; in England pamphlets and broadsheets by the score extolled his feats of arms and romanticised his character, while a special new periodical, *The Swedish Intelligencer*, gave week-by-week news of his progress. (One of his most devoted admirers was an earnest young Huntingdonshire squire, Oliver Cromwell, who had never heard a shot fired in anger.) Deep was the gloom in England when he was killed at Lützen in 1632, on the verge of another splendid victory.

From our vantage point it is clear that by now the Thirty Years' War was approaching a position of stalemate. The Swedish army, under able though less charismatic generals like Wrangel and Baner, hung on; the Imperialists were exhausted, and the Emperor did little to help by ordering the assassination in 1634 of his most accomplished general, Wallenstein, on suspicion of treason; in 1635 France threw her weight against him. But at the time, and from afar, this was not apparent; indeed, it seemed lamentable that the leading Catholic nation, under a Roman cardinal (Richelieu), should be left to bolster up the Protestant cause, while Charles I, arguably the senior Protestant ruler in Europe, did nothing. When the Elector Palatine died in 1632, still an exile at The Hague, his widow pointedly refused Charles's suggestion that she and her children make their home in England.

To be fair, Charles's obligations to his sister, and to his nephew, the titular Elector Charles Lewis, were never far from his mind, but without financial support from Parliament, which even now was not likely to be forthcoming, he could do little. He subsidised his friend the Marquess of Hamilton, who went over to Germany in 1630 with a couple of regiments of volunteers, one Scottish, the other English, and as late as 1638 he was discussing the possibility of a more substantial expedition with Alexander Leslie, recently retired from the Swedish service, but Leslie then went north to head the Army of the Covenant (p. 16 below). In any case, the main bent of his foreign policy was towards a closer liaison with Spain; in fact, he had fallen back on his father's policy of using Spain to put indirect diplomatic pressure on the Emperor, but as his father had found, this kind of relationship with the traditional enemy of the Protestant religion and national independence was unacceptable in the eyes of the English public.

In fact, the whole drift of Charles's policy in the 1630s seemed increasingly 'un-Protestant', even anti-Protestant. Laud, whose apparent aim was to force the English Church back in the direction of Rome, was appointed Archbishop of Canterbury in 1633 and now loomed larger than ever in the King's councils. In 1635 his faithful ally William Juxon, Bishop of London, was even appointed Lord Treasurer. He and Laud dominated the Privy Council and its judicial arm, the Court of Star Chamber, which they used to launch a series of vindictive prosecutions against the opponents and critics of episcopacy which only served to damage their reputations (and that of Star Chamber itself) still further. Meanwhile thinly disguised papal emissaries, the Irishman George Con and after him Gregorio Panzani, were cordially received at the Court of St James, where the busy, glamorous Catholic Queen did much to set the tone, inspiring a number of conversions which Charles regarded with apparent indifference. Henrietta Maria even took her infant sons, the future Charles II and James II, regularly to mass.

Only in this context can we understand the crisis which arose in 1637 and 1638 when Charles and Laud made the fatal error of trying to impose a modified version of the English Prayer Book on the Presbyterian Church of Scotland. To the English as well as the Scots it seemed that the crypto-papalism typical of the present government was expanding relentlessly north. But the Scots were prepared to do much more than protest. Precisely because Scotland was at an earlier stage of development, her nobility and her priesthood independent, rebellious and active, her parliamentary institutions rudimentary and little regarded, the rule of law imperfectly imposed by a weak central government, she was able to mount the kind of spontaneous rebellion never achieved south of the border. Riots against the new liturgy broke out in Edinburgh in July 1637 and spread rapidly across the Lowlands; a National Covenant, pledging resistance to church reform, was hastily drawn up; the original was signed by a large gathering of noblemen, ministers and burgesses at the Greyfriars Church, Edinburgh, in February 1638, and copies were distributed up and down the country. The local presbyteries, comprising the leading laymen as well as the minister in each parish, provided a ready-made revolutionary organisation; they were soon grouped in areas, each area sending representatives to Edinburgh to form a kind of 'anti-administration' known as 'The Tables'. The Covenant, though it emphasised their loyalty to the King, implied a dark suspicion of his real motives, beginning as it did with a long diatribe against 'papistry'; and though Charles suspended the new prayer book he was at the same time mobilising for war, and the Scots followed suit, calling Alexander Leslie from retirement to organise and lead the Army of the Covenant.

In March 1639 the King left for York to lead the campaign in person. He had ordered a special levy of 6,000 foot and 1,000 horse, and mobilised the trained bands, or militia, of Yorkshire, Durham and Northumberland, counties with a centuries-old tradition of warfare against the Scots. These numbered about 4,000. In his role as feudal lord he also called upon his tenants-in-chief to aid him by their personal attendance, each with a suitable retinue of horsemen. This extraordinary medieval revival was technically legal, and even the Puritan lords felt obliged to comply. By June he had an army, on paper at least, of 18,000 foot and 3,000 horse.

The subsequent débâcle was due not so much to shortage of money as to a disastrous failure in administration, a shortage of arms and equipment which no amount of money could have made good in time, and a total failure in morale. Jacob Astley, a retired veteran of the Flanders war recalled to command the infantry, was confounded to find many of the trained bands armed with bows and arrows, and the pikes sent to re-equip them were too short. According to Sir Edmund Verney, the King's standard-bearer: 'Our men are very raw, our arms of all sorts naught, our victuals scarce, and provisions for horses worse.' Few of the newly appointed officers had the ability or the experience to bring their men up to battle readiness in the short time available, and most of the nobility, conscripted by what they could only regard as a confidence trick, were resentful and obstructive. This was true even of the high command, where the Queen persuaded Charles to demote the highly experienced Earl of Essex from command of the horse in favour of one of her courtiers, the lightweight Earl of Holland.

Moreover, though the English as a nation regarded the Scots with contempt and aversion, they were loath to see them defeated. The conquest of Scotland, and the need to hold it down, would give Charles a weapon no previous monarch had enjoyed, a regular army, which might well be maintained, like the Navy, by an extra-parliamentary tax levied on the plea of national emergency.

In fact, this remained an unlikely scenario. Plans for amphibious operations against Aberdeen in the east and Kintyre in the west were abandoned early; the royal castles dominating the Lowlands at Edinburgh, Dalkeith, Stirling and Dumbarton capitulated one by one; and when it came to a direct confrontation on the Border it was no contest. Leslie had now recruited as many as 20,000 men, and he had been drilling them for six months; by a prodigious feat of organisation the puny Scots manufacturing industry had also been geared to supply him with the necessary arms and ammunition. He had the great advantage of an aristocratic officer corps devoted to his cause and obedient to his will, and he could draw on a considerable reservoir of battle-hardened officers, NCOs and men who had returned from Germany on the news of the crisis. In fact, he was in a position to insist that, though well-born amateurs might be appointed colonels of regiments, they must be supported by professional under-officers and NCOs. This was also the ideal in the English armies raised during the Civil Wars, but it was rarely achieved and when it was it was not much publicised.

On 3 June the Scots arrived at Kelso, clearly bound for England, and Lord Holland was despatched with a 'forlorn hope' of 3,000 foot and 300 horse to turn them back.* Finding himself hopelessly outnumbered, he naturally retreated, but this broke the flimsy morale of the rest of the royal army. Whether Leslie would have risked a pitched battle at this stage, with Scotland's independence at stake, is doubtful, but when he boldly advanced to Dunshaw, ten miles from the Border, Charles decided to negotiate, helped on by a letter from Lord Deputy Wentworth warning him that he could expect no help from Ireland for the time being, and advising him to *reculer pour mieux sauter*. By the Pacification of Berwick he agreed to disband his army, which was falling apart anyway, and to allow a meeting of the General Assembly of the Church of Scotland and the election of a new parliament to negotiate peace; its first task was to pass an act of indemnity for the Covenanters.

But neither side regarded this as more than a truce. Charles's first thought was to send for Wentworth from Dublin. Wentworth was the most resolute and ruthless of his ministers, and his Irish army of 8,000 men (its numbers, its ferocity and its devotion to popery the subject of exaggerated rumour) might well prove an invaluable reserve force. As for the Scots, they refused to disband their provisional government, and the General Assembly of the Church of Scotland provocatively voted that the office of bishop was contrary not only to the constitution

---

* 'Forlorn hope' was a semi-technical term, denoting a small unit of crack troops sent on ahead to harass or distract the enemy, or, in a siege, to divert his attention from the main point of attack. It was not a suicide or 'kamikaze' mission, as its name might suggest.

of the Church of Scotland but to that of Christ's church in general, thus passing judgment on the Church of England. The Scots Parliament was no more amenable, and in November 1639 Charles ordered it to adjourn until the following June; it reluctantly complied, but it left behind in Edinburgh an interim committee to lend a certain legal authority to the provisional government. In January Charles announced his intention of embarking on another campaign that summer.

Before that, however, Wentworth, recently promoted Earl of Strafford, urged Charles to summon a parliament to Westminster, the first for eleven years, confident that it would rally to the King against the national enemy. But he was woefully mistaken. The Short Parliament, as it was later called, assembled on 13 April 1640. It was very ready to vote taxation for a 'patriotic' war; in fact, it offered Charles the unheard-of sum of twelve subsidies. But it refused to pass the necessary subsidy act until its manifold grievances, ecclesiastical and civil, had been settled. Strafford at once swung round, and on 5 May, after a mere three weeks, we find him urging the King to dissolve them. 'Go on with a vigorous war', he told him, 'as you first designed. [You are] loosed and absolved from all rules of government. Being reduced to extreme necessity, everything is to be done that power might admit, and that you are to do. They refusing, you are acquitted towards God and man.'

In fact Strafford's subsequent actions did not match his words. Charles did not even attempt to levy a forced loan, as in 1627, and attempts to coerce the county sheriffs into collecting ship money or to bully the City of London into offering a loan were counter-productive. When Strafford went down with a disabling attack of 'the stone' (gallstones) in June the government lost what little driving force it possessed. The Scots Parliament reassembled that month, defying Charles's orders to dissolve, and the Irish Parliament, subservient enough in Strafford's presence earlier in the year, now turned mutinous and obstructive. The King secretly appealed to Spain for a loan, promising to declare war on the Dutch as soon as he had brought the Scots to heel. The Queen even appealed to the Pope, also in vain. Her own brother, Louis XIII of France, pleaded poverty.

Before he fell ill Strafford had decided to stand down the northern militia, whose performance in 1639 had been unimpressive, and levy a new army in the South. But these levies, conscripted from the off-scourings of society, untrained and ill-disciplined, tended to seep away on the long march north, and those who did not were prone to mutiny; two Catholic officers were simply lynched by their own men, who then dispersed. By the beginning of August, already late in the campaigning season, about 12,000 men had assembled at Selby, but 3,000 of them had no arms at all, and all of them were unpaid, short of food and thoroughly discontented. Lord Conway and Sir Jacob Astley were stationed on the River Tyne with another 12,000 foot and 2,000 horse, in rather better shape but by no means entirely reliable. The Scots meanwhile had massed an army of 25,000 men on the Border, but Charles took heart from the news of a bitter feud between the two leading Covenanting noblemen, the Earls of Argyll and Montrose, and his advisers did not believe that the Scots Border counties could support an army of this size for more than a week or two.

They were right, but this cut both ways. Only by advancing into England could Leslie suppress the divisions in the Covenanting leadership and commandeer fresh supplies to feed his troops. He crossed the Tweed on 20 August, the day Charles left London for York, and meeting with no resistance he marched south through Northumberland. But the time Strafford rejoined the King at York on the 27th the Scots were at the Tyne. Leslie forced a crossing of the river next day, brushing aside Conway's feeble attempt to stop him at Newburn, and on the 30th he took the city and fortress of Newcastle without firing a shot. Conway and Astley could only retreat before him as he marched irresistibly south through County Durham, but he was content to call a halt at the River Tees.

Reaching desperately for another forgotten medieval device, Charles now summoned a Great Council of the peerage to York on 24 September, obviously hoping to bypass the commonalty by an appeal to what in effect was the House of Lords. But the peers almost unanimously advised him to call a truce with the Scots and summon another parliament, and he had no choice but to comply. By the Treaty of Ripon, signed on 14 October, negotiations for a permanent settlement were adjourned to London, but meanwhile the Scots army was to occupy Durham and Northumberland. The army was to be paid £850 a day maintenance during the occupation, and the Scots provisional government was to be reimbursed its expenses in prosecuting war against the King. These sums only Parliament could provide.

*    *    *

The Long Parliament met on 3 November 1640, launched on a stormy and oft-interrupted career which was to take it up to 16 March 1660. In its early sessions our attention is captured by the high drama of Strafford's impeachment, culminating in the tragedy of his execution in May 1641. The other dominating theme of the first session, in the eyes of liberal historians, was a series of reform statutes, passed in the summer of 1641, which abolished the courts of Star Chamber and High Commission, declared ship money illegal, abolished distraint of knighthood and established the limits of the Royal Forests. This legislation, which formed the basis of the Restoration Settlement, arguably set England on the road to constitutional monarchy and parliamentary democracy.

But in 1640 parliamentary democracy was far in the future; present circumstances were dominated by military power. After all, Parliament was sitting only because of the military threat posed by the Scots army. Strafford was marked for death, not merely because he was suspected of advising the King to unconstitutional courses, but because he was the chief exponent of ultra-royalism, and he had a weapon to hand in the English army which he had raised in 1640, which was still in being and uneasily stationed in south Yorkshire. George Goring, another royalist extremist, was governor of Portsmouth, with a large garrison and a full arsenal. Until all these men could be paid off and demobilised, and until the Scots had been paid off, too, and had retired across the Border, the civilian politicians in Parliament had to operate under the threat of a military *révanche*. The Triennial Act in February 1641, which obliged the King to meet all subsequent parliaments at least once every three years, and an even more radical act in May forbidding him to prorogue or dissolve the present Parliament without its own consent, were avowedly designed to enhance the stability of the government, and thus facilitate the floating of loans on the London market to pay off the English and Scots armies. Not until this problem was in sight of a solution, and Strafford was destroyed, could Parliament turn to the task of constitutional reform, in June and July 1641.

Meanwhile there were persistent rumours, with some basis in fact, that the King was still looking for assistance from abroad. Spain had finally bowed out, after desultory negotiations with Charles for much of 1640, but this was not generally known. It was not to be expected that Louis XIII would ignore the Queen's sisterly appeals (though in fact he did). In February 1641 Charles negotiated a marriage treaty between his elder daughter Mary and William, the son of the Dutch

Stadholder, Frederick Henry, Prince of Orange, which it could plausibly be assumed contained a secret proviso for military assistance (though in fact it did not). Even more ominously, from early January through to 7 May Charles stubbornly ignored the Commons' repeated requests to disband the Irish army, mostly Catholic and reputed to be 9,000 strong (actually nearer 3,000) which was still stationed in Ulster. The belief that Strafford had been ready to bring this army over to England in 1640 had been the main count in his indictment.

As it was, the officers of the English army, meeting regularly together at Boroughbridge, were growing increasingly restless. In March they sent a letter to their nominal commander, the Earl of Northumberland, outlining their grievances and calling for a renewal of the Scots campaign. In fact there was a secret plan afoot to replace Northumberland by a much firmer loyalist, the Earl of Newcastle, and march the army on London to overawe Parliament, and on 2 May one Captain Billingsley, who had been recruiting troops in London, ostensibly for the Portuguese service,* suddenly appeared with a hundred of them at the Tower, demanding entrance in the King's name. The Constable, Sir William Balfour, refused, and the Lords ordered the garrison to be strengthened by the addition of 500 militiamen from the Tower Hamlets. Whether the King was really behind Billingsley or not was unknown.

The Commons leader, John Pym, soon got wind of this 'First Army Plot', and revealed it to an alarmed House on 5 May. Pym undoubtedly played it for all it was worth, and his melodramatic exaggeration has tended to obscure the seriousness of the situation. By the end of May another officer, Daniel O'Neill, was conspiring afresh to bring the Northern army to London, and Charles's announcement at the end of June that he planned an early visit to Edinburgh, passing through the English and Scottish armies on his way north, naturally heightened the tension. The result was a frenzied effort to dispose of both armies. Five English regiments stationed at Hull were paid off in mid-July, and the Scots withdrew to the Tyne. Charles reached Newcastle on 13 August without incident and pressed on to Edinburgh. A week later the Scots retired to Morpeth, and on 25 August they withdrew across the Tweed at last, and Parliament called a day of thanksgiving on 7 September to celebrate the great disbandment.

---

* Portugal's rebellion against Spain in 1640 attracted much sympathy in England, and was obviously of interest to unemployed professional soldiers.

The nation was demilitarised at last, and with the threat of the sword removed Parliament returned on 20 October, after a short recess, to resume the programme of legal and ecclesiastical reform it had left unfinished in the summer. It was at once regaled by exaggerated reports of 'the Incident' at Edinburgh, a bungled attempt by Charles to arrest the Earl of Argyll, the leader of the Covenanting nobility. At this fresh evidence of the King's perfidy Pym persuaded the Commons to bring in contingents of the London trained bands to guard the Palace of Westminster, but this was merely a provocative gesture. However, a few days later came the shattering news that Catholic Ireland had risen in revolt.

# 3

# THE DESCENT
# TO WAR

On 23 October 1641 a sudden uprising of the Irish Catholics in Ulster put most of that province into their hands, though luckily a plot to seize Dublin failed. The news reached London on 1 November, closely followed by circumstantial accounts of the horrendous atrocities committed on the Protestant settlers, accounts which were wildly exaggerated, in some cases entirely untrue, but not susceptible to immediate disproof. The resulting trauma coloured England's attitude to the Irish for generations.

No one in London had expected such a revolt. The last rebellion in Ulster had lasted five years, but it had apparently been quelled for good in 1603, in the last week of the old Queen's life, when her Deputy Lord Mountjoy had taken the surrender of Hugh O'Neill, Earl of Tyrone. In 1607 Tyrone and the remaining nationalist leaders had fled to Spain for good, and in 1610 Ulster had been declared a plantation, and had been partly settled by Protestant immigrants, mainly from Scotland. Strafford's rule in Ireland in the 1630s had caused concern in opposition circles, but only because he seemed intent on exalting monarchical authority by the most unscrupulous means, not because any reaction was anticipated from the Irish. Once he was removed the Long Parliament assumed that the Irish problem was solved.

But the situation was not so simple. There were three power groups in seventeenth-century Ireland. First, the native Irish, staunchly Roman Catholic, anti-English and pro-Spanish; Mountjoy had destroyed their aristocratic leadership, but it was impossible short of genocide to eradicate the gentry class and the peasantry, even in Ulster. They deeply resented their position as an under-class. At the opposite pole stood the New English, descended from the Protestant immigrants of the previous century, who were naturally entrenched in the permanent government at Dublin, the 'Castle', and blankly hostile to the Irish. Between them stood the Old English, descended from the medieval settlers and never fully absorbed into Irish society; most of them were loyal Catholics, but they were desperate to assert their 'Englishry' and distance themselves from the 'Old Irish'.

Successive Lord Lieutenants or Lord Deputies had done their best to hold the ring, but in trying to conciliate the Old English they had often found themselves at odds with their own aides in Dublin. In 1628 the Castle had won the latest struggle, when it had frustrated Lord Deputy Falkland's attempt to give legal substance to the 'special position' of the Old English, and as soon as Wentworth arrived in 1634 he threw himself wholeheartedly on the side of the New English. Narrow and dogmatic Protestantism was now the only touchstone of loyalty, and he began to extend the English Plantation westwards into Galway and Connaught, encroaching in the process on the estates of some of the leading Old English nobility, especially those of Ulick Bourke, Earl of Clanricarde.

The Castle was seriously weakened by Strafford's fall, and the failure of the new Lord Lieutenant, the Earl of Leicester, to take up his post, and in the first half of 1641 the Irish Parliament, dominated by the Old English, made another determined attempt to secure recognition of their status. But Charles, ignorant of Irish conditions, and lacking a Lord Lieutenant on the spot who might have advised him, refused again. Alarmed by the King's weakness in the face of his violently anti-Catholic parliament at Westminster, the Old English decided it was now or never.

The Long Parliament's horror was infinite, but its power to act was limited. The rebels claimed to be acting on the King's behalf against the Dublin government, and they even displayed a forged commission from Charles under the Great Seal of Scotland, dated 1 October at Edinburgh, and with his usual fatal hesitation he did not disown it until 1 January. He had in fact been in correspondence with some of the Old English lords that summer, and rumours of this were beginning to leak out, causing consternation in Parliament, which in any case made no distinction between one Irish Catholic and another. However, the King took charge of whatever resistance there was, and on 10 November, from Edinburgh, he appointed as his Lieutenant-General James Butler, Earl of Ormonde, one of the few Old English noblemen who had been raised as a Protestant.

Ormonde acted with vigour; he remobilised the Irish army, numbering on paper 2,297 foot and 943 horse, and began raising three new regiments of 1,000 each, most of them embittered refugees from Ulster. His hated second-in-command, Sir Charles Coote, was soon mounting punitive raids from Dublin on the scorched-earth principle which had proved so successful under Mountjoy, destroying crops, burning down houses and killing any Catholic he met, loyal or not. But the only result was to antagonise men who might otherwise have remained neutral, and by the end of the year the rebellion was spreading inexorably south and west. Ormonde was soon confined to the Pale, an area of a few hundred square miles round Dublin.

In London the reform programme of the Long Parliament ground to an abrupt halt. Parliament's first priority was to reconquer Ireland and this time finally protestantise it, but this called for a new army, just when the previous armies, so troublesome and dangerous, had been disbanded. By custom, law and long tradition only the King could lead such an army, but it was doubtful if he could now be trusted with it. With Charles still at Edinburgh they temporised; on 12 November they voted to send 2,000 troops to Dublin without consulting him, inviting the Scots, who were directly concerned in the Ulster Plantation, to contribute another thousand. Three days later Pym gave the Commons details of a 'Second Army Plot', this time to use the Portsmouth garrison, under George Goring, to coerce Parliament, which heavily underlined the unwisdom of raising another army for the King to command. On the 22nd they passed the Grand Remonstrance, which amongst much else reaffirmed their belief in a longstanding conspiracy amongst the King's advisers to overthrow the Protestant constitution, and requested him to appoint no one to high office, civil or military, who was not approved by them.

On his return from Scotland three days later, however, Charles dismissed the Remonstrance with contempt, and while he now accepted the support of the 'constitutional loyalists', including the Earl of Bristol and his erratic son George, Lord Digby, and Edward Hyde, the future Earl of Clarendon, who were working for a negotiated compromise with Parliament, some of his other actions were decidedly sinister. He removed the armed guard posted round the parliament buildings and dismissed Parliament's trusted general, the Earl of Essex, from the command of the county militia south of Trent, to which he had been appointed only in August. Meanwhile since October a disturbing number of 'reformadoes', officers of the demobilised Northern army, had been gathering in London, ostensibly looking for employment in the Spanish or Portuguese service, or in Ireland. Since their only recreation seemed to be drinking, and picking squabbles with all and sundry, they constituted a growing public-order problem. On 8 November Parliament was informed that as many as forty of them, fully armed, were in lodgings near the Tower, apparently recruited into the Spanish service by an Irish captain, Robert More, and his financial agent, John Bourke, though they showed no signs of going abroad. The matter came to a head on 21 December. Charles suddenly dismissed his Lieutenant of the Tower, Sir William Balfour. Balfour was a skilled Scots professional who had left the Dutch service in 1627 to serve on the Île de Rhé expedition under Buckingham; he had been a prime favourite with the Duke, whose posthumous influence had brought him this plum appointment at the Tower in 1630, but he was now beginning to show a fatal inclination towards Parliament. In fact, he was to become one of the senior colonels of cavalry in the parliamentary army raised in 1642. Charles's right to dismiss him was incontestable, but he rashly replaced him with one of the most notorious of the reformadoes from the Northern army, Sir Thomas Lunsford, a blustering rakehell who had narrowly escaped an indictment for murder in 1637, and whose reputation in his native Sussex was so unsavoury that he was rumoured to have eaten babies. Such was the uproar that he was replaced only five days later by the loyal but more acceptable Sir John Byron; but next day he reappeared at the head of a band of officers which cleared a group of incipient rioters out of Westminster Hall with drawn swords. The King's only answer to subsequent complaints was to hold a public dinner for these officers, who now formed a kind of praetorian guard round Whitehall, with a detachment guarding Westminster Abbey.

Understandably Parliament shrank from Charles's offer to raise 10,000 men for Ireland, to be officered by these bravos; instead it raised £11,000 by voluntary subscription, which enabled it to send 1,100 foot to Dublin under Sir Simon Harcourt; these arrived on 30 December, followed in February by George Monck with another 1,500 foot, and

Sir Richard Grenville with 400 horse. An impressment bill for Ireland was blocked in the Lords, but abortive proposals in the Commons to mobilise the militia nationwide and place it under an unnamed general of their own choosing, and then, when this failed, the introduction of a bill 'for a better settling of a military power for the defence of the kingdom', betray their real fears. (They were both introduced by the Cambridge MP Oliver Cromwell.) The Commons then asked Charles to appoint the Earl of Essex to command the London trained bands, but this attempt to encroach on his hereditary authority was rejected by the City itself. In response Charles ordered Byron to purge the Tower garrison of all officers of suspect loyalty, and strengthened it by the addition of thirty or forty professional artillerymen.

There was now every sign that Charles meditated a *coup d'état*, or at least that it was high on his list of alternative policies, but early in the new year he was panicked into moving too far too fast. Alarmed by threats against the Queen for her supposed share in the Army Plots and the Irish Rebellion, he impeached the five leading members of the opposition, headed by Pym and John Hampden, and on 4 January 1642 he took a posse of cavalry – some said 400 strong, others forty – down to Westminster in an abortive attempt to arrest them in the Commons' own House. This unprecedented breach of parliamentary privilege lost him London. The Lords at once rallied to the Commons, and so did the City government, followed by the Inns of Court. (The Inns of Court regiments, which had been put at the King's disposal only a few weeks before, ended up as the Earl of Essex's lifeguard; they included amongst their officers three future Cromwellian generals, Edmund Ludlow, Henry Ireton and Charles Fleetwood.) The City now took as commander of its trained-band regiments Philip Skippon, a staunch Puritan who had served under Sir Horace Vere in the Palatinate in the 1620s as a pikeman and had subsequently risen to commissioned rank in the Dutch army, retiring in 1639; he at once mounted a new guard on the Houses of Parliament. Lunsford wanted to lead a strike force into the City, where the five impeached Members had taken refuge, but this would have meant civil war there and then. Instead on 10 January Charles left Hampton Court with his wife and children, ignoring a personal plea from the Earl of Essex that he remain. He did not return until January 1649, when he was brought up from Windsor for his trial.

\*    \*    \*

From the moment Charles left London the leaders on both sides were preparing for war, whatever they told their more timid supporters, and their first thought was to secure the only military force available. On 14 January Parliament ordered the militia nationwide to assume a state of readiness; sheriffs were ordered to take over any castles, forts or magazines within their jurisdiction, and not to surrender them 'without his Majesty's authority signified by both Houses of Parliament'. On the 31st they began to draw up a bill appointing new lord lieutenants in every county, the future Militia Ordinance.

The royalists were much slower off the mark. Charles secretly named the Earl of Newcastle as governor of Hull, which still held a huge cache of arms and ammunition stockpiled for the 1640 campaign, but he found that Parliament had already ordered in one of its strongest local supporters, Sir John Hotham. He then sent Lord Digby and Thomas Lunsford to seize a similar arsenal at Kingston-on-Thames, but they were repulsed by the local militia. His Lieutenant at the Tower of London, Sir John Byron, was virtually besieged there, and had to be replaced in February by the neutral Sir John Conyers. Men were reluctant to come in to Charles, and he was wandering in a desultory fashion up and down the southern counties with only a hundred or so followers. Lengthy exchanges with Parliament over the militia came to nothing. On 23 February he escorted the Queen to Dover, whence she sailed for the Continent with the Crown Jewels, in search of men and guns; he then began to wend his way slowly and rather indecisively north. On 9 March at Newmarket he received a parliamentary delegation headed by the Earl of Pembroke, who pleaded with him to surrender control of the militia 'for a time'. 'By God!' said Charles, 'Not for an hour. You have asked that of me in this never asked of a king, and with which I will not trust my wife and children.' As a result the Lords abandoned their opposition to the Militia Ordinance, which passed without his consent. The argument used, then and later, was that the King was so much under the sway of his 'evil councillors' that he was unfit to execute his office, and Parliament had no choice but to act on his behalf, in order to protect his own interests. More practically, Parliament on 15 March ordered the Earl of Warwick to take command of the Navy, a detail Charles left until he arrived at York three days later – too late.

The original cause of the whole dispute, the Irish Rebellion, had receded into the background, but it could not be entirely ignored. The Scots were eager to help, but they were not entirely trusted at

Westminster; if they reconquered Ireland, or large parts of it, they might try and hold on to it for themselves, and Parliament insisted on strict parity of effort. After the King left London these negotiations languished, while Ireland retreated into what one of her historians calls 'a red mist of blood'. Given the notorious unwillingness of the English taxpayer to back words with action, Parliament decided in February to put the Irish campaign on a commercial basis. It passed a bill setting up a Company of Adventurers in Ireland empowered to raise £1 million by public subscription, the investors to be compensated at the end of the war by a proportional share of two and a half million acres of confiscated land. The King gave his assent in March. This was calculated to stiffen the resistance of those whose estates were in jeopardy, but the scheme had the simple beauty that the farther the rebellion spread the more land would become available. However, subscriptions came in slowly, as the mounting English problem displaced the Irish problem in the public mind.

Scotland now decided to go it alone, and in April 1642 Robert Monro, a long-serving veteran of the Swedish army, landed at Carrickfergus with an army of 2,500, which by August had increased to 10,000. He traversed the counties of Down and Antrim almost at will, but he could not bring the guerrilla forces opposing him to pitched battle, and the blank hostility of the local population left him dependent on supplies by sea and unable to penetrate the interior. Moreover, in July Owen Roe O'Neill, nephew to the great Hugh, Earl of Tyrone, and a veteran of thirty years in the Spanish army, landed at Donegal to head the rebellion, and he was followed in September by Thomas Preston, another hispanicised veteran, with other exiled Irish mercenaries and five shiploads of arms and ammunition. They not only offered the rebels first-class military training and leadership, they brought to Ireland the confrontational spirit of the Counter-Reformation in Europe. On 24 September, at a historic meeting at Kilkenny, the rebels formed an Irish Confederation with an elected executive Council, and took as their motto, 'Irishmen unanimous for God, King and Country'; they were now committed to religious freedom and national independence.

Back in England, King and Parliament were engaged in a furious public debate on the fundamentals of the constitution and the interpretation of their respective powers: remonstrances and counter-remonstrances, declarations and counter-declarations, proclamations and counter-proclamations, flooded from the press. On a technical level the King emerged the victor from this high debate; in the Middle Ages it had been common for committees of noblemen, sometimes assisted by Parliament, to restrain and even depose unsuitable or erratic kings, like Edward II, Richard II and Henry VI, but the autocracy of the Tudors, reinforced by the new doctrine of the Divine Right of Kings, had put such action out of court. However, on a practical level such was Charles's public reputation that it virtually nullified the enormous inertial prestige of the institution he represented. The nation watched with mounting concern, but when he arrived at York on 19 March he still had less than 200 loyal followers and (it was estimated) no more than £600 in cash. In fact, without the Welsh landed millionaire the Earl of Glamorgan he would have been in dire straits; by the end of June Glamorgan had lent him £22,000, and early in July his son, Lord Herbert, arrived at York with another £95,000 – sums which must be multiplied by at least ten, probably more, to bring them up to twentieth-century values. But money in itself could not buy supporters, it could only pay and equip them when they presented themselves; the Yorkshire nobility and gentry remained lukewarm, and on 5 April they sent the King a petition earnestly begging him to seek an accommodation with 'his' Parliament.

In fact, if he had been seeking immediate support Charles would have done better to go to Lancashire or the West Country. He was influenced by the fact that York was conventionally regarded as the capital of the North, and he still had his sights on the arsenal at Hull. However, on 29 March Parliament ordered this arsenal to be transferred by sea to London, and when he appeared before the gates of the city on 23 April Sir John Hotham denied him entry. This provoked a new flurry of protests and counter-protests, but the brute fact was that the King was losing military control. On 2 May Parliament launched a national campaign to enforce the Militia Ordinance, and on 10 May it held a mass parade of the London trained bands on Finsbury Fields. The sun shone on a gala occasion, the Londoners were out *en fête*, and the salute was taken by the Earls of Essex, Warwick and Holland. Holland, the Queen's favourite, had defected, and Essex had refused a direct order from Charles to join him at York and had resigned his post of Lord Chamberlain.

On the other hand at York only a further 200 gentry volunteers had joined the King, and one militia regiment, and here as elsewhere the militia was so divided in its allegiance that Charles's only resort was to disarm them and reserve their weapons for better motivated volunteers, but these were still slow to come in. On 3 June he took the rather desperate step of calling a mass meeting of the county freeholders on Heyworth Moor, just outside York. Perhaps he underestimated the size of Yorkshire; as many as 40,000 men presented themselves, and the whole occasion soon lapsed into chaos. In any case, at least half of those present had only come to petition him, yet again, to reach a compromise with 'his' Parliament. In the mêlée there was at least one inauspicious incident. Young Sir Thomas Fairfax of Denton tried to present a petition to the King and was nearly ridden underfoot for his pains. It would be ridiculous to suggest that the conduct of the future commander of the New Model Army was decided that afternoon, but not for the first or the last time it showed that Charles did not know who his friends were.

Parliament, conscious of its strength, now put forward the Nineteen Propositions, which were effectively terms of unconditional surrender, requiring the King to give up not only the militia but the right to appoint his own ministers and even the care and control of his own children. Taking his refusal for granted, on 6 June it issued a proclamation claiming to exercise sovereign power in view of the King's demonstrable incapacity.

However, from now on the tide began to turn. Parliament's intransigence, its insistence on terms which no man of honour could accept, began to work against it. On 13 June Charles issued a statement denying any aggressive intent, and pleading self-defence, which was endorsed by a large group of peers who had now joined him at York. On the 18th he issued a dignified and statesmanlike answer to the Nineteen Propositions in which he warned the nation, with prophetic insight, of the social chaos which would result from Parliament's policy of mobilising the people against the monarchy. Meanwhile royalist sheriffs using commissions of array, and local magnates on their own initiative, had begun to enlist men right across the country; in Cheshire, Lancashire and Wales in particular, but also in Herefordshire, Lincolnshire, Dorset and Somerset, even Norfolk and Kent. Scuffles were breaking out all over. In mid-June Lord Henry Hastings was rebuffed when he tried to execute the commission of array in Leicestershire, and again on 1 July, when he tried to commandeer the county magazine, though no blood was shed. A similar attempt on the magazine at Chester, containing munitions destined for Ireland, also failed.

Parliament chose to regard these incidents as acts of war, and at once appointed a Committee for Defence consisting of five peers (the Earls of Essex, Northumberland, Pembroke and Holland, with Viscount Saye and Sele) and ten MPs headed by Pym, Hampden and Denzil Holles. Their remit was 'to take into consideration whatsoever may concern the safety of the kingdom, and opposing any force that may be raised against Parliament'. On 6 July it recommended the raising of an army of 10,000 men, preparations for which were already far advanced, and on the 11th a state of war was declared. Next day Essex was appointed Lord General, and the members of both Houses took an emotive oath to live and die with him, 'in this cause; for the safety of the King's person, and the defence of both Houses of Parliament'.

Parliament's choice of general was perhaps inevitable, but Robert Devereux, 3rd Earl of Essex, was a strange man. Any summary of his career reads like a psychiatric case-study.

He was only ten when his father, Queen Elizabeth's favourite, went to the block for treason, in 1601. Two years later his mother married Richard Bourke, Earl of Clanricarde, and retired to Connaught, leaving him behind. James I, who – provided it caused him no trouble – liked to favour those whom Elizabeth had disfavoured, restored the boy to his father's lands and titles, but then pitchforked him into marriage with the wanton and irresponsible Frances Howard, daughter of the Earl of Suffolk, which ended in 1613 in a humiliating annulment on the grounds of impotence.

Thereafter he took to the military life, but given his great wealth he did not have to make a career of it, and by 1642 his experience of war was extensive but sporadic. Thus he went with Sir Horace Vere to the Palatinate in 1620, but came back after a year. He served with the Dutch in 1623 and 1624 for short periods, and he was offered high command on the Cadiz expedition in 1625, only to be publicly slighted when Buckingham demoted him from the Vice-Admiralship to command of a regiment. The same thing happened in 1626, when he was appointed to lead the English contingent sent to the aid of Christian IV of Denmark, then passed over in favour of the Welsh career soldier, Sir Charles Morgan. Again in 1639, as we have seen, he was appointed Lieutenant-General of Horse for the Scots campaign, then superseded by the Earl of Holland. In 1640 he declined to serve.

His second marriage, to Frances Powlett in 1632, was now breaking down. Tongues began to wag again when no children were forthcoming, and in 1636 he caught her *in flagrante* with Sir Thomas Uvedale (who incidentally was to emerge as Charles I's Treasurer-at-War in 1642). The lady subsequently announced herself pregnant, and though Essex grudgingly acknowledged the child, a boy, it was perhaps fortunate that the baby lived only a few months. Totally estranged from his wife, who was to live on until 1691, he found an alternative family with his favourite sister, another Frances, and her husband William Seymour, 3rd Earl (later Marquess) of Hertford, who in 1639 took up residence with him in his palatial town house on the Strand. But his household was broken up again in the autumn of 1642, when Lord Hertford joined the King.

Essex was a particular favourite of the Long Parliament, and the darling of the London mob, though he was the last man to court popularity. Charles I clearly distrusted him and may have disliked him, but in 1641 he tried to win him over by making him Lord Chamberlain and General of the Militia south of Trent. However, when he returned from Edinburgh in November he found him so deep in the counsels of the opposition that he had to dismiss him from the Generalship, though he retained the Lord Chamberlain's wand into the new year.

His deficiencies are more obvious to us than they were to his contemporaries in 1642. His vast estates – he was one of the wealthiest men in England – and his high rank put him above criticism; stubborn, aloof and inward-looking, he had cultivated a melancholy reserve which was mistakenly assumed to conceal deep wisdom. In a way he was one of those men who are famous for being famous; for what they are, not what they do. Time was to show that though he could inspire his officers and men with an intense and unwavering loyalty, to the extent that many of them refused to serve under anyone else, he was a poor tactician and a worse strategist. His military experience was neither deep nor continuous, and he was the prisoner of the military dogmas he had absorbed in the Flanders war. To him the step-by-step manoeuvres, the cautious catch-as-catch-can campaigns waged by Spinola and Maurice of Nassau, represented the acme of the military art. Unfortunately for him Charles I was no Spinola, and the rather scrappy, improvised warfare of 1643 and 1644 in England posed problems not to be resolved by textbook formulae.

Meanwhile the King was on the move. He made another pass at Hull early in July, then rode down to Lincoln, across to Newark and on to Leicester, where the townsmen again refused to give up their magazine. He had to retreat, but Herefordshire, Worcestershire and Warwickshire had now declared for him, and more volunteers were trickling in. On 16 July he returned to Beverley and made another attempt on Hull, twelve miles away. But the city had now been reinforced by 1,500 troops shipped from London under the redoubtable Scots professional Sir John Meldrum, who cut the embankments on the rivers Hull and Humber, flooding the low-lying countryside.

In the meantime over in Manchester Lord Strange, trying to prevent the execution of the Militia Ordinance, was repulsed in a burst of street-fighting which conferred an unlucky immortality on one Richard Percival of Kirksmanshulme, linen weaver, the first fatal casualty of the Civil Wars. Early in August fighting was breaking out all over: in Warwickshire, where the royalist Earl of Northampton was besieging Lord Brooke in Warwick Castle; in Dorset, where Essex's brother-in-law Hertford was besieged in Sherborne Castle; and in Oxfordshire, where John Hampden was sparring with the Earl of Berkshire. The Portsmouth garrison under George Goring was also under siege.

With Hull manifestly impregnable, and the county at the best luke-warm, there was no reason for Charles to linger in Yorkshire. Early in August he marched south, calling his supporters to a general rendezvous at Nottingham on the 22nd, but even now he had no more than 500 horse and scarcely any infantry, and they 'the scum of the county' (Yorkshire), and a diversion to Coventry only resulted in another humiliating rebuff, as at Leicester and Hull. He raised his standard at Nottingham on the 22nd, but it was a dismal occasion. The high, exposed field before the Castle was swept by rain, and the herald stumbled over the wording of the proclamation of rebellion, fussily amended by the King at the last moment. According to Clarendon 'a general sadness covered the whole town', and Charles was so ill-supported still that Astley warned him 'that he could not give any assurance against his Majesty being taken out of his bed if the rebels should make a brisk attempt to that purpose'. In the night the standard blew down in the wind. Four days later, in a mood of self-doubt, Charles sent emissaries to Westminster to negotiate a truce, but they were rebuffed, as was a further delegation, headed by Lord Spencer and Lord Falkland, on 6 September. The Commons leaders were swept up in the momentum of revolution.

Nevertheless, volunteers were now arriving at Nottingham in larger numbers, and by 10 September Charles's little army had grown to 2,000 horse and 1,200 foot. Nor did he lack seasoned officers to lead them. Astley was already there, in charge of the foot, and the Catholic

Sir Arthur Aston, who was to command the dragoons at Edgehill. Aston's professional experience was more varied than most; he had served in the Russian army from 1613 to 1618, from then until 1631 in the Polish army and 1631–9 in the Swedish army. But the most spectacular recruit to arrive at Nottingham was the King's German nephew, Prince Rupert, a younger son of the Princess Elizabeth. With him came his brother Maurice and a number of other foreign professionals, notably the great engineer Bernhard de Gomme and the munitions expert Bartholemew de la Roche. They landed at Newcastle in July and reached Nottingham on 21 August.

Rupert's immediate appointment as the King's Lieutenant-General of Horse is often taken for granted, but, apart from his princely rank, it was not an obvious step at the time. He was certainly a dedicated professional soldier, daring, courageous and much in love with war, but he was only twenty-three and his actual military experience was negligible. As a teenager, on vacation from Leyden University, he had served briefly on the staff of the Stadholder Frederick Henry in the Flanders campaigns of 1633 and 1635; he was also found at the siege of Breda in 1637. In 1638 he and his elder brother Charles Lewis had raised a small force to invade the Upper Palatinate, taking with them the Scotsman James King, seconded from the Swedish army. But Rupert was captured at Vlemgo, on the Weser, after an impetuous cavalry charge which went wrong, and he and King did not meet again until the eve of Marston Moor, in 1644. He spent three years in an Imperial prison, and was only released on the personal intervention of King Charles, who had taken a liking to his young nephew during his occasional visits to England in the 1630s. Gratitude apart, he had taken an oath not to fight against the Emperor again, so it was natural enough that he should offer his sword to Charles.

Rupert's strength lay in the unusual affection he inspired in his shy, diffident uncle, and the respect he won from the troops under his immediate command. But from the first he was a 'swordsman', unhappy except in the company of other swordsmen and contemptuous of Court politics. This and his foreign birth, and the fact that he was of the blood royal, put a distance between him and the King's civilian advisers, like Sir Edward Hyde and Lord Falkland, spokesmen for constitutional royalism. But he also alienated the principal advocate of ultra-royalism, George, Lord Digby, whom many regarded as the King's evil genius. Digby fancied himself as a soldier, though with little reason; Rupert affronted him at the siege of Lichfield in 1643 and he returned to Court, where a few months later he succeeded Falkland as Secretary of State. Thereafter he made every effort to loosen the Prince's hold on the King. Even more surprising is the fact that Rupert was soon at odds with his second-in-command, Henry Wilmot, Commissary-General of Horse, though Wilmot, another swordsman, on the face of it seemed a natural ally. All in all, his presence set up disruptive polarities in the Court and Council, which were already divided enough.

As for his military abilities, he was thoroughly versed in the technicalities of war, but most of his learning was from books, and it is surprising that he could translate it into action to the extent that he did. In the early years of the war his reputation grew to prodigious heights, and he inspired in the enemy a terrified respect, building up by 1644 into an astonishing moral ascendancy. News of his coming would put armies to flight, just as it would raise men to serve him, apparently from nowhere. But his grasp of strategy, or even battle tactics, was weak, and he mismanaged the only battle in which he took sole command, Marston Moor. Nor can his reputation as a trainer of men be taken seriously; his cavalry disastrously overshot the field of battle at Edgehill in 1642, and they were still committing the same fault three years later, at Naseby. Both Wilmot and Goring were arguably his superiors as cavalry commanders, but it was the parliamentary generals, Fairfax and Cromwell, Ireton and Lambert, who learned to control their battle-happy troopers, and pull them back from the charge and into the main battle again.

At last, in mid-September, Charles abandoned the East Midlands for the time being and marched west through Leicestershire and Derbyshire to Shrewsbury, whence he could gain access to the heartland of royalism, in the Marches, Wales and Lancashire – a decision he might well have taken a month or so before. This time he insisted on disarming the county trained bands and distributing their equipment amongst his own followers, and as they went Rupert began to make cavalry sweeps down into Northamptonshire and Warwickshire, demanding money with menaces from the local magnates and 'beating up' the mansions of prominent parliamentarians, like the Earl of Stamford's at Groby near Leicester and George Marwood's at Nun Monckton – an unwelcome introduction to ruthless Continental-style warfare, for which the Prince and his brother Maurice soon became notorious. Moreover, it had been evident for some time that Charles was taking on Catholic officers, even Irish Catholics like Lord Robert Dillon and Lord Theobald Taffe, despite protestations to the contrary. On 27 September he authorised it publicly, first in the Army of the North, now being raised by the Earl of Newcastle in Northumberland and Durham, and then generally. As many as one-third of Newcastle's officers were Catholic, and so were two of the infantry regiments raised further south for the King's field army, Sir John Byron's and John Belasyse's; Belasyse himself was a prominent Yorkshire Catholic. This was a triumphant vindication of Parliament's case: that he had been led by his advisers into a popish conspiracy against his own subjects.

However, there were compensating factors. In August and September a wave of riots swept the southern clothing towns of Colchester, Cirencester and Long Melford, spreading across the Midlands to Coventry and Birmingham, then north to Manchester, Leeds, Bradford and Wakefield. The root cause was unemployment, due to a marked recession in trade, but in many places mobs spilled out into the countryside, sacking the houses of local gentry on the plea that they were royalists or papists, pulling down enclosure fences and unlawfully killing deer. It all went to confirm Charles's momentous prophecy in his Answer to the Nineteen Propositions, in June, that an attack on the Crown would only encourage the common people, the *mobile vulgus*, to 'set up for themselves, call parity and independence liberty, destroy all rights and properties, all distinctions of families and merit', and plunge the whole nation into 'a dark equal chaos of confusion'.

His considered stance as protector of the Church as by law established also paid mounting dividends. A typical royal proclamation on 12 August asked how the Church could be regarded as safe from harm 'when such licence was given to Anabaptists, Brownists and sectaries, and while coachmen, feltmakers and such mechanic persons were allowed and entertained to preach, [and] when such barbarous outrages and uproars, even in the time of divine service and the administration of the blessed sacrament, were practised without control', and the point was driven home when Parliament's army of working-class Londoners emerged from the capital in September and swarmed over the Midlands, desecrating churches, overturning altars and rabbling clergymen with manic glee.

In general terms, the question why this man or that fought on one side or the other is difficult to answer. Moreover, it is estimated that less than half the nobility and gentry, the class we know most about, played more than an involuntary part in the wars at all, and it is reasonable to suppose that this held good for the classes below them.

Many tried to temporise. In her scathing account of the Nottinghamshire nobility Lucy Hutchinson remarks that the Earl of Clare 'was very often of both parties, and I think never advantaged either' (though his brother Denzil Holles was one of the Long Parliament's leading spokesmen), and the Earl of Kingston 'divided his sons between both parties and concealed himself'. He said in 1642, 'When I take up arms with the King against Parliament, or with Parliament against the King, let a cannon bullet divide me between them.'* In fact, it was common enough, whether by accident or design, for fathers and sons, brother and brother, to choose opposite sides and stick to them. In broader terms no less than twenty-one counties tried to preserve their neutrality, by agreements between the different factions; some even tried to make their county a 'no-go area'. They all failed, of course, but in the end very few counties were wholeheartedly for one side or the other. The far northern counties, Cumberland, Westmorland and Northumberland, were solidly for the King, and so was North Wales and one or two of the Marcher counties, such as Monmouthshire and Worcestershire, and eventually Cornwall; East Anglia was pretty solidly for Parliament, though Norfolk was only secured after a tough struggle. Elsewhere John Morrill's comment on Wiltshire is generally applicable:

> Neither side can be said to contain more than a small number of determined partisans, and allegiance within both parties was a shifting rather than a stable condition. To call someone a 'royalist' or a 'parliamentarian' may mean no more than that he superficially acquiesced in a series of orders for which he had no stomach.

One thing is clear, the towns and cities, industrial or not, were solidly for Parliament; in fact, it is difficult to call to mind any towns which could be described as 'naturally' royalist: Worcester, and perhaps York. Even towns which became royalist strongholds, like Oxford, Chester and for a time Bristol, did so only after a strong opposition element had been suppressed or expelled, and Shrewsbury, despite its reputation for spotless loyalty, suddenly 'turned' in 1644. In many areas this had serious repercussions: in Devon, Lancashire, the East and West Ridings of Yorkshire, and in South Wales, the stubborn resistance and obstruction of the towns weakened the royalists' grip on counties which were otherwise loyal.

The attitude of the towns can safely be attributed to Puritanism,

---

* Which unfortunately it did. Belatedly declaring for the King in 1643, he was taken prisoner, and was being carried down the Humber in a pinnace to Hull when a shot from the royalist artillery on the north bank cut him neatly in two at the waist.

which for legal and social reasons had always flourished best in an urban environment. On the other hand, anti-Puritanism was a powerful inducement to royalism, and it has even been argued that the party which Charles I led into the first Civil War was not so much royalist as Anglican. But gut loyalty to the King, either as a person or as an institution, could often override religious doubts. Sir Edmund Verney, in a famous letter to his friend Edward Hyde, later Earl of Clarendon, said:

> My conscience is only concerned in honour and gratitude to follow my master. I have eaten his bread and served him near thirty years, and will not do so base a thing as to forsake him, and choose rather to lose my life, which I am sure to do, to preserve and defend those things which are against my conscience to defend, for . . . I have no reverence for the bishops, for whom this quarrel subsists.

He fell at Edgehill later that year, his son at Drogheda in 1649. At the other extreme was Sir Thomas Salusbury, who followed the constitutional debate conducted in the public press with close attention and an open mind, and deeply 'pondered the role of monarchy in scripture, history and the modern world', before finally deciding to join the King.

No doubt many more pondered the issues just as deeply, and the inertia in favour of monarchy was so strong that it weighed even on convinced Puritans. Captain John Hodgson said later, 'When I put my hand to the Lord's work I did it not rashly, but had many an hour, day and night, to seek God to know my way.' With this in mind it is difficult to explain why so many noblemen and gentlemen, often men of great wealth, ranged themselves against the King; on the face of it they ought to have been as rare as socialist stockbrokers or merchant bankers are today. Only a few seem to have been driven by religious fanaticism, and those who were tended to be disillusioned by the experience of defeat, like the Earl of Manchester in 1644 (p. 121 below). It is doubtful if many of them were Puritan at all, the Earl of Essex amongst them. Their real motive was a profound personal mistrust of and dislike for Charles I, which it was neither polite nor politic to voice too openly. Parliament continued to insist that its aim was to rescue an innocent monarch from the evil advisers who held him in thrall, just as the opposition to Sir Robert Walpole a century later accused him of having George II 'in chains'. Almost to the end of the first Civil War the official battle cry of the parliamentary armies was 'King and

Parliament', and in August 1643 Henry Marten was expelled from the House of Commons for proposing Charles's deposition. But it was a pretence which grew steadily thinner.

This produced an extraordinary instability. Lord Savile, for instance, was one of the most aggressive leaders of opposition right up to the very eve of the war, when he declared for the King and was expelled from Parliament. But in 1643 he was arrested at Newark on suspicion of treason; Charles pardoned him, but he reneged again in 1645 and was outlawed. Parliament reluctantly took him back in 1646. At the other extreme was the Queen's favourite, the Earl of Holland, who declared for Parliament in 1642, then fled to Oxford a year later; meeting with a cool reception there he returned to London, trusted by neither side. But on the outbreak of the second Civil War in 1648 he declared for the King again, was captured and executed (pp. 184–5 below). As for the Scotsman Sir John Urry, his name became a byword for treachery. Starting on Parliament's side in 1642, he changed his allegiance twice in the first Civil War, then returned to Scotland, where he switched sides again. Defeated by Montrose at Auldearn in 1645, he joined his second expedition in 1650, only to be captured at Corbisdale and beheaded by an exasperated Edinburgh government. Urry was obviously a natural turncoat, but the weakening of the social structure evident quite early in the war caused some parliamentarians to think again. The defection of Sir John Hotham, governor of Hull, in 1643 was a *cause célèbre*, ending in his execution together with his son. The son said that if the war went on 'the mutinous people of the whole kingdom will presently rise in mighty numbers', and 'set up for themselves, to the utter ruin of all the nobility and gentry'. Earlier that year the mere arrival of Queen Henrietta Maria at Bridlington was enough to 'turn' the parliamentary governor of Scarborough, Sir Hugh Chomley. It is not surprising that by 1644 the faith of the rank and file in its upper-class leadership was seriously eroded.

As for the motives of the rank and file themselves, they are largely unreachable, though there is plenty of evidence for Puritan feeling in the towns, as we have seen, down to quite a low social level. This was particularly evident in London. But in the absence of muster rolls, except for the militia, we can only guess at the composition of the main field armies on either side.

The King recruited mainly by commissions of array, another medieval revival which Parliament regarded with scorn, but which seems to have been reasonably effective in the beginning, when it was accompanied by the promise of pay. Noblemen and gentlemen on both sides were also encouraged to raise cavalry regiments, or troops, equipped at their own expense, though not paid by them. As early as January 1642 Sir William Waller provided 'four bay horses with star on their foreheads, their riders John Chambers, James Hosier, Thomas Ward and Thomas Cooper, armed with carbiners [carbines], pistols, buff coats and swords, each horse and arms valued one with another at £26 apiece'. Wealthy men like Sir Arthur Haselrigg and John Hampden raised their own regiments. There is also no doubt that in outlying areas of royalist ascendancy, the northernmost counties, parts of Wales and the Marches, where seigneurial authority was still taken for granted, landowners simply led their tenants into action, though in a more settled area like Cheshire the Earl of Derby had to threaten them with eviction, not always successfully. It is reasonable to suppose that parliamentary grandees like Lord Brooke, the Earl of Warwick and the Earl of Denbigh used similar methods, though after Edgehill Oliver Cromwell dismissed Hampden's troopers as 'most of them old decayed serving-men and tapsters, and such kind of fellows', in contrast with the royalists, who could call on 'gentlemen's sons, younger sons and persons of quality'.

In fact, such evidence as we have points to the fact that even in 1642 both sides were recruiting into the infantry the surplus elements in the population: younger sons or brothers, the bankrupt, the chronically unemployed, the local bad hats and ne'er-do-wells. In his classic *History of Myddle* Richard Gough lists fourteen men who went to war from this tiny Shropshire hamlet; they included a notorious tearaway whose father had been hanged for felony, one of the Gough family servants, a bastard nephew of the village blacksmith, a younger brother of the village innkeeper, a wandering tailor of no fixed address, and four complete drop-outs, a father and three sons who lived in a cave outside the village with no visible means of support. (One of the sons was later hanged by the army for horse stealing.) Of only two others, 'a very hopeful young man' and 'a pretty little fellow', had Gough anything good to say.

Unsatisfactory as they were, men like this were drilled into shape, and when they were lost, by death or desertion, they were extremely difficult to replace. As we shall see, by the autumn of 1643, only a year into the war, both sides were suffering from a shortage of infantry, and in 1644 this anaemia began to spread to the cavalry, on the royalist side at least. We know as little of the social composition of the cavalry as of the infantry, but cavalry troopers must have been drawn from the yeomanry or above; working-class labourers would not have had the same ability to handle a horse, especially in combat conditions. Oliver Cromwell was accused of deliberately recruiting the Eastern Association cavalry from the artisan or 'blue-collar' classes in East Anglia, but essentially he was taking what he could get; he was on record as saying that he preferred gentlemen when he could get them (p. 77 below). It is significant that the most enduring royalist cavalry units were the Northern horse, which boasted an unusually high proportion of troopers from gentry families, they and their officers drawn from the same region, and Rupert and Maurice's brigades of horse, well-staffed with professional officers and, it seems, a stiffening of foreign troopers.

We shall meet foreign officers on both sides in the Civil Wars, probably, though not certainly, accompanied by foreign soldiers. We must suppose that this was one reason why both sides were able to lick their armies into shape so quickly in the autumn of 1642. But there were other reasons. Charles I's drive for an 'Exact Militia', unpopular as it was, had been far from fruitless. Beginning in January 1626, eighty-four experienced NCOs were brought over from the Low Countries and shared out amongst the counties for three months; their task, to teach company officers the basics of drill and tactics, which they could then hand on to their men. Some of them stayed on into 1629, and the counties did not jib at paying them their six shillings a day plus expenses. The attempt to carry this 'muster-master' system over into the 1630s roused resentment, but it may well be that the recalcitrant, as usual, have attracted more attention than the compliant. Some towns, we know, took defence very seriously: Great Yarmouth hired a foreign professional, 'Captain de Eugaine', to drill its trained bands, and Manchester engaged a German engineer, Johann Rosworm, at £60 a year, which proved an excellent investment. Moreover, beginning in 1635 the government made a determined effort to bring militia weapons up to standard in quality as well as quantity, and the eagerness of both sides to commandeer the county arsenals in 1642 suggests that they were well worth having. It is rather astonishing, too, that many noblemen reported for duty in 1642 bringing with them light artillery pieces, sakers and even drakes. There was also a buoyant market for books on the military art. William Barriffe's *Military Discipline*, explaining the Swedish system of war, was published in 1635, second edition 1639. This was matched in 1637 by Henry Hexham's *Principles of the Art Military as Practised in the Wars of the United Netherlands*, and the Irish mercenary Gerrard Barry had already outlined the tactics of the victorious Spanish tercios in his *Discourse of Military Discipline* (1634).

Moreover, the refusal of successive British governments to undertake direct military intervention on the Continent after about 1598 did not hinder the participation of English volunteers on quite a large scale. Ever since 1572 there had been an English contingent in the Netherlands, and when Elizabeth pulled out in 1598 the English brigade, now numbering about 8,000 men, a quarter of them Scots, under Sir Francis Vere, was simply taken over into the Dutch army. In fact, Maurice of Nassau regarded this brigade as one of his finest, and Vere one of his best lieutenants; he gave him most of the credit for the Dutch victory over the Spaniards at Nieuport in 1600, and he led the defence of Ostend in the first crucial months of the Spanish assault, from July 1601 to March 1602. The epic siege of Ostend, which lasted into September 1604, caught the imagination of the English public in a big way, and volunteers poured over by the shipload. (Which was just as well: for three years 20,000 Spaniards hammered away at 3,000 English and 3,000 Dutch, and during that time at least 200,000 men died.)

Francis Vere was succeeded by his younger brother Horace, who had been fighting alongside him since 1592. During the Spanish–Dutch truce of 1609–21 Sir Horace led a contingent of 2,000 men to the aid of Venice in the War of Gradisca against Austria (1615–17),* and in 1621–3, as we have seen, he was commissioned by James I to lead an expeditionary force to the Palatinate. On both occasions he was accompanied by the young William Waller, son of the Constable of Dover Castle and just down from Oxford. Waller was one of 300 volunteers who rode half-way across Europe in 1621 to escort the Princess Elizabeth, *soi-disant* Queen of Bohemia, to safety in the Netherlands, a service for which he was knighted. Waller, Essex, Goring, almost all the Civil War generals we care to mention, had had hard experience in the Low Countries war; in fact, the siege of Breda in 1637 was a kind of 'pre-union' of Civil War notables: Philip Skippon was there, George Goring, the spoilt son-in-law of the millionaire Earl of Cork, the Princes Rupert and Maurice, and George Monck. Monck, born of a middling gentry family in Devon, joined the Cadiz expedition

---

* There seems to have been no objection to Englishmen serving in Catholic armies, except those of Spain. As soon as Waller laid down his command in 1645 he was seeking to command a Venetian expedition against Crete, Puritan as he was. The runaway London apprentice Sydenham Poyntz rose to high command in the Imperial army before returning in 1645 to take over Parliament's Northern army.

in 1625 as a volunteer in the regiment of his kinsman Sir Richard Grenville, and went on to the Île de Rhé in 1627 under Buckingham, when he was commissioned in the field. In 1629 he enlisted in the Dutch army, but he returned in 1639 to take up a commission as Lieutenant-Colonel of Foot in the Scots campaign, and in 1642 he was offered his own regiment in Ireland.

As for Sir Horace Vere, he was now the living embodiment of the English military tradition; James I appointed him Master-General of the Ordnance in 1623 and Charles I raised him to the peerage as Lord Vere of Tilbury in 1625. But in that same year he is found at the siege of Breda, where he had to take command of the whole Dutch army on Maurice's sudden death. He was back in the Low Countries in 1629 and again in 1632, though he died in his bed in London in 1635.

He had no male heir, and his peerage died with him, but his daughter Anne married young Thomas Fairfax, of Denton in Yorkshire, scion of another fighting clan. His grandfather, Thomas Fairfax the elder, was knighted at the siege of Rouen in 1591, and stayed on in the Low Countries for a few years under Sir Francis Vere; but under James I he took up a diplomatic career, and on his retirement in 1627 he purchased a Scots peerage, Fairfax of Cameron, for the comparatively modest sum of £1,500. Of his twelve sons four are known to have died in action: William and John in the Palatinate in 1621, Peregrine at La Rochelle in 1627, and Thomas, rather mysteriously, in Turkey that same year. He died in 1640, and his eldest surviving son, Ferdinando, 2nd Lord Fairfax, was appointed commander of Parliament's forces in Yorkshire in 1642. Ferdinando's son Thomas, the future commander of the New Model, followed the family tradition; he served in the Low Countries campaigns of 1626 and 1629, and though his plan to join the Swedish army in 1632 was vetoed by his father he mustered a troop of dragoons from his Yorkshire estates for the Scots campaign of 1639 and was knighted by the King.

Both sides could also call on the services of a number of Scots professionals who were left stranded by the withdrawal of the Covenant army in 1641 and its subsequent demobilisation. Many of them enjoyed the cachet of having served the great Gustavus; indeed, it is estimated that there were as many as 20,000 Scots serving in Germany in the 1630s, and Gustavus is said to have had three generals, eight colonels, five lieutenant-colonels, eleven majors and more than thirty captains, all called 'Munro' or 'Monro'. But there were at least a few Scots officers in the Imperial army, too, for three of them had the dubious distinction of participating in the murder of their former commander, Wallenstein, at Eger in Saxony in 1634. (The other assassins were an Italian, a Spaniard and four Irishmen.)

King Charles was particularly delighted when he was joined at Shrewsbury in September 1642 by Patrick Ruthven, with twenty-nine other Scots officers. Ruthven had entered the Swedish army as a young man in 1606, and rose by merit to the rank of colonel in 1630, lieutenant-general in 1635. He was one of Gustavus Adolphus' favourite drinking companions as well as one of his most trusted officers, and he was created Count Kirchberg in the Swedish peerage in 1632. He retired in 1638 but was called out the following year to act as the King's Muster-Master-General in Scotland; he had precious few Scots to muster, but he sustained a nine-week siege in Edinburgh Castle and was raised to the peerage as Lord Ruthven. At Shrewsbury he was created Earl of Forth, and a few weeks later, on the eve of the battle of Edgehill, he was appointed to command the King's main field army, a post he held until the autumn of 1644.

James King was another Scots veteran of the Swedish service; by 1636 he had risen to the rank of lieutenant-general, and he commanded the foot under Marshal Baner at the battle of Wittstock later that year. In 1642 he offered to serve Charles I in return for a peerage and a pension of £1,000 a year. Predictably, he received his peerage, as Lord Eythin, but not his pension, and he withdrew to Hamburg. However, Charles gave way, and in January 1643 King joined him at Oxford as Lieutenant-General of Foot, though he was almost immediately sent north to act as second-in-command to the Earl of Newcastle.

But most Scots officers, understandably, offered their services to Parliament. We have already seen how Sir William Balfour, high in the King's favour as he was, courted dismissal from the Lieutenancy of the Tower in December 1641 (p. 26 above). In 1642 he joined Essex's army as a colonel of horse. Sir John Meldrum, a Scots entrepreneur and professional soldier who had been something of a favourite with James I, sent a public letter to the King in 1642 explaining why he was withdrawing the allegiance he had given his father. He was to prove one of Parliament's most enterprising and successful generals, though he was never given command of a field army. In fact, jealousy and suspicion of the Scots militated against such an appointment, but Scots officers were much sought after by all the parliamentary generals; Sir William Waller had five Scots colonels out of eleven in 1643, as well as many Scots captains, and there were thirteen Scots colonels in the

Army of the Eastern Association. It is significant that in 1644 the commander of the Eastern Association, the Earl of Manchester, unhesitatingly accepted the newly arrived Scots professional Lawrence Crawford as his second-in-command, though it meant demoting Cromwell (p. 114 below).

In fact, Manchester, Cromwell, the Earl of Newcastle and King Charles were the only senior field officers in the first Civil War who lacked any previous military experience, but they were well served by their professional officers. It is reasonable to suppose, though difficult to prove, that they could also call on a cadre of seasoned NCOs and men returning from the German and Low Countries wars. The Anglo-Scots brigade in the Dutch army numbered 6,000 in 1621, 12,000 in 1624 and 17,000 in 1625. Here was a huge reservoir of trained men, and as we have seen Charles I called back some of their NCOs in the 1620s to act as muster-masters to the militia. It is safe to assume that some, perhaps many, of them returned to England in 1642. Certainly the idea that the Civil Wars were little more than a series of amateur scuffles will not stand up to serious examination.

Men who were bred to war, and who in the case of officers and NCOs were being well paid for it, had little interest in the speedy termination of the struggle, but this feeling was not confined to the professionals. We must beware of assuming that the war was obnoxious to all those who took part, and too much emphasis has been placed on the views of famous individuals who hated 'this unnatural war', as Clarendon called it more than once, or 'this war without an enemy', in Waller's memorable phrase. The moral revulsion which prompted the Earl of Leicester to think in 1642 that 'it would be a shame for any private man to be happy, and a sin to think himself so', which apparently drove the young Lord Falkland to ride straight into a hail of enemy fire at First Newbury, knowing he would be killed, was certainly not universal. Many officers and men are found wandering from area to area in 1643 and 1644 in search of fighting and loot, and it is apparent that many of the leaders on both sides positively enjoyed the war – Rupert, for instance, George Goring and Oliver Cromwell, for all his pious protestations. Many local worthies eagerly seized the opportunity for a more active life, enhanced fame, plunder and personal aggrandisement – like Sir John Gell, for example, in Derbyshire, Sir William Brereton in Cheshire, Sir Richard Grenville in Cornwall and Sir Anthony Weldon in Kent. Cromwell reminded the Commons in December 1644 that many outside the House thought they were prolonging the war for their own advantage, and that acerbic veteran Thomas Birch later remembered, 'When I was in the Army some said, "Let us not go this way, lest the war be ended too soon."'. This is an aspect of the Civil Wars we too easily overlook.

# 4

# THE OPENING
# CAMPAIGN

The year was ebbing fast, and winter approaching, but the King stayed on at Shrewsbury through September, waiting for recruits. Nor did he wait in vain. Men soon began to pour in from North Wales, Cheshire, Denbighshire and Lancashire. Money poured in, too, and plate; a mint was soon set up, and volunteers were offered an acceptable 4s 4d a week. By the end of the month he had over 6,000 foot and 2,000 horse, with more arriving every day.

Meanwhile the Earl of Essex left London on 9 September, preceded by about 6,000 foot and 4,000 horse, drawn from London, Surrey and Middlesex. At Northampton they rendezvoused with contingents from the Midlands and the Eastern counties, including a troop of horse led by Captain Oliver Cromwell, MP for Cambridge. (Most of the celebrities of later years were present on this campaign, though few distinguished themselves; Cromwell's role at Edgehill is obscure, Waller's ignominious.) A rebel army it might be, but its regimental and brigade commanders rivalled the King's in social status; amongst the colonels of regiments were the Earls of Peterborough and Stamford, Lord Brooke and Viscount Mandeville, soon to succeed to the earldom of Manchester, Viscount Saye and Sele and Lord Rocheford, as well as MPs Denzil Holles, John Hampden and Sir Arthur Haselrigg. They were well supported, too, by seasoned professionals; in fact, Parliament had done its best to recruit as many such officers as it could that summer, ostensibly for service in Ireland, and as early as July it had 168 of them in its pay. Thus the inexperienced Earl of Bedford, Lieutenant-General of Horse, was backed up by the Scots professionals Sir William Balfour and Sir James Ramsay, and the Commissary-General, commanding the left wing of the cavalry, was the Dutch mercenary, Hans Behre, with his own troop of Dutchmen. Similarly, the Earl of Peterborough was technically in charge of the artillery, but he was advised by a Dutch (or French) expert, Philibert Emmanuel de Boyce (or du Bois). We also catch a glimpse of the exotic Captain Carlo Fantom, a Croatian who spoke thirteen languages; Essex held him 'in high esteem, for he was an admirable horse officer, and taught the cavalry of the army the way of fighting with horse'.

Essex's stately farewell to the two Houses, and his ceremonial exit from London, suggest a cult of personality which the King himself encouraged by making the Earl the principal target of his propaganda. Essex himself wanted to assume a proconsular role; he asked Parliament not only for the authority to wage war as he saw fit but also for plenipotentiary power to conclude peace. Parliament refused, of course, but for two years his critics were unable to weaken its blind faith in his leadership, however manifest his incompetence. Indeed, he blundered at the very outset, in allowing his new army, its troops mostly raw and inexperienced, its command structure yet to shake down, to precede him to Northampton. On the way they pillaged the towns and countryside as ruthlessly as Rupert's notorious troopers, and they arrived in disorder, with one City regiment already threatening to desert for lack of pay – a recurrent theme in later years.

Moreover, once he had pulled the army together, Essex found it difficult to decide on his future strategy. The King was still at Shrewsbury; once he had enough troops he would presumably march on London, but Essex was not anxious to bring him to a pitched battle in Shropshire, far from his own base, and after advancing tentatively on Coventry on 19 September, as if to block Charles's anticipated advance, he turned away towards Worcester, though there seemed little point in harassing a royalist town which if captured could not be held.

Charles responded by detaching Rupert with about a thousand horse to go to Worcester's aid. Arriving first, Rupert ordered the governor, Sir John Byron, to withdraw the garrison, but in the process he clashed with Essex's advance guard of a thousand horse and dragoons, under Sir John Brown, at Powick Bridge, south of the city. In this, the first

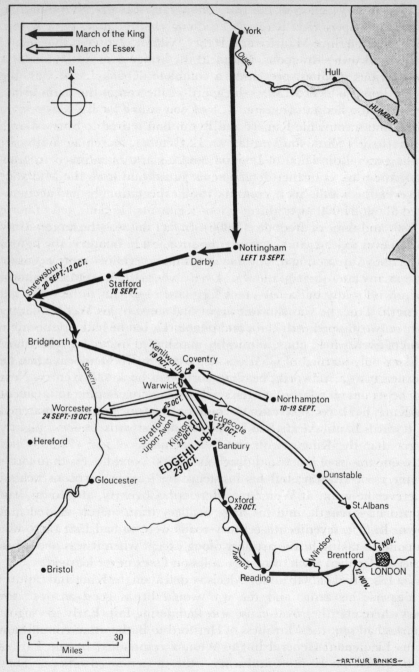

**THE CAMPAIGN OF EDGEHILL**

Within the map:

March of the King
March of Essex

N

York

Hull

HUMBER

Ouse

Nottingham
*LEFT 13 SEPT.*

Derby

Shrewsbury
*20 SEPT.-12 OCT.*

Stafford
*18 SEPT.*

Bridgnorth

Severn

Kenilworth
*19 OCT.*

Coventry

Warwick

Worcester
*24 SEPT.-19 OCT.*

*25 OCT.*

Northampton
*10-19 SEPT.*

Stratford
-upon-Avon

Kineton
*22 OCT.*

Edgecote
*22 OCT.*

EDGEHILL
*23 OCT.*

Banbury

Hereford

Gloucester

Dunstable

St.Albans

Oxford
*29 OCT.*

Thames

Windsor

Brentford
*8 NOV.*

Bristol

Reading

LONDON
*12 NOV.*

0    30
Miles

~ARTHUR BANKS~

formal military action of the war, the royalist cavalry established an immediate superiority. Rupert's headlong charge, along with Byron, Lord Digby, Prince Maurice and Henry Wilmot, shattered the enemy, and only Brown's dragoons, who held the bridge over the Teme for a few precious minutes, prevented a complete débâcle. As it was, the fleeing horse panicked Essex's lifeguard in the van of the main army, and they also fled in confusion. It took some time for Essex to restore order, and meanwhile Rupert and Byron had retired to Shrewsbury.

Charles left Shrewsbury at last on 12 October, marching south-east in the general direction of London, and his army continued to grow along the way, as further detachments joined him from the Midlands and even the South. Soon, contrary to all expectation, he had accumulated about 24,000 men: thirteen foot regiments (15,600), ten of horse (5,000) and three of dragoons (3,000). In fact this was the largest army he was ever to lead, and certainly the strongest in infantry; the figures given above are notional, but they are almost certainly more accurate than at any later stage of the war. Even a year later it would be almost unknown for any but a few crack lifeguard regiments to be up to full strength. True, he was short of arms, and some of his Welsh infantry were only equipped with clubs and pitchforks, but he had a respectable train of twenty field guns, admirably marshalled by Sir John Heydon.

Essex only learned of Charles's departure on 18 October, when he was nearly at Kenilworth, heading north-east back to Coventry. Next day he set out on a forced march south to Kineton, hoping to intercept the King, but he was too late; he could only pursue him as he marched on towards Banbury. He had left Northampton with an army slightly larger than the King's, with eighteen regiments of foot (21,500) and sixty-one troops of horse and dragoons (4,200), and no less than forty-six pieces of artillery; but his insistence on leaving garrisons behind wherever he went, at Worcester, Hereford, Coventry, and so on, had sapped his strength, and his huge artillery train merely slowed him down. In fact, seventeenth-century roads were so bad that there was no point in taking heavy artillery along except when it was needed to besiege a fortified town or castle – a lesson Essex never learned.

Yet Essex had only to inflict a decisive defeat on the King and capture or disperse his army and the war would be as good as over, for everywhere else the royal cause was foundering fast. Early in August Charles had sent the Marquess of Hertford to Bath with a commission as his Lieutenant-General in the West, accompanied by the Earl of Bath, Sir Ralph Hopton and a few other experienced officers. They quickly recruited about a thousand infantry from the Dorset trained bands, and a few volunteer troops of horse, and at first carried all before them. But Somerset, with its depressed clothing industry and its militant Puritanism, soon threw up levies estimated at 10,000 (no doubt an exaggeration), and Parliament despatched another 7,000 men from London under the Earl of Bedford. Hertford's forces melted away, and he was soon reduced to two hundred horse and four hundred foot. He decided to march them to Minehead on the coast and ship them over to South Wales; he then set off at all speed to join the King, arriving in time for the battle of Edgehill. Bedford, similarly, turned back to rejoin Essex's army. Hopton and a small group of officers rode on down the north coast of Devon and into Cornwall, but they were apparently of no account.

Nor was the situation much better in the North. In June the Earl of Newcastle had been appointed Lieutenant-General in the North; he had seized Newcastle and Tynemouth, giving the King an invaluable port of entry as well as control over the valuable Newcastle coalfield, and he had begun to recruit a well-drilled force of 2,000 horse and 6,000 foot from the staunchly conservative Border counties of Durham, Northumberland, Cumberland and Westmorland. But his departure from Yorkshire, followed by the King's, left that county wide open, and the woollen towns of the West Riding (Leeds, Bradford, Wakefield and Huddersfield), a prey to the same recession which had hit Somerset, were aggressively parliamentarian, and offered a reservoir of potential fighting men who were speedily organised by Ferdinando, Lord Fairfax, and his son Sir Thomas. At the same time Hotham and Meldrum, still ensconced in Hull, were mounting cavalry sweeps as far east as Selby and as far north as Driffield. The royalists at York could only appeal to Newcastle for help. He agreed, but on a semi-mercenary basis; they were to provide £8,000 a month to pay his troops, raised by a county assessment. Even so, it was 1 December before he started south. In Lancashire the position was much the same; the countryside, deeply conservative and here strongly tinged with Catholicism, was a prime recruiting-ground for the King, but the local royalist grandees could never overcome the stubborn resistance of the towns long enough to gain control of the county as a whole. In September Lord Strange made another unsuccessful attempt on Manchester; the defences organised by Rosworm were too strong for him. Early in October he gave up, and retreated north to his family home at Lathom House, near Ormskirk.

Nevertheless, Essex still had to dispose of the King's field army. He caught up with Charles on the afternoon of 22 October at Edgehill, between Stratford-on-Avon and Banbury, but Charles was barring the road to London, instead of vice-versa, as intended, and was occupying a slight ridge (the 'hill' in 'Edgehill'), which gave him ground advantage.

Come the morning of the 23rd neither side was eager to begin hostilities. Essex was still waiting for his artillery and some of his infantry to come up, and the royalist high command was disrupted by a quarrel between Rupert and the commanding general, the Earl of Lindsey, over whether the infantry should be drawn up on the Dutch or the Swedish pattern – symbolic of their dependence on Continental example, and symptomatic of Charles's inability to control his staff. The Sergeant-Major-General of Foot, Sir Jacob Astley, who had longer experience in Europe than Lindsey or Rupert put together, prudently stood aside. Lindsey, overruled by the King, promptly resigned, put himself at the head of his foot regiment, and was killed in the subsequent battle. The Scottish veteran Patrick Ruthven, Earl of Forth, took over, and held onto the post for two years. He kept a low profile, but it must be assumed that he was the principal director of the royalist field army until he gave way to Rupert in 1644.

Both armies were drawn up in the conventional way, more or less standard in Civil War battles thereafter where numbers permitted. In the centre stood the infantry brigades, drawn up in two lines six deep, with the pikemen in the centre of each brigade, musketeers on the flanks, and with the cavalry regiments drawn up on each wing in roughly equal numbers. (By convention the right wing was led by the senior cavalry officer, the lieutenant-general, the left by the officer immediately below him, the commissary-general.) The heavy artillery was at the rear, where it could fire over the heads of its own troops; the light field pieces, from 'sakers' (firing a 5-pound shot) downwards, were stationed in the front line between the infantry brigades, sometimes firing 'case shot' or primitive shrapnel, usually nails and scrap iron in canvas bags.

Ideally all the infantry were provided with some sort of armour, at the minimum the famous buff leather tunic or coat, capable of turning a sword thrust; they might also have steel helmets ('pots') and back and breast plates ('backs' and 'breast'), though these were obviously onerous on long summer marches.* The musketeers were equipped

---

* In October 1644 Sir William Waller, a poor disciplinarian, asked the Committee for Both Kingdoms to replace five hundred backs, breasts and pots discarded by his men 'in the heat of summer'. The Committee's reply is not recorded.

with the matchlock, a crude and inaccurate weapon, but capable of killing or maiming at two to three hundred yards. (Almost any shot wound was ultimately fatal, though men commonly recovered from sword or pike thrusts.) Its main disadvantage was the time it took to reload after each shot: first, the powder was dropped down the barrel and tamped down with a rod (though paper cartridges were coming into use), then the ball, followed by a wad to hold it in place. The powder was then ignited by a length of match (flax soaked in saltpetre and dried) which the musketeer carried lit at both ends when in sight of the enemy. Gustavus Adolphus had introduced the tactic of making his front rank kneel, the second crouch and the third stand, this achieving a mass volley; their place was then taken by another three ranks coming from behind while they reloaded. Alternatively the first rank would fire, then retire to the rear to reload, followed by the second rank and so on. It is not usually possible to determine which tactic was being used in any particular Civil War battle.

The superior flint-lock musket, whose action resembled that of a modern petrol lighter, was issued to the companies guarding the artillery train, where lighted match was not permitted. Because of the expense it was not made the standard infantry weapon until 1685. Some cavalry troopers carried a flint-lock carbine, or short-barrelled musket, and Cromwell re-equipped the army with this weapon in 1649, but in the first Civil War they usually carried a pair of flint-lock pistols, or sometimes the more advanced wheel-locks, fired by a clockwork device wound up with a spanner.

The pikemen, conventionally regarded as superior in status to the musketeers, though they were often paid less, carried a steel-shod pike at least sixteen feet long, though it was not unknown for troops on long marches to saw a foot or two off, to the fury of their officers. Infantrymen also carried a short sword, for in-fighting, but since they all too often damaged them by using them to chop firewood and the like, some units were re-equipped with axes, which were equally effective in battle. The pike was usually thrust forward at an angle of about fifty degrees, so that it would meet the chest of an oncoming horse, with the hilt jammed against the instep, but more complex formations were sometimes used, with a second rank holding their weapons horizontally at shoulder height. The theory was that after a few musket volleys the opposing infantry would advance to 'push of pike', but the pikes were more commonly used as a defence against cavalry attacks, with the musketeers sheltering behind or between the pikemen.

As we have seen, a cavalry trooper usually carried two pistols, plus a short sword or cutlass; he wore the basic armour of back, breast and pot, and usually some protection for his thighs, if only thigh-length boots. A few regiments of 'cuirassiers' were equipped with articulated plate armour and a lobster-tail helmet with nose guard; Sir Arthur Haselrigg's 'Lobsters', equipped at his own expense, are well-known. Many rejected such armour as too hot and heavy, but it proved its worth to Haselrigg at Roundway Down in 1643; unhorsed, he took three point-blank pistol shots and several sword-thrusts before being rescued. However, one wonders how many armourers were readily available who could service or repair such equipment.

Dragoons were essentially mobile support troops, equipped with flint-lock muskets or carbines and mounted on inferior nags; they dismounted and fought on foot. (In 1645 the standard price for a dragoon horse was £4, as against £9 for a cavalry horse; a dragoon saddle cost 7s 6d, a troop saddle 16s 6d.) But their increasing usefulness, particularly as marksmen posted along the side of a battlefield to harass enemy cavalry, enhanced their status, and in 1645 the New Model Army boasted a crack regiment of 1,000 dragoons under John Okey.

As for tactics, the theory was that a cavalry troop (of sixty to eighty men, six troops to a regiment) advanced at a quick trot in six or seven ranks, each rank firing off its pistols at the infantry as they came within range, then wheeling away, to return *en masse* with their swords. This was the Dutch tactic, apparently used by Parliament's cavalry at the beginning of the war, though it is difficult to be sure. The Swedish tactic, supposed to have been introduced in England by Rupert, was to charge at full gallop in three ranks, forming a kind of phalanx, each man's knee locked behind his neighbour's to prevent the horses rearing away, pistol fire being reserved for the moment of impact or just before.

This was the theory. In actuality, in all the great set-piece battles of the Civil Wars, beginning with Edgehill, the cavalry were drawn up on each wing facing each other, and charged at each other first, almost as if engaged in a separate battle. Only when the opposing cavalry had been routed, by the impact of the charge, backed up by pistol and sword, did the victors turn on the enemy infantry; but by then their pistols were discharged, and it is not clear that they were reloaded in the saddle; we know that many troopers just threw them away, hoping to retrieve them, or their equivalent, later. In a cavalry *v.* cavalry encounter the horse which charged first had a clear advantage, and Waller was to insist that his men advanced at the trot rather than receive an enemy charge standing still. However, it is clear that the victorious cavalry often found it very difficult to break down a well-disciplined infantry formation with their swords alone, and at close range the toll on horses was horrendous; at Lansdown Captain Hardy's troop lost two men and ten horses charging against pikes, and at Naseby, to take another random example, Sir Philip Monckton had three horses killed under him and survived the battle on a fourth.* The cavalry lance had now been discarded, except on ceremonial parades, but it is apparent that it was still the best weapon against infantry. It had been retained by a few Scots regiments, and Lord Balgonie's lancers inflicted heavy damage on one of the royalist foot regiments at Marston Moor in 1644. Another such regiment gave Cromwell a few awkward moments at Preston in 1648. In fact, after two hundred years of fruitless experiment the lance was readopted in the early nineteenth century as the standard cavalry weapon in the British army. However, once the enemy's cavalry had been defeated his infantry was doomed, though it was often subdued only after a desperate hand-to-hand mêlée, with heavy casualties on both sides.

At Edgehill the proceedings began about one o'clock in the afternoon with an exchange of artillery fire lasting about an hour. Little damage was done, but it induced the royalist army to move down the hill so as to bring their guns to bear. (It was difficult to depress the guns sufficiently to fire down hill without the shot rolling out of the barrel or landing amongst one's own troops.)

The battle proper then began with a thunderous cavalry charge by Rupert on the right wing, his men riding at full tilt and reserving their pistol fire until the last moment. The inexperienced enemy cavalry fired off their own pistols then fled, taking with them in the rout four of their own infantry regiments on the left flank. (Some infantry officers, mounting their horses, only drew rein when they reached London, with news of a total defeat.) But instead of wheeling about and attacking the remaining enemy infantry from the flank Rupert galloped on regardless as far as Kineton village, a mile or more in the rear, where he fell on Essex's baggage train, which was of no military importance whatsoever at this stage. It was at least an hour before he returned, his men tired and his horses blown. Much the same could be said of the

---

* Horses were entirely expendable, and no sentimentality was wasted on them. Thus we know the name of Prince Rupert's poodle, 'Boy', a casualty of Marston Moor, but of none of his horses, and the same could be said of Cromwell, Fairfax, the King and so on. A senior officer would have six to ten horses available anyway.

royalist left wing, under Henry Wilmot; sweeping away the opposing cavalry and at least one foot regiment, he too disappeared into the wild blue yonder. Only Sir Charles Lucas had the sense to rally about two hundred men and launch them at the rear of Essex's army, only to be involved in a general mêlée. Lucas was to display similar self-discipline at Marston Moor in 1644, and he was one of the few royalist cavalry officers who did.

Meanwhile Astley, encouraged by the cavalry's obvious success, ordered the royalist infantry forward against the enemy, assuming that the cavalry would soon return to support him. Alas, this is what would have happened in Pomerania or Swabia, but not in Warwickshire. Instead, the infantry were left to slog it out by push of pike, and to make matters worse Wilmot had failed to take out the two enemy cavalry regiments of Sir William Balfour and Sir Philip Stapleton, who now led their troopers, pistols reloaded, through the gaps between their own brigades of foot and fell on Lord Feilding's brigade and broke it, then charged up the hill right to the royalist gun positions. Essex now ordered in his reserves, and they began to push the whole royalist army back. The royal lifeguards, the 'King's Red Regiment', suffered grievous losses, and for a time the King himself was in some danger; his standard-bearer, Sir Edmund Verney, was killed and the standard captured, though it was fortuitously recaptured soon after by Lucas's troopers, still hacking about in the rear of the parliamentary positions. By now the Earl of Lindsey had been killed and Lord Feilding captured, and all the remaining royalist infantry commanders – Byron, Gerard, Belasyse and Astley himself – had been wounded to a greater or less degree.

However, Charles went about personally rallying his men, and the belated return of the runaway royalist horse about five o'clock checked the enemy infantry. Night was falling, and both sides were probably short of ammunition. Another full cavalry charge at this stage might have given the royalists an overwhelming victory – so it was later said – but men and horses were exhausted. The two sides drew off from one another, but they spent the night on or near the battlefield. No one was clear who had won, and some of Charles's advisers urged him to retreat towards South Wales in search of reinforcements. But he refused. At daybreak the two armies were still in sight of one another, but neither of them had the stomach for another fight; it had been a damp, wretchedly cold night, few of the men on either side had eaten for more than twenty-four hours, and it is doubtful if their horses had been watered either.

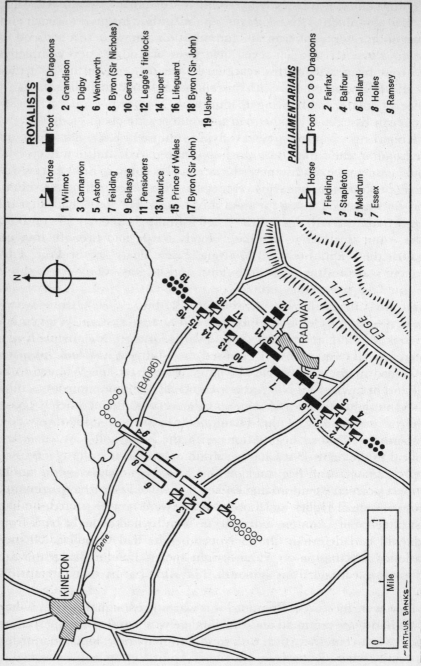

**ROYALISTS**

▲ Horse  ■ Foot  ●●● Dragoons

| 1 Wilmot | 2 Grandison |
| 3 Carnarvon | 4 Digby |
| 5 Aston | 6 Wentworth |
| 7 Feilding | 8 Byron (Sir Nicholas) |
| 9 Belasyse | 10 Gerard |
| 11 Pensioners | 12 Legge's firelocks |
| 13 Maurice | 14 Rupert |
| 15 Prince of Wales | 16 Lifeguard |
| 17 Byron (Sir John) | 18 Byron (Sir John) |
| | 19 Usher |

*PARLIAMENTARIANS*

▲ Horse  ▢ Foot  ○○○ Dragoons

| 1 Fielding | 2 Fairfax |
| 3 Stapleton | 4 Balfour |
| 5 Meldrum | 6 Ballard |
| 7 Essex | 8 Holles |
| | 9 Ramsey |

N

(B4086)

19
18
16
15
14
13
12
11
10
9
8
7
6
5
4
3
2
1

RADWAY

EDGE HILL

KINETON

Dene

0 ——— Mile 1

~ARTHUR BANKS~

THE BATTLE OF EDGEHILL

Eventually it was Essex who retreated, due north towards Warwick. He had lost much of his baggage train, including his private coach and most of his reserves of arms and ammunition, which were a godsend to the royalists. He also left seven field guns behind. Rupert completed the rout by a raid on his rearguard next day, capturing a further twenty-five wagons laden with miscellaneous booty, including the Lord General's plate, and blowing up four more. Most important, by retreating north Essex had left the road to London wide open.

Rupert now wanted to send a flying column of 3,000 horse straight for London; the capital was woefully unprepared, and in any case he could easily have outdistanced the news of his coming. But Charles was reluctant to divide his army, especially with Essex still in the offing, and he was in no mood for fresh adventures. His losses had after all been comparatively slight – the usual estimate is about 1,500 on both sides – but this heavy, mauling, bloody battle had brought him up against the realities of war. A strong 'Peace Party' in the Long Parliament was pressing for negotiations, and he was not averse to this if he could get reasonable terms.

At any rate, he now struck south to Banbury, then Oxford, where he arrived on 27 October. Only then did he turn east; on 4 November he took Reading and marched on towards London. Meanwhile Essex, steering well clear of trouble, crossed the Chilterns and took his army by forced marches south via Daventry, Towcester and Woburn to St Albans, arriving on 6 November. Afraid his London regiments would desert in sight of home, he then sent them round the perimeter to face Charles on the line of the Thames. Parliament's position was now desperate; it opened negotiations with the King and sent a fruitless appeal to the Scots. But Charles, afraid of losing the initiative, refused a preliminary armistice, and on the 12th his advance guard under Rupert stormed Brentford and sacked it. Two of Essex's best regiments, those of Denzil Holles and Lord Brooke, were now shattered, he had lost fifteen more cannon, and half the men he had brought back from Edgehill had deserted. On 13 November he had to pull 3,000 men stationed at Kingston-on-Thames right back to London Bridge to ward off a possible attack from the south. The King's army rolled irresistibly on.

However, the sack of Brentford was warning enough. In fact, civilian losses had been minimal, and the damage was mainly to property; but 'sack' was an emotive word, with connotations of rape, loot and murder, especially where Rupert was involved. An urgent appeal was issued to the deserters from the army, and the response was overwhelming. The London trained bands under Skippon paraded 6,000-strong on Chelsea Fields on the 12th, supplemented by the auxiliary City regiments and a host of sketchily armed volunteers. Next day at Turnham Green, just upriver from Putney, the royalists found their way blocked by an army of about 24,000, perhaps twice as large as theirs. (The royalists were not immune to desertion in the aftermath of Edgehill.) The armies stood face to face all that day, Sunday 13 November, but during the night the King withdrew to Hounslow.

Turnham Green has been called 'the Valmy of the first Civil War', and certainly no such opportunity presented itself again. But even Rupert agreed that a frontal assault would incur unacceptable losses, and if it succeeded it would only lead to mile after mile of bitter street fighting. Perhaps Charles ought to have crossed the Thames and swung in an arc eastwards, to link up with the active and numerous royalists of Kent, who would have helped him storm London from the south. There were voices raised in favour of such a plan. However, the degree of support Charles could expect from Kent was difficult to assess from a distance; what he did know was that the adjacent counties of Sussex and Surrey were deeply divided. Winter was setting in, and an invasion of London across the Thames was a daunting prospect; he might easily find himself penned up in the extreme South East, cut off from his natural recruiting grounds in the West. Finally he withdrew tamely enough to Oxford, which he had decided would be his main base, and on 9 December he sent his troops into winter quarters. Essex followed suit, setting up his headquarters at Windsor.

If Charles had muffed his one chance of finishing the war quickly, the Earl of Essex had scarcely distinguished himself, and he had been extremely lucky to emerge from the Edgehill campaign with honours more or less even. Parliament's faith in its Lord General was unshaken – publicly at least – but the fickle London public were already acclaiming a new star.

In August the Committee of Safety had given Sir William Waller, MP for Andover, a regiment each of horse and dragoons, and sent him down to harass George Goring at Portsmouth, a major royal arsenal and the obvious port of entry for assistance from France, which might yet arrive. He did better than that. He at once displayed that daring and tactical skill which was to be his hallmark, and he could call on the help of Sir John Meldrum, that indomitable Scots freebooter recalled temporarily from Hull. Together they pounded Portsmouth into submission; Goring surrendered on 5 September and went abroad.

Goring, eldest son of the Earl of Norwich, was a former professional soldier, and his decision to surrender, with only sixty effectives left and the townspeople in a state of mutiny, was a professional's decision. He was accused of cowardice and treachery, and not for the first time – for reasons incalculable he had betrayed the First Army Plot to John Pym in the spring of 1641 – but he always bounced back into favour. He was a man of considerable charm and address, and when sober he was to prove one of the King's most able field generals. Unfortunately, as Clarendon censoriously noted, he was drunk as often as not, even in the face of the enemy, which cast a blight on his military prowess. Thus he was taken by surprise at Wakefield in May 1643 by a much inferior force, and he was blamed in some quarters for the escape of the parliamentary horse from Lostwithiel in 1644 (pp. 112–13) below). The strange thing is that such reprobates – for Henry Wilmot, the King's Commissary-General of Horse, if anything exceeded him in debauchery – should have captured and held the confidence of a strictly sober, rather prudish man like Charles I; certainly it was not with the approbation of his civilian advisers like Lord Falkland or Sir Edward Hyde, his Chancellor of Exchequer, nor for that matter Prince Rupert. In his *History of the Rebellion* Hyde (now Earl of Clarendon) denounced Goring in much stronger terms than he used on the King's overt enemies, John Pym or even Cromwell. Goring would, he said,

> without hesitation, have broken any trust, or done any act of treachery, to have satisfied an ordinary passion or appetite; and in truth wanted nothing but industry (for he had wit and courage, and understanding, and ambition, uncontrolled by any fear of God or man) to have been as eminent and successful in the highest attempt in wickedness of any man in the age he lived in, or before.

Waller, too, was a complex character. He had inherited from his father the post of Chief Butler of England, a sinecure which brought in a handsome income from the 'prisage and butlerage' of all wine sold. He had fought with distinction under Sir Horace Vere in the Palatinate campaign of 1620–3 (p. 43 above), and he was a close friend of Sir Bevil Grenville and Sir Ralph Hopton, who seem to have chosen the royal side almost automatically. He was, it seems, a convinced Puritan, but in his memoirs he wrote:

All the ends I had were but to bring things to a fair and peaceable issue, that there might have been a general payment of all duties. That God might have had his fear; the King his honour; the Houses of Parliament their privileges; the people of the kingdom their liberties and properties; and nothing might have remained upon the score between us, but that debt which must be for ever paying, and ever owing, love.

In a way he was the common man's general, brilliant but fallible. He was full of daring and cunning, a supremely able improviser with an instinctive feel for the lie of the land, a master of small-group operations, raids and sorties. Like Rupert he preferred to operate with cavalry only, and he seems to have had difficulty handling infantry at all; flaws which became apparent once he had to take charge of a full field army. Time and again he would fall over his own feet, as it were, on the brink of success. But in this, his first campaign, he carried all before him. Having taken Portsmouth in record time, he proceeded to Farnham Castle in Surrey, which was to be his favourite base for much of the war. Having no artillery with him, he blew in the main gate with a petard and took it by storm. He was then ordered north to join Essex in the Midlands; at Edgehill he and his men were swept away in the general rout of Parliament's left wing, and he counted himself lucky to survive. However, on 3 December, the King having retired to Oxford, Essex gave him a larger detachment, four regiments of horse and two of dragoons, and sent him to retake Winchester, which had been captured by the royalists in a surprise attack. There began his long association with fellow MP Sir Arthur Haselrigg and his 'Lobsters', and a London wood-merchant called Richard Browne and a precocious nineteen-year-old Scots professional, John Middleton, both of whom rose to field rank in 1644.

Winchester fell on 14 December, and Waller was then ordered to Chichester. Taking Arundel Castle on the way, he laid siege to Chichester and starved it out; it surrendered on 6 January. Only then did he dismiss his men to winter quarters and return to London. It had been a small-scale campaign, but he had taken three towns, two castles and over 2,000 prisoners with minimal losses, and he had consolidated Parliament's grip on the wealthy counties of Surrey and Sussex, particularly important for their powder mills and iron foundries. The London public took him to their hearts as their 'William the Conqueror'.

# 5

# THE WAR FOR
# THE CENTRE: 1643

Negotiations for peace continued for much of the winter; in fact, until mid-April 1643. Parliament demanded that the Church be reformed on the advice of a synod of Puritan divines it had summoned to Westminster that summer, and that Charles surrender all control over the army. But the real stumbling block, which was to wreck subsequent negotiations at Uxbridge in 1645 and Newcastle in 1646, was Parliament's demand for the proscription of the King's leading supporters – Hertford, Digby, Wilmot, Newcastle and many more. In any case, Charles was in no mood for compromise; he insisted on his right to command the armed forces, stood out for an armistice without immediate demobilisation and demanded that Parliament establish the Book of Common Prayer by statute.

In February Parliament, ignoring these negotiations, began to fortify London on an enormous scale. Its 'Lines of Communication' consisted of a ditch nine feet wide and nine deep, with a rampart nine feet high; they ran from the present Vauxhall Bridge west and north over what are now the gardens of Buckingham Palace, north-east to the present line of Oxford Street at Wardour Street, then east through Bloomsbury and Hoxton to Shoreditch, and south to the river again at Wapping. On the south bank they ran from Rotherhithe through Newington and Kennington back to the river at Vauxhall. They were punctuated by twenty-four main forts, made of packed earth held up by timber, in the approved Continental star formation; between them were various half-moon redoubts and counterscarps. Dutch engineers were brought over, with a small force of professional navvies, but most of the work was done by unpaid volunteers, who worked with hectic enthusiasm. (The Venetian Ambassador was amazed to see these earnest Puritans working on a Sunday.) The forts were completed by May, the lines by July. No trace of them now remains.

If the aim was to prevent another Turnham Green, then it was a complete success; thereafter no royalist general seems to have contemplated an attack on London. But whether its eighteen-mile circumference could ever have been adequately manned, even by untrained volunteers, is doubtful, and it represented an enormous investment in time, money and matériel; for instance, its forts held 212 cannon of various sizes at a time when guns were in short supply. It reminds us of the fact that though Parliament reaped many advantages from its possession of the national capital it posed enormous problems, not least that of feeding and employing its huge population of at least 400,000 during an acute depression in trade and manufactures. In December 1642 the King explicitly authorised the continuation of the wool trade between the West Country and London, but the following July he closed it off; in any case it had already been severely disrupted by marauding war bands in the Midlands. Similarly, when he took the Tees and Tyne ports in 1642 he left them open, but he imposed a duty of 1s a chaldron on coal and a further £30–50 on each collier which sailed. Rather than subsidise the royalist cause in this way, Parliament imposed a total blockade from January 1643, which was so effective that only 876 chaldrons slipped through in the next twelve months. But the effect on London, so heavily dependent on 'sea-coal' for industrial as well as domestic use, was devastating. The Scots coalfields were quite unable to take the strain, and by May 1643 the price of coal in London had risen to 50s a chaldron, 20s above the legal maximum, and a parliamentary ordinance in June admitted that coal was 'absolutely necessary to the maintenance and support of life' and that the current shortage 'is like to be of very dangerous consequence in the influence it may have on the necessities of the meaner sort'. By this time, in fact, 'the meaner sort', including many women, were besieging Westminster crying for an early peace.

So it is not surprising that the new campaigning season was a matter of fits and starts. One effect of the fortification of London was to shift the epicentre of the whole war westward. If we draw an imaginary line from Boston on the Wash due south to Brighton on the south coast, we can see that after 1642 the area east of that line was never directly involved in the war. It was largely fought in an area to the north and west of Oxford, in the counties of Gloucester, Stafford, Oxford, Northampton and Wiltshire. These counties guarded the approach to the royalist strongholds in the far West and Wales, and offered the quickest route to other royal enclaves in the North, given that the Great North Road (the A1) was impassable over much of its length. As a result the paths of the rival field armies crossed and recrossed again and again. Edgehill (1642) is only a few miles from Cropredy Bridge (1644), and Naseby (1645) only forty miles north-east. They clashed at Newbury twice in successive years (1643 and 1644), though at opposite ends of this little town. Only two major battles, Marston Moor and Langport, took place outside this charmed area, and at the centre of its web of roads lay Stow-on-the-Wold. Here Essex and Waller met in June 1644 before Essex left for the West, and it was here that Charles, Rupert and Goring met in May 1645 before Goring in his turn departed for the West. Here the last royalist army, under Lord Astley, surrendered a year later.

In fact, Rupert opened the new campaigning season in February 1643 by storming Cirencester. This presaged an attack on one or the other of the great western cities of Bristol or Gloucester, at the moment held by Parliament. Waller was hastily appointed to command a new auxiliary army to be raised on the counties of Gloucester, Wiltshire, Somerset and Worcester, grouped in a 'Western Association'. Parliament had begun forming these county associations the previous December in an attempt to break down the reluctance of local levies to venture outside their own counties. The only one to enjoy any permanence was the famous Eastern Association, consisting of Norfolk, Suffolk, Cambridge, Hertford and Essex.

As soon as Waller took over the Western Association he acted with vigour and decision. Mustering about 2,000 horse and dragoons, he threw them across the River Severn on a bridge of boats to confront Lord Herbert, who was advancing from Glamorgan with 1,500 newly raised Welsh foot and 500 horse. He surprised Herbert at Newnham in Monmouthshire on 24 March, took two-thirds of his men prisoners and pressed on to take the towns of Monmouth, Chepstow and Ross-on-Wye, barring the way into South Wales. But further north a fierce struggle was raging for Staffordshire. Lichfield Cathedral made an unlikely strongpoint, but the close was surrounded by a deep ditch, and the royalists had pierced the walls of the clergy houses overlooking this moat to take muskets and light guns, with more guns perched on the cathedral tower. It was a tough nut to crack, and Lord Brooke, commander of the Midlands Association and one of the most highly regarded leaders of the Long Parliament, was killed in the first assault. Sir John Gell, the unpopular but irremovable county 'boss' of Derbyshire, took over and forced the town's surrender on 4 March.

Unfortunately Lichfield, together with the town of Stafford, straddled two crucial royalist 'corridors', from Oxford to Lancashire and North Wales, and from Oxford to Yorkshire, where the Queen had landed on 22 February with badly needed money and munitions. The Earl of Northampton was promptly despatched to Stafford with two regiments of horse and a few companies of foot, only to be killed at the moment of victory in a hard-fought action at Hopton Heath on 19 March. Gell had to withdraw, leaving his guns behind, though he retrieved them, typically enough, by trading them for Lord Northampton's body. Stafford was now secured, but Rupert had to be brought up to recapture Lichfield. On the way he took and sacked Birmingham, a solidly parliamentarian industrial town which had already provided Essex with 15,000 sword blades; according to Clarendon it was 'as famed for hearty, wilful, affected disloyalty to the King as any place in England'. When Rupert arrived before Lichfield on 10 April, even he found it a daunting prospect, and he at once sent for professional miners from Cannock Chase. Their mine was exploded on the 21st, but the royalists still suffered heavy casualties in the subsequent storm.

In fact his brother Prince Maurice was doing rather better. He had been sent out from Oxford to rescue Lord Herbert. He was too late for that, but he surprised Waller the master tactician at Ripple Field, just north of Tewkesbury, on 13 April and routed him. Waller, as was his way, commanded what was virtually an all-mounted force of cavalry and dragoons, his only infantry a small contingent supplied by the governor of Gloucester, Edward Massey. He was short of artillery and (so he said) of skilled gunners, and for once his keen eye for the ground failed him. His run of unbroken success came to an abrupt end and Massey's infantry were virtually wiped out, an unlooked-for event which seems to have caused some coolness between the two commanders. Unfortunately, at this promising juncture the King recalled Maurice and Rupert to Oxford to meet the impending threat from Essex's main field army, and with the pressure off him Waller took Hereford on 25 April. But there he remained, licking his wounds and considering his options.

Essex had chosen to wait until he was sure the peace negotiations had foundered, but on 13 April he pushed his army forward from Windsor towards Reading, which was in no position to resist him. The royal governor, Colonel Richard Fielding, negotiated a truce, and Charles agreed to terms of capitulation on 26 April; but Fielding was darkly suspected of treachery, especially since his elder brother Basil, Earl of Denbigh, had just succeeded Lord Brooke as commander of the Midlands Association.* On Charles's orders he was court-martialled, found guilty and sentenced to death, and he was only reprieved at Rupert's direct request. Charles was now in a thoroughly neurotic mood, insisting that he dare not trust his person inside any closed town, even Oxford, for fear of treachery. He had begun to build a ring of fortifications round Oxford, in emulation of London, but they were still far from complete; he lacked the manpower available in London, and the solid support; the University of Oxford was firmly behind him, but the town was not. He was also critically short of arms and ammunition, though this was to some extent relieved on 13 May, when an advance convoy arrived from York, sent by the Queen.

Fortunately at this juncture Essex's army was pinned down at Reading by a serious epidemic of fever, perhaps typhus. He was also short of cavalry and short of money to pay his infantry. On 10 June he advanced as far as Thame, twelve miles due east of Oxford, but there he stuck. A week later he detached 2,500 men in an unsuccessful attempt to take Islip, about five miles north of Oxford, and this left him wide open to the kind of lightning cavalry raid which Rupert mounted next day against a convoy bringing up money from London. Rupert missed the convoy, but he skirmished with John Hampden's regiment of horse at Chalgrove, between Thame and Abingdon, and there Hampden sustained a wound from which he died six days later. It was a heavy moral blow to Parliament's cause. In a similar raid on the 25th Sir John Urry circled round the helpless parliamentary army and raided the town of High Wycombe, throwing London into near-panic. The Commons complained bitterly to Essex – Pym told him roundly that

---

* Ironically, Parliament also looked askance at Denbigh; after all, he was a nephew of the late Duke of Buckingham; his father, one of Rupert's officers, had been killed at Birmingham, and his mother was a close friend of the Queen's.

men were safer under the King's protection than his – and he tendered his resignation, which was refused. All the same he could not be moved.

Meanwhile contrary to all expectations a formidable little royalist army had arisen in the West. It will be remembered that when the Marquess of Hertford shipped his troops from Somerset across to South Wales in September 1642 (p. 52 above) Sir Ralph Hopton and a few other officers had ridden off down the north coast of Devon and into Cornwall. Cornwall was one of the most individualistic of the shires, with its own unique traditions and even its own language, and the success of a 'foreigner' like Hopton (from Somerset) in raising men for the royal cause was quite remarkable. The trained bands came out at his summons, 3,000-strong, and he began to raise further volunteer regiments, headed by the flower of the Cornish gentry: Sir Nicholas Slanning, John Trevannion, William Godolphin, Lord Mohun, and above all the near-legendary hero Sir Bevil Grenville, six foot two inches tall, who always led his regiment on foot. Moreover, this army was distinctly unusual in its willingness, at this early stage of the war, to serve outside its home area. Even the trained bands, though they were usually employed in internal duties, left Cornwall from time to time; they are found, for instance, at the siege of Lyme in Dorset in 1644.

Not that Hopton had it all his own way. By October local parliamentarians had managed to raise a thousand foot in Cornwall and five hundred dragoons in Devon, and the Committee of Safety hastily ordered the Earl of Stamford in from Dorset with another 1,500 men. Plymouth held out for Parliament under a local magnate, Lord Robartes, its garrison headed by a Scots professional, Colonel William Ruthin, and it could not be taken without artillery. In November Hopton pressed on to Exeter, but this held out for Parliament, too, and by 30 December Ruthin, emerging from Plymouth, had forced him back to the River Tamar, marking the boundary between Devon and Cornwall, and on into Cornwall, as far as Liskeard. However, he was then routed by Hopton at Braddock Down, near Lostwithiel, on 19 January. The outnumbered royalist cavalry could only hold their own, but the Cornish infantry rolled down the hill into the valley between the two armies and up the other side, flattening the enemy. They hotly pursued Ruthin to Saltash, where he was routed again on the 22nd, losing forty guns, and so back to Plymouth. The Cornishmen followed, but by this time Lord Stamford had at last arrived. He mauled Hopton's advance guard at Modbury, twelve miles east of Plymouth, on 21 February, and pushed him north to Tavistock. Then, to the fury of the Committee of Safety, he agreed to a forty-day truce.

As soon as this truce expired, on 22 April, Stamford sent 1,500 foot and 600 horse into Cornwall under James Chudleigh, a professional soldier with experience in Ireland and a major-general at the age of twenty-five. After some preliminary skirmishing he lured Hopton back into Devon, where he ambushed him on Sourton Down near Tavistock on 25 April. Half the army simply panicked – the high sheriff of Devon fled in women's clothes – and though Hopton, Grenville and Lord Mohun made something of a stand, and drenching rain brought the proceedings to a premature end, they had to retreat across north Cornwall, almost to Bude, on the coast, leaving behind their guns and much of their stores. Stamford now advanced for the *coup de grâce* with 5,400 foot and 200 horse, ordering Chudleigh to meet him at Stratton, three miles inland from Bude, on 15 May. Hopton, with only 2,400 foot and 500 horse, was heavily outnumbered, but next day, the 16th, he ordered a desperate attack on the joint enemy army at Stratton which came off, again due to the heroism of the infantry, who advanced uphill against the enemy in three converging columns, apparently without cavalry support at all. Stamford fled as far as Exeter, leaving behind 300 dead and 1,700 prisoners.

This kind of see-saw struggle could well continue indefinitely, but now Hopton learned that Prince Maurice, released from Oxford by Essex's supine inactivity, was heading west to join him. So he decided to ignore the parliamentary garrisons holding out at Exeter, Plymouth, Bideford and Barnstaple, and marched on into Somerset, joining up with Maurice at Chard on 4 June.

Their first task was to deal with Waller, who was still lurking in the Severn valley, recruiting infantry from Wiltshire and Gloucestershire. Maurice had three crack regiments of horse from Oxford, about 1,500 men, and 1,000 foot recently levied in the Oxford area. Hopton could contribute about 3,000 Cornish foot, well-blooded and formidable, plus 500 horse and 300 dragoons. Stamford had now sent Waller 1,200 horse and dragoons rounded up after Stratton, to supplement his own cavalry which had survived his defeat at Ripple Field. In numbers the two armies were fairly evenly matched, though Waller would have been foolish to rely too much on his raw infantry.

The two armies then spent the best part of a month in a complex game of military chess focused on the city of Bath, neither side willing to risk a head-on battle except on its own terms. In the middle of all this Hopton wrote to his old friend Waller suggesting that they meet under a flag of truce to arrange an exchange of captured officers. Waller refused, but his reply is justly famous:

> The experience I have had of your worth, and the happiness I have enjoyed in your friendship, are wounding considerations when I look upon this present distance between us. Certainly my affections to you are so unchangeable that hostility itself cannot violate my friendship to your person, but I must be true to the cause wherein I serve . . . and where my conscience is interested all other obligations are swallowed up. . . . That great God, which is the searcher of my heart, knows with what a sad sense I go upon this service, and with what a perfect hatred I detest this war without an enemy, but I look upon it as *opus domini*, which is enough to silence all passion in me. The God of Peace in his good time send us peace, and in the meantime fit us to receive it; we are both upon the stage, and must act the parts assigned to us in this tragedy. Let us do it in a way of honour, and without personal animosities. Whatever the issue be, I shall never willingly relinquish the dear title of, Your most affectionate friend and faithful servant.

This was on 16 June. On 4 July, after further tortuous marching and counter-marching in the hilly country round Bath, Waller seized the advantage. He took up his position on the top of Lansdown Hill, a steep-sided ridge some three miles long, with a flat top. From this vantage point he was in a good position to harass the royalist army, and the morning of 5 July was taken up with some vigorous but inconclusive cavalry actions on the valley floor, after which Waller's horse regained the top of the ridge. Nevertheless, at about two o'clock Hopton ordered his horse and foot up the hill in the face of withering musket and artillery fire, Waller having depressed his field guns sufficiently to fire case shot down the slope. The casualties were horrific, and it is not surprising that the horse broke and fled; Hopton said later, 'Of two thousand there did not stand above six hundred.' But the day was saved by Sir Bevil Grenville, leading his regiment of pikemen, who pushed relentlessly up the hill and gained a foothold on the rim. Grenville, in the van as always, was killed on the brow of the hill, where his monument now stands. His men stood firm, but their position was precarious in the extreme; as one of them said later, they were 'like a very heavy stone upon the very brow of the hill, which with one lusty charge might well have been rolled to the bottom'. But at this stage

Waller seems to have lost confidence, and he withdrew his troops along the ridge to the middle, where it was traversed by a stout stone wall. With his musketeers ensconced behind this wall he was still in a strong position, but about one in the morning he simply pulled out, ordering his men to leave their match burning on the wall to deceive the enemy.

Who 'won' this battle is still debatable. Waller still commanded the approaches to Bath, into which he now withdrew. Hopton was left in possession of the field, but he was short of ammunition, he had suffered heavy infantry casualties and his Cornishmen were demoralised by Grenville's death, and two-thirds of his cavalry had fled he knew not where and were slow to reassemble. Worse still, as he got on the move next morning one of his ammunition wagons accidentally blew up, killing several senior officers outright, and leaving Hopton himself, who was standing nearby, temporarily blind and half paralysed. Waller was quick to take advantage. Rallying his men, and sending for reinforcements from Bristol, he pursued the royalists, now looking a thoroughly beaten army, north-east to Chippenham, then south-east to Devizes, where they arrived late in the evening on 9 July. He came up next day and penned them in the town.

At a council of war held that night round Hopton's sick-bed it was decided that Maurice and Lord Hertford, with the horse, should break out at once and ride to Oxford for help, while the infantry hung on as best they could. They escaped that same night, before Waller could properly invest the town, and rode hard for Oxford. We know that they rode south-east to elude pursuit before swinging north again towards Oxford; presumably they took the line of the present road to Upavon, then north and east to Burbage, continuing north-east across the Thames and on to Oxford via Wantage; a ride of more than fifty miles. They arrived early next morning, 11 July, the horses reeling and the men grey with fatigue.

The King, alerted to the general situation, had already ordered Henry Wilmot to leave for Bath with a brigade of cavalry; he now ordered another brigade, under Sir John Byron, after him; they joined forces at Marlborough, Wiltshire, together with the remainder of Maurice's horse, no doubt remounted. This gave Wilmot about 1,800 horse, and a pair of light guns which could keep up with them. After a forced march, presumably west on the A4, then south-west on the A361 (though the modern road takes a different track to the old), he approached Devizes early on the morning of the 13th. Waller regrouped to face him in front of the town. He had about 2,500 foot and 2,000 horse; in other

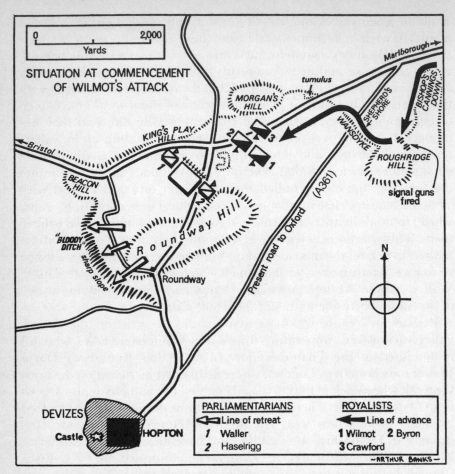

THE BATTLE OF ROUNDWAY DOWN

words, he was superior to Wilmot in cavalry alone, and the Western infantry, which could have done much to redress the balance, ignored prearranged cannon signals from Wilmot, not believing that help had arrived so soon, and fearing some devious plot of Waller's.

This left Wilmot with no alternative but to come on, and luckily he was always an attacking general, Waller a defensive one. Come on he did, and his troops, who had ridden all night, simply went straight through. Wilmot's own regiment met Haselrigg's 'Lobsters' head on on the left wing and broke them after a fearsome struggle in which Sir Arthur was unhorsed and left for dead (p. 55 above). Byron, confronting Waller's own regiment on the right wing, ordered his men not to fire until the enemy had discharged their pistols, and then, in his own words, 'We fell in with them, and gave them ours in the teeth.' In fact, he pushed Waller's regiment back into the reserve regiment behind, which also broke and fled. As a result the whole of the parliamentary cavalry streamed off across nearby Roundway Down in disorder, with the royalists in hot pursuit. No doubt many of them would have lived to fight another day, as mounted troopers usually did, had they not plunged headlong over a concealed escarpment, ending up in a shattered tangle of flesh and bone, equine and human, at the bottom of what is still known as 'Bloody Ditch'. Then Wilmot and Byron, despite the frenzy of the chase, rallied their men and returned to deal with Waller's infantry, left marooned on the field. Their doom was sealed when Hopton's infantry at last began to debouch from the town behind them. This was no occasion for heroics, nor were they, enlisted only a few weeks before, the men for it; most of them surrendered after a token resistance. Apart from a few horsemen who had escaped 'Bloody Ditch' Waller's whole Western Association army had been wiped out in one of the most conclusive battles of the whole Civil War.

Parliament's cause was now at its nadir. Its grip on the Severn valley was broken, imperilling Bristol and Gloucester; Essex was still immobilised in the Thames valley. In fact, after Roundway Down Waller rode hotfoot to London, where he blamed his defeat on the Lord General, whose lack of initiative had enabled the King to deploy troops from Oxford at will. There was much truth in this, and he was backed by many of his fellow MPs. The firebrand Henry Marten said, 'It is summer in Devonshire, it is summer in Yorkshire, and only winter at Windsor.' The war party in Parliament continued to back Essex (though he did not look very warlike), but when the City of London offered to raise a new army for Waller they agreed to perpetuate his command, not as the leader of a county association but as a field general. After furious arguments Essex agreed that he could serve as a lieutenant-general, under his nominal control, but he delayed issuing his commission as long as he could, and in any case by this time new armies were proving difficult to raise. In July Essex withdrew to Reading again; he had only 3,000 foot and 2,500 horse fit for service, and he declined to advance until he was substantially reinforced.

In the North, too, Parliament's power was tottering. The Earl of Newcastle had reached York early the previous December, with an army of 8,000, as many as 6,000 of them crack infantry, the famous

'Whitecoats'.* The cavalry, led by the Yorkshireman Sir Marmaduke Langdale, were almost entirely yeomen troopers or even members of the lesser gentry. Until the bitter end the 'Northern horse' were always conscious of being an elite force. In January he was joined by James King, Lord Eythin, who landed at Tynemouth 'with 200 experienced officers and 3,000 stand of arms'; with him was George Goring, unabashed by his humiliation at Portsmouth a few months before. They were placed in command of the foot and the horse respectively. Another tough professional soldier, Sir Thomas Glemham, was appointed governor of York.

Newcastle had already captured Tadcaster and Pontefract, cutting communications between Hull and the West Riding cloth towns. He also sent a detachment south to seize and fortify Newark, the key to his communications with Oxford. Newark and Oxford, though strictly besieged for long periods, were to hold out until the end of the war. At this stage, towards the end of December, Newcastle put his army into winter quarters round York in the conventional way, but in this first winter of the war conventions were at a discount, and Sir Thomas Fairfax suddenly emerged with a force of volunteers to storm Leeds on 23 January, giving him and his father an important foothold once more in the West Riding. On the other hand the Queen's arrival at Bridlington on 22 February with 2,000 cases of pistols, £80,000 cash and 'over a thousand old, experienced soldiers', was a boost to royalist morale, and resulted in the immediate surrender of Scarborough.

There was some talk of Henrietta's remaining in the North, as 'she-generalissima', but in any case for the time being she could not risk the journey to Oxford with Lincolnshire and Derbyshire in the hands of the rebels. In fact, in late February a scratch force of 6,000 men raised in Lincolnshire, Nottinghamshire and Derbyshire launched an attack on Newark, though they were repulsed with heavy losses by the Scots veteran Sir John Henderson. (The parliamentary commander, Sir Thomas Ballard, was promptly replaced by another Scotsman, Meldrum.)

Newcastle was slow to leave winter quarters, and in March Lord Fairfax concentrated his forces at Leeds, and told his son to make a diversion at Tadcaster, near York. This brought forth Goring with about 1,200 horse, and he fell on the retreating Thomas Fairfax at

---

* In fact, only two regiments out of four were dressed in white, Sir William Lambton's 'Lambs'. Newcastle's own regiment wore red, the fourth regiment black.

Seacroft Moor on 30 March, swept aside his thin cavalry screen and smashed in his infantry, who were short of pikes. Fairfax lost about 200 men killed and another 800 captured, and it was an incident he did not care to discuss in his later years of fame. Meanwhile Newcastle detached a small contingent under Charles Cavendish, who picked up reinforcements from the Newark garrison and drove south into Lincolnshire; on 23 March he took Grantham, and on 11 April he defeated a hastily assembled force of local levies at Ancaster Heath, near Sleaford.

A wave of alarm swept the Eastern Counties and spread to London, which drew most of its beef and mutton from the lush acres of Lincolnshire. After some shillyshallying a joint force under the local magnate Lord Willoughby of Parham, with Sir John Hotham from Hull and Oliver Cromwell from Cambridge, gathered at Sleaford early in May. On the 13th they clashed with Cavendish's horse at Grantham, an incident notable only for the fact that it was Cromwell's first independent action as a cavalry commander. Its importance has therefore been exaggerated, and in fact an attack on Newark, which had been the original purpose of the expedition, had to be abandoned. Much more significant, further north, was Thomas Fairfax's night attack on Wakefield on 24 May, Whitsunday. Fairfax always preferred a frontal attack to a siege, despite the concomitant loss of life, but here he had no choice; any delay and royalist reinforcements would sweep in from York, only ten miles away. As it was, he thought he was leading his little force of 1,500 volunteers against a garrison of about 900. When the dust settled he found he had routed 2,000 foot and 500 horse led by Goring, who was taken prisoner and despatched to London.

Meanwhile Parliament decided that the Eastern Association must be protected at all costs. If this area could be isolated from the war, then its huge agricultural wealth, its prosperous cloth industry, its burgeoning trade with the Continent from Colchester, Harwich, Yarmouth and King's Lynn – not to mention its fishing industry – would make it a prime source of men and money. On 25 July, an ordinance was passed for the creation of a new cavalry force of 5,200 under the Earl of Manchester, with Cromwell second-in-command, to be levied not only on the Eastern Counties but on Kent, Surrey, Sussex, Berkshire, Northamptonshire and London. But on 9 August Parliament changed direction, perhaps realising that this would impede the creation of a new army for Waller. Instead, it appointed Manchester to command an army to be raised exclusively on the Association, with

Cromwell as Lieutenant-General of Horse. Next day a Commons committee was appointed to oversee the Association and its own directing
committee, established at Norwich. On 16 August the Association was
ordered to raise an army of 20,000 men 'in constant pay', though
initially its purpose was defensive; Manchester was ordered to see that
'all the frontiers be supplied with fitting forces to resist all sudden
surprises and invasions, and from time to time send out scouts, to
discover how and in what manner any enemy approacheth near the
frontiers'. (This concept had already appeared in an ordinance of 29
July, which referred to Huntingdon as a 'frontier county'.) In September the Association's frontiers, and its war capacity, were extended
by the addition of Lincolnshire.

Oliver Cromwell may be said to need no introduction, but in a sense
this can be dangerous. The stupendous glory he later achieved casts a
retrospective glow over his earlier career, and gives him an importance
he did not then possess. He was born in 1599, the son of a minor
Huntingdonshire squire, Robert Cromwell, a younger son of Sir Oliver
Cromwell of Hinchingbroke, after whom he was named. The Cromwells
were not descended from Henry VIII's great minister, Thomas
Cromwell, Earl of Essex, but from one of his hangers-on, Richard
Williams, son of a Welsh innkeeper, who took his patron's name. In
his marriage settlement, in 1620, Cromwell is still named as 'Oliver
Cromwell *alias* Williams', and it is not too fanciful to ascribe his fervent,
and towards the end of his life interminable, eloquence to his Welsh
ancestry. In the 1620s the senior line of the Cromwells fell on evil days,
and Hinchingbroke, with much of their local influence, fell to
the Montagus, Earls of Manchester. It was presumably the Montagu
influence which secured Cromwell's election to the Parliament of
1628–9 as MP for Huntingdon. The same influence may well have
ensured his election for the city of Cambridge in 1640, first in the Short
then in the Long Parliament, for though he was a perfectly respectable,
economically sound member of the lower gentry, he was certainly not
of that class which normally aspired to such an honour.

In the Long Parliament he emerged as an active Puritan, and an
opponent of episcopacy, which was probably what endeared him to the
Montagu family, and he was one of those Members, though only one
of many, who never had the least doubt of the propriety of restraining
the King and ultimately fighting him. In July 1642 he seized the
county magazine at Cambridge Castle and frustrated an attempt by the
colleges to send their plate to the King, though under what authority,

except as a member of the county committee, is not clear. By now he had raised a troop of horse and assumed the rank of captain, and henceforward he seems to have taken over Cambridgeshire, Hertfordshire and Huntingdonshire, partly through determination and strength of character, partly because there was no one prepared to challenge him. He took his troop to Edgehill, but was deeply disappointed by what he saw and experienced there (pp. 41, 48 above). He returned to East Anglia and over the winter and following spring expanded his troop into a regiment, most of his troopers composed of men heartily committed to the cause, usually for religious reasons. These were the famous 'Ironsides', though the name was subsequently to be attached to the whole army. He was not choosy about his men's social class, but his enemies' gibe that he deliberately chose working-class recruits and 'Anabaptists' (a catch-all term of religious abuse) was exaggerated, to say the least. Wherever possible he chose men of the kind he admired in the royalist army; but they were not always available, and as he said later: 'It had been well that men of honour and worth had entered into these employments, but seeing it was necessary the work should be done, better plain men than none.' Also, though he did not say so, 'plain men' were more amenable to the strict discipline he imposed, on and off the field. Despite his total lack of experience he emerged in 1643 as a superb cavalry general, capable of leading his men in a headlong charge like any Rupert or Byron, but capable, too, of controlling them and pulling them back into the main action. Moreover, in the attenuated House of Commons he was coming to prominence as an active and aggressive radical, and no respecter of persons. After the bungled attempt to secure Newark in May he complained to Parliament of his commander, Lord Willoughby of Parham, and forced his resignation, an omen of things to come.

With his new commander, however, his relations were close. Edward Montagu, 2nd Earl of Manchester, had no more than a routine military capability, and no previous experience in war, but he was a sound administrator, he enjoyed an assured social ascendancy in the Eastern Counties, and he was deeply committed to the cause of Parliament. Under his then title of Lord Kimbolton he had been impeached with the Five Members in January 1642, and he was now prominent amongst that dwindling band of peers which constituted the House of Lords. What he had in common with Cromwell was close local and familial associations and strong left-of-centre Puritanism, and despite Cromwell's personal gifts his meteoric rise in 1642 and 1643 is explicable only on the assumption that he enjoyed Manchester's active support. Over the next twelve months religion was to drive them apart; Manchester opted for an authoritarian or oligarchic Presbyterian Church, Cromwell for a much more loosely structured organisation, with the broadest possible religious toleration. Nevertheless, they seem to have subsisted on a basis of mutual respect until the second Newbury campaign in the autumn of 1644.

But this was for the future, and so was the new Eastern Association army, which had to be recruited and trained over the winter. Meanwhile the royalists were not idle. By the beginning of June, with Waller heavily engaged in Somerset, and Essex still becalmed in Berkshire, the route from York to Oxford was as clear as it ever would be. The Queen left on 4 June, with an escort of 4,500 men under the Hon. Charles Cavendish, including two new lifeguard regiments raised for her in Lancashire. (Gossips detected a *tendresse*, perhaps more than a *tendresse*, between her and her handsome young guard commander, second son to the Earl of Devonshire.) They went via Newark and Burton upon Trent, and on 11 July Rupert came out to meet them at Stratford on Avon; two days later Charles was solemnly reunited with his wife on the field of Edgehill – an example of his crashing insensitivity.

It was an exploit calculated to demonstrate Parliament's helplessness, and particularly the ineffectuality of its Lord General. Tormented by Rupert's regular cavalry raids from Oxford, Essex now tried to bring him to an engagement near Buckingham, but that failing he could only draw back into Bedfordshire. Even then, a delegation of MPs sent out to confer with him had to run the gauntlet of enemy patrols. On 9 July he wrote to Parliament suggesting that they sue for peace, or that he and the King should withdraw, and the issue be decided by a kind of formal trial by battle between selected contingents of their two armies. It was the kind of idea which undermined the best efforts of his friends and was seized on with glee by his enemies, who were growing in number.

Meanwhile the Queen's departure had relieved Newcastle of a grave responsibility, and he could now risk a once-for-all encounter with the Fairfaxes. His chance came on 30 June, at Adwalton Moor, near Bradford. It was an unusual battle. It began with an exchange of cavalry attacks in which Thomas Fairfax, perhaps because of Goring's absence, had rather the better of it. In fact, despite Newcastle's superiority in numbers – perhaps as many as 10,000 to 4,000 – he was thinking of withdrawing when one of his infantry colonels, Posthumous Kirton, yet another veteran of the Dutch wars, threw his regiment of pikemen against the Fairfaxes' infantry, who were still mainly armed with muskets. They broke, and so did the left wing of the horse, cut to pieces by Newcastle's field guns. At this stage Lord Fairfax pulled out without telling his son, who had to retreat on Bradford, but could not hold it. He escaped that night with only one troop of horse, leaving the garrison to surrender next day. At Leeds the garrison was overwhelmed by 700 royalist prisoners who broke out of gaol. The Fairfaxes, father and son, fled with a few hundred men to the shelter of Hull, now Parliament's only stronghold in Yorkshire; and only just, for Sir John Hotham and his son had just been detected in a plot to betray the town to the King. They were arrested on 29 June and sent under armed guard to London.

The Queen's safe arrival at Oxford also left Rupert free to tackle Bristol, the second city in the kingdom, an important manufacturing centre and a vital port of entry from Ireland and the Continent. He left Oxford on 15 July with three brigades of foot (about 9,000 men), 3,000 horse and 900 dragoons; near Bath he also took over Hopton's army, full of confidence after its stunning victory at Roundway Down. Bristol was now ringed by a chain of elaborate fortifications, and though they were largely built of wood and earth they could absorb a great deal of artillery fire. But its garrison of 300 horse and 1,500 foot was quite inadequate to man a perimeter three miles in circumference, especially if the enemy attacked at more than one point. Inevitably, it also contained far too many civilian non-combatants to sustain a long siege. The governor, Nathaniel Fiennes, complained that in the past few weeks Waller had drawn off 1,200 men from the garrison to restock his own army; after protests he had returned with five or six hundred, but then he had slipped away with them again, 'not loving to be cooped up in a siege'. (However, he asked Fiennes to sign a chit approving his conduct, which he did.)

The initial royalist assault, at first light on 26 July, was soon brought to a standstill for lack of scaling ladders, and the Cornish foot, already decimated at Lansdown, suffered further heavy losses, as did the brigade of Oxford infantry under John Belasyse, who was wounded. However, another Oxford brigade, under Lord Wentworth, took advantage of the diversion to force an entry on the western side, between the forts at Brandon Hill and Windmill Hill, and they flooded in; Fiennes brought up his cavalry, but they were at a disadvantage in street fighting and were repelled by blazing pikes. Rupert was soon on the spot, pushing more and more troops through the breach, but before he could attack the citadel Fiennes asked for terms. On his return to London he was court-martialled and sentenced to death. Essex argued successfully for his reprieve, but he was expelled from the House of Commons in black disgrace. Ironically enough, Rupert was to face similar treatment when he surrendered Bristol to the New Model in 1645.

At this stage a combined royalist pincer movement might have finished the war. In theory the Oxford army could have advanced on London, backed up by the Western army, brushing aside Essex's enfeebled army, the only one at Parliament's immediate disposal, while Newcastle advanced down the Great North Road to complete the rout. However, there is no sign that the King's Council of War considered such a plan, and the provincial armies were barely under its control at all. The Western army, for instance, had shown a remarkable willingness to forsake its home ground, but the West was now crying out for help, and in August it turned back to Devonshire under the command of Prince Maurice; Hopton remained at Oxford. Maurice took Bideford and Barnstaple in late August, and Exeter on 4 September; then he settled down before Plymouth, a much harder nut. In fact he lifted the siege just before Christmas and retired into winter quarters.

As for Lord Newcastle, his attempts to secure Lincolnshire had been frustrated by Cromwell, who captured Stamford in July, stormed Burleigh House and on the 28th at Gainsborough defeated and killed Charles Cavendish, newly returned from Oxford. On the same day Parliament appointed Cromwell governor of the Isle of Ely, and a few weeks later he began to organise the Eastern Association horse. But in any case Newcastle's army was financed by the taxpayers of Yorkshire, and he could not possibly march south while the Fairfaxes held out in Hull, ready to pounce again as soon as his back was turned. Hull's landward defences were formidable, and it was next to impossible to cut off its supplies by sea or from across the Humber. Nevertheless, Newcastle opened the siege on 2 September, sending a small detachment round into Lincolnshire to police the south bank of the Humber.

There is no evidence that this was unwelcome to the King, or that he ever envisaged ordering Newcastle south. He and his Council were still intent on consolidating his power in the west Midlands, and there, after Bristol, the next logical step was the capture of Gloucester. This would open up the Severn valley and divert the lucrative wool trade from the Marches and North Wales through Bristol; as it was, it was still filtering across the Midlands from Gloucester to London. Above all, it would be an appalling blow to Parliament's morale.

Charles appeared before the town with his Oxford field army on 10 August. Rupert was all for a quick storm; the governor, Edward Massey, had only 1,500 men at his disposal, and apart from the medieval castle the fortifications consisted of a few hastily dug earthworks. But Charles was still appalled by the heavy casualties sustained at Bristol, and he insisted on a siege. By the end of the month Massey was running short of food, water and ammunition, but Charles still hesitated to apply the *coup de grâce*; moreover, whether because of over-confidence or the persistent rain, he had neglected to dig himself in – that is, to build lines of circumvallation which would have enabled him to defy a relieving army.

And that relieving army was on its way. Parliament gave Gloucester top priority. The City released six of its trained-band regiments, and Essex was authorised to levy another 2,000 conscripts. Essex himself was on his mettle, for it was his failure to maintain the pressure on Oxford over the summer which had freed Charles's army for this expedition. He left on 26 August and proceeded by forced marches, undeterred by the occasional cavalry raid mounted by Rupert or Wilmot. He came in sight of Gloucester on 6 September, and Charles retired south-west to Painswick, barring the road back to London.

Gloucester had been saved, and enough men and supplies had been brought in to make it tolerably safe, but Essex's position was now deadly dangerous. He faced a long march back to London with tired troops, their numbers depleted by the need to reinforce the Gloucester garrison, much of the way through hostile territory, with food and fodder pre-empted ahead of him, and Charles's army hanging on his flanks or even barring his way. Moreover, if Essex lost this army, as Waller had lost his at Roundway Down, there was still no other available; London's best trained-band regiments had been removed, the formation of Waller's new army had been halted, and the Eastern Association army only existed in embryo.

In this predicament he behaved with unwonted cunning and decision; this was the kind of war of manoeuvre he had known in the Low Countries. First he made a feint north to Tewkesbury, as if intending to swing north-east to Evesham then run for London via Banbury, well to the north of Oxford; but when Charles tried to block this route by advancing to Pershore, between Tewkesbury and

Evesham, Essex abruptly turned back, giving him the slip, and marched almost due south, through Cheltenham and on to Cirencester, which he reached on 15 September, then Cricklade (on the 16th) and Swindon (on the 17th), taking a wide arc south of Oxford and on to Reading. The King followed as best he could on a parallel course ten or twenty miles to the east but some way behind. Despite almost incessant rain Essex made excellent time, and he captured an ample store of food and ammunition at Cirencester; in fact, if Rupert had not checked him by a full-scale cavalry raid at Aldbourne Chase on the 18th he might have got clean away. That same day the main royalist army reached Wantage, then swung due south, and as Essex approached the town of Newbury on the evening of the 19th, within striking distance of Reading and home, he found it drawn up across his path. To reach London he had to fight.

The two armies were evenly balanced at about 14,000 men each, and while Rupert's cavalry were still markedly superior, the London trained-band regiments, with the psychological advantage of striking for home, were a match for the Oxford foot. Moreover, by failing to catch Essex earlier Charles had forfeited the advantage his horse would have enjoyed on the open downs of the Cotswolds, and he was now fighting across hummocky arable land. True, Rupert's horse on the left wing faced the open ground of Wash Common (or Enbourne Heath), but on the right Sir John Byron had to cope with the worst possible cavalry ground, a cluster of small fields enclosed by hedges and ditches, and overlooked by a slight ridge know as Round Hill. Altogether, the royalists' deployment of their forces for this crucial battle was seriously defective, and, as Rupert's biographer remarks, 'The battle was as confused in its action as in its narrations; we find no trace of tactics on the King's side, where there were so many generals, or any order of battle deserving the name.'

For a start, the royalists had failed to occupy the slight ridge immediately in front of them, a quite inexplicable omission. Essex promptly planted his guns on it, so that instead of simply awaiting his attack in entrenched positions, the royalists had to take the initiative. Rupert soon cleared the enemy cavalry from Wash Common, but the two trained-band regiments refused to budge, holding off wave after wave of horse with musket and pike. They gave ground very slowly, retiring north in good order onto cultivated ground in the middle of the battle line, where their position was not seriously disputed. Meanwhile they had prevented Rupert from swinging round to support his right wing,

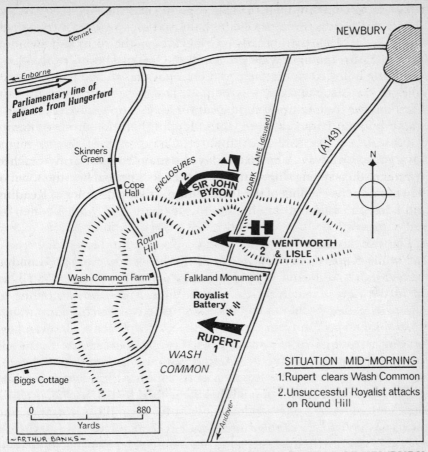

**THE FIRST BATTLE OF NEWBURY**

where Byron's cavalry, forced to work across farmland, one field at a time, and up Round Hill, were being decimated by musket fire from the infantry on the hill and from dragoons planted in the hedges. Troopers fell in droves; Byron lost more than a hundred from his own regiment alone, including some of the flower of the cavalier nobility: the Earl of Sunderland stopped a cannon ball, the Earl of Caernarvon and Lord Falkland were cut down as they tried to negotiate the gaps in the hedges – though Falkland's conduct was so reckless as to raise suspicions of suicide. Even then their sacrifice was in vain: whenever the cavalry succeeded in topping the ridge they were thrown off again by Essex's infantry. They received little support from their own foot, whom Byron denounced as 'poltroons'.

When darkness fell neither side had made any significant advance, and the royalists had suffered heavy losses and their powder was running dangerously low; they had expended a great deal in the siege of Gloucester, and had never been able to make it up. (Here Essex's capture of their magazine at Cirencester may well have been decisive.) Charles had no choice but to order a withdrawal under cover of darkness, and daybreak found him marching north, back to Oxford. Essex resumed his march on London, making light of the occasional royalist cavalry raid. He reached Reading on the 22nd, where he left the 'regular' nucleus of his army, and took the trained-band regiments on to London for a heroes' welcome three days later. Unfortunately his army was so weakened that he could not hold onto Reading, which fell to the royalists again on 3 October, but his reputation was for the time being restored, and his critics silenced.

The Marquess of Newcastle (newly promoted in the peerage) was still besieging Hull, but in September Parliament again sent Sir John Meldrum back to organise its defence. On the way he was joined by Cromwell, who accompanied him across the river and into Hull, where he met Thomas Fairfax for the first time. They decided to ship Fairfax's cavalry, now swollen to twenty troops, over into Lincolnshire to join Cromwell's, and on 11 October they defeated a strong royalist detachment from Newark at Winceby, near Horncastle. That same day Meldrum sallied forth from Hull and captured the besiegers' main siege cannon, a monster weighing 5,790 pounds and firing a 36-pound shot.* Next day, 12 October, Newcastle raised the siege. Apart from anything else, he had learned that the new Eastern Association army was on the move. On 20 October the Earl of Manchester took Lincoln, and proceeded methodically to reduce the remaining strongpoints in the county, saving Newark until last.

Meanwhile Parliament resumed the task of providing Waller with a new army, a plan temporarily abandoned because of the crisis at Gloucester. His independent commission as a major-general had at last been extorted from Essex, who objected, so he said, to the creation of

---

* This was a celebrated and much-used piece of ordnance. The royalists called it the 'Queen's Pocket Pistol', but it was now re-christened 'Sweet Lips', after a well-known Hull whore. Rupert recaptured it at Newark in March 1644, then lost it again at Marston Moor in July. It was almost certainly the gun used by Meldrum to batter down Scarborough Castle in 1645, and, transhipped to Portsmouth, it may well have been used by Cromwell in the final assault on Basing House.

subordinate commanders not under his direct control. However, he had given Manchester a similar commission without demur, and in Waller's case he was clearly activated by personal jealousy and perhaps class consciousness; the personal animus between the two men was to have a disastrous effect the following year. Even so, it was easier to plan a new army for Waller than to find it; both sides were now having acute difficulty raising fresh troops, especially infantry, and it was not until November, with winter setting in, that he was appointed to lead a force levied on the counties of Kent, Surrey, Sussex and Hampshire, with its headquarters at Farnham. Even then the conscripts from this area – for both sides had now resorted to conscription – had to be supplemented by the Red Regiment of the Westminster trained bands, and two City of London auxiliary regiments, the Green and the Yellow. His own foot regiment, and such horse as had survived Roundway Down, completed what was very much a scratch force. To deal with this threat the King, too, had decided to raise a new army south of the Thames, under the command of Sir Ralph Hopton (now Lord Hopton). But, like Parliament, he was finding it difficult to raise new recruits. He could give Hopton 1,580 horse, but only 2,000 raw, conscripted foot (and this is a paper figure) plus about 500 Irish troops who were now beginning to arrive from Munster.

Late as it was in the season, Waller began on 7 November by attempting to lay siege to Basing House, near Basingstoke in Hampshire, a Norman castle strengthened in the sixteenth century and lying within an Iron Age earthwork. Its strategic importance was slight, but it was uncomfortably near the main road west from London to Salisbury and Winchester (the present A30 and M3) and well within what Parliament liked to regard as its own sphere of influence.

In theory such medieval relics were no match for seventeenth-century artillery. On the Continent they had long ago been replaced by star-shaped fortifications, with sloping walls to deflect cannon shot, and revetments which allowed the defenders to enfilade the enemy gun emplacements; but the only examples of this in England were the south-coast forts built by Henry viii, and the elaborate fortifications of Berwick-on-Tweed. Nor was Parliament short of heavy artillery for siege operations; it had commandeered the Wealden iron industry of Kent and Sussex, and with it the services of the Browne family, makers of heavy ordnance for the Crown from the reign of Elizabeth up to the Revolution of 1688 and beyond. Also, though Lord Admiral Warwick objected, its forces could and often did borrow heavy guns from the

Navy. Nevertheless many royalist castles and fortified manor houses – Basing, Donnington, Sudely, Lathom, Pontefract, Scarborough – defied their besiegers for months, even years on end. So did several parliamentary strongholds; Berkeley Castle under Edmund Ludlow, for instance, and the manor house of Brampton Bryan under Brilliana, Lady Harley.

Why was this so? First, medieval castles, with walls as much as ten feet thick, were simply much stronger than previous experts had calculated, and paradoxically, the softer the stonework the less vulnerable they were; cannon shot merely dented it instead of cracking it. Secondly, there were serious problems facing any besieging army. Only the cannon royal, firing a 66-pound shot, was in any way effective against medieval stonework, and this weighed three tons and needed a team of seventy draught horses – always in short supply – to drag it slowly along the unmetalled roads of seventeenth-century England, which in the wet summers of 1643 and 1644 rapidly degenerated into a sea of mud. Such guns also called for a heavy cavalry escort. Moreover, they were useless in a pitched battle, which left them with no subsidiary function, and many commanders, particularly Waller and Fairfax, preferred to march with as few guns as possible, and those light, anti-personnel pieces. In fact, the trouble and expense involved in bringing these huge siege guns into action was prohibitive, yet the alternative, of sitting down to a siege of attrition, represented a huge commitment in manpower, which neither side could usually sustain for very long.

So it was now with Waller at Basing. The guns he had with him, the largest a demi-cannon, made no impression on the castle, and two nights camped out in the open, in the wind and the rain, were enough for the London regiments; their officers warned him that they were on the point of mutiny and he withdrew on the 9th to Basingstoke. After two nights under cover he tried again, this time by storm, but the Red Regiment fled at the first salvo from the castle, and the others refused to advance within range. After another wet night in the park, 11–12 November, he had to march his men back to Basingstoke, though he had forsaken his own tent to sleep alongside them on a straw mattress. Threatening to pistol the next man who raised the cry 'Home! Home!', he then marched them to Farnham, where he waited for Hopton, whose new army was now assembling. Hopton duly arrived on 27 November, but it was another wet, misty day and Waller, understandably, given the troops he had, was not to be lured out from beneath the guns of

Farnham Castle. Eventually Hopton had to retire; he then scattered his men in winter quarters across Hampshire, at Winchester, Alresford, Alton and Petersfield.

Such scattering was necessary to spread the burden on the civil population, but it was a distinctly unwise move with Waller still nearby at Farnham, and anxious to recoup his reputation after the fiasco at Basing House. On the night of 12–13 December he took advantage of a hard frost which solidified the muddy roads to lead 5,000 of his men, infantry and dragoons, in a surprise attack on Hopton's nearest outpost at Alton – only ten miles from Farnham, in fact, and just off the main Guildford–Winchester road (the A31). On his sudden arrival the royalist cavalry under Lord Crawford hastily decamped for Winchester, leaving their infantry to slog it out in the streets of the little town. One of the most savage encounters of the Civil Wars ended in the parish church, where the cornered royalists made a last stand behind a barricade of dead horses. There their commander, Colonel Richard Bolle, killed seven of the enemy before he was bludgeoned to death. According to Waller he lost only ten men in all, the royalists more than a hundred, plus 875 captured, most of whom re-enlisted under Parliament. Hopton was short of infantry as it was; he had now lost nearly half of them at one blow. Moreover, Waller was not yet done. He now turned back to Arundel; he occupied the town on 20 December, and sat down before the castle. Hopton had to have more infantry if he was to raise the siege, but his desperate appeals to Oxford only brought forth Henry Wilmot with a thousand of his crack horse, who were certainly not going to soil their hands with siege operations. Arundel surrendered on 6 January 1644, and Waller at last retired to winter quarters.

Both sides were now nearly at the end of their tether. Parliament in fact held a trump card in the Army of the Eastern Association, but its enormous potential was not yet apparent. The Earl of Essex retained the nucleus of the dedicated army raised in the autumn of 1642, but it was proving difficult to supplement it or make good its losses; Waller's scratch army, after initial difficulties, was functioning well in small-scale operations in Hampshire, Sussex and Surrey, but it was doubtful if it would hold together in a major campaign. The London trained-band regiments, in theory Parliament's most effective weapon, had shown their worth at Newbury, but refused to march far from home without some crucial end in view, such as the relief of Gloucester. The King was in no better shape; he, too, had acute problems of recruitment. His attempt to raise a new army for Hopton had gone off at half cock, and he was having difficulty keeping his main field army at Oxford up to strength. Newcastle's army, though its continued occupation of the Tyne and Tees coalfields exerted useful pressure on London, was tied up in Yorkshire, Maurice's Western army in Devon. It was natural that both sides should look for outside help in the campaign of 1644.

# 6

# DEADLOCK: 1644

Ever since the autumn of 1642 the Long Parliament had been trying to persuade the Scots provisional government to intervene again in English affairs, as it had so effectively in 1640. As for the King, he had always looked for support from his fellow monarchs, and particularly his brother-in-law Louis XIII of France. But such hopes were illusory, and they were finally dashed by Louis' death early in 1643 and the accession of a minor, the boy king Louis XIV. Charles's thoughts then turned to the Irish army, now swollen to nearly 20,000 men. The bulk of it had been recruited by Parliament in 1642, but it had been sent over to Ireland in the King's name, and its officers held his commission. It was under the command of his Lieutenant-General, the Marquess of Ormonde (promoted from Earl in 1642).

By mid-1643 the Irish war had reached deadlock. Parliament, given its commitments in England, could not reinforce the Irish army sufficiently to defeat the Confederates, and such was the hostility of the native population that its sphere of operations was limited by supply and transport difficulties. The same applied to the small Scots army clinging on in Ulster. On the other hand the Confederates, though they had made much of the country a 'no-go area', were not strong enough to tackle the English strongholds centred on Dublin and Cork. Ultimate authority was wielded by the Lords Justices in Dublin, appointed by

Parliament in the absence of a Lord Lieutenant, and they insisted on a policy of 'frightfulness', involving savage military reprisals against the civilian population, which Ormonde and his senior officers found morally repugnant and politically counter-productive. So he had no qualms when in April 1643 Charles ordered him to open negotiations for a 'Cessation', a one-year armistice with the rebels pending a final settlement. The Cessation was duly signed on 15 September; negotiations for a peace treaty were to begin at Oxford that winter, and Irish regiments began to leave for England at once.

Between September 1643 and March 1644 about 17,600 men, mainly experienced and battle-hardened infantry, were shipped over to join the King. The accession of this number of troops, led by first-class officers like Henry Tillier and George Monck, must have strengthened the royalist forces, but it is a process very difficult to quantify. Unlike the Scots army brought in by Parliament, they never functioned as a national unit under a central command; in fact, in order to avoid parliamentary naval patrols in the Irish Sea they were shipped over piecemeal, some landing at Chester, others at Bristol, and one contingent as far south as Weymouth. Thus they tended to be parcelled out amongst the various royalist armies as occasion served; as we have seen (p. 85 above), some were allocated to Hopton's Southern army in November 1643, others seem to have been employed on garrison duties in the Midlands. The bulk of those which arrived at Chester before the turn of the year were allocated to Sir John Byron, who had been sent north to recruit a new army in Cheshire and Lancashire, an army which was unfortunately destroyed or dispersed at the battle of Nantwich in January 1644, and the Irish with it. Moreover, though it suited Parliament's book to describe these men as Irish papists, the great majority were straightforward Protestant Englishmen, who had opted for Irish service in 1642 on religious or ideological grounds. As a result many of them mutinied when they arrived in England and found they were expected to fight against Parliament, and though discipline was restored it is doubtful if they could have been trusted to operate as an independent unit, supposing that had been possible.

In fact, it is arguable that any military advantage the King may have gained by the Cessation was offset by the political damage he sustained as a result. It was a blatant appeasement of Roman Catholicism and Irish nationalism, and Charles was going into the final peace negotiations with his hands tied. The token military force remaining in Ireland could only defend a narrow strip of territory running along the east coast from Dublin to Belfast, while in the south the Earl of Clanricarde and Lord Inchiquin hung onto a small enclave round Cork, using mainly local troops. This left the Scots army under Robert Monro marooned in Ulster, and in October 1643 Parliament agreed to assume financial responsibility for its maintenance.

This paper promise, never fulfilled, eased negotiations which had been proceeding since August between Parliament and the Scots. The Solemn League and Covenant, adopted by the Scots Estates on 17 August and the Westminster Parliament on 1 September, was to be taken under oath by the members of both bodies and by all officers and officials in their employ. It pledged them, with studied vagueness, 'to preserve the rights and privileges of the parliaments, and the liberties of the kingdoms, and to preserve and defend the King's Majesty's person and authority'; in fact, it denied that they had any 'thoughts or intentions to diminish his Majesty's just power and greatness'. Moreover it pledged them to work for the establishment in England of a Presbyterian church on the Scottish model, for this is what was meant by 'the reformation of religion according to the word of God and the example of the best reformed churches'. To many parliamentarians, Oliver Cromwell amongst them, this was almost as great a religious betrayal as the Irish Cessation. However, the immediate advantage gained was likely to prove decisive, and John Pym died of cancer that December content that he had fulfilled the trust imposed on him as leader of the Long Parliament. Under the terms of a military convention signed soon after the League and Covenant, the Scots undertook to invade England early in the new year with an army of 20,000 men, to be financed out of the profits of the North East coalfield, once it was liberated.

In fact, the old Earl of Leven, summoned once more from retirement, crossed the Tweed on 19 January 1644, with an army which was formidable indeed – at least on paper. He had 18,000 foot, 3,000 horse, 500 dragoons and 120 guns. But many of his men were described as 'raw, untrained and undisciplined; their officers for the most part young and inexperienced', and some of his cavalry were mounted on 'the veriest nags'. Moreover, they now faced the worst of the winter weather in the North; every night snow fell, every day it half melted, filling to the brim the many streams and rivers which traverse Northumberland roughly east–west, so that the water 'oftentimes came up to the middle, sometimes the armpits'. In these conditions progress was slow and arduous, and the sheer size of the army and the difficulty of supplying

it in this under-populated region dictated a kind of caterpillar movement. It reached Morpeth on 28 January, where it had to wait until 2
February for supplies to arrive from Berwick, and by this time the
Marquess of Newcastle was hastening north from York. He reached
the town of Newcastle just in time, on 7 February, and flung a garrison
into it. It was another fortnight before Leven decided to leave a small
siege force there and press on; he forced a crossing of the Tyne on 28
February under cover of a snow storm, and reached Sunderland on 4
March, where he was held up again, this time because of a shortage of
fodder for his horses. Newcastle held out until October, but the rich
Durham coalfield was now open, and the fuel crisis in London averted.
However, the coal duties never met the whole of the Scots army's costs,
which as much as anything explains Leven's reluctance to advance
farther south than York later in the year.

The Scots marched steadily on through Durham and into Yorkshire,
with Lord Newcastle in constant attendance. On the face of it he
was heavily outnumbered, but his 8,000 men were all crack troops,
defending their home region against a traditional foe, and as they slowly
retreated they were joined by another 2,000 men from Cumberland,
and two Yorkshire cavalry regiments under Sir Charles Lucas. In fact
Leven showed no desire to tangle with them, rather the opposite; on at
least two occasions, on the Bowden Hills on 7–8 March, and at Hilton
on the 24–5th, he used all his experience and tactical skill to avoid a
battle Newcastle did his best to provoke.

Meanwhile Newcastle's precipitate abandonment of Yorkshire had
left that county in some confusion. John Belasyse was hastily detached
from the Oxford army and sent north to take over. He at once decided
to establish his main base at Selby, centred between Hull and the West
Riding towns; there he transferred 5,000 foot and 1,500 horse from
York, and he began recruiting another 1,000 horse and 500 foot in the
East Riding. Fortunately for him Thomas Fairfax was absent. On
29 December he had been ordered out of his winter quarters near
Nottingham and sent over to Cheshire to help the local parliamentary
commander, Sir William Brereton, deal with the new royalist army
raised by Sir John Byron, supplemented by five recently landed Irish
regiments. In fact, he and Brereton virtually destroyed this army at
Nantwich on 29 January, and he went on into Lancashire, mopping
up. The whole of the North West was now in peril, as much as the
North East.

Charles's immediate reaction was to appoint Rupert President of the

Council of Wales and the Marches and Captain-General in Lancashire, Cheshire, Worcestershire and Shropshire, and the Prince arrived at Shrewsbury on 19 February. By this time Fairfax had retired to Yorkshire, to assess the new situation there, but Rupert was still picking up the bits, trying to reorganise the remnants of Byron's army and seeking new recruits, when news came that the ubiquitous Sir John Meldrum was besieging Newark with an army of about 7,000 men raised in Nottinghamshire.

Rupert at once threw together what we would call a special operations division; he took 1,100 Irish infantry from the local garrisons in Shropshire and Cheshire and asked Lord Loughborough to raise another 2,700 men in Leicestershire. He himself rode north into Cheshire in search of more men, and at Nantwich he found a new element of frightfulness; the governor chose to designate thirteen of his prisoners as Irish and hanged them from the battlements before the Prince's eyes. Rupert was the last man to stand for this; he promptly hanged thirteen of his own prisoners and sent the fourteenth south to Essex's headquarters with a warning that he would henceforth execute two parliamentary prisoners for every royalist. This led to a sharp exchange of letters, but though it was Parliament's official policy to give Irish troops no quarter – it was even embodied in an ordinance that October – this was no longer strictly enforced. Professionals like Meldrum simply ignored it.*

The Prince finally left Shrewsbury on 15 March, picked up Lord Loughborough's men on the 18th at Ashby de la Zouch, and pressed on by forced marches to Newark, collecting further recruits along the way. He arrived unexpectedly on the 20th with about 3,300 horse and 3,000 foot, and by his skilled use of the ground and the sheer fury of his attack he pinned Meldrum back against the town fortifications, captured most of his troops and dispersed the rest. Considering the scratch nature of his force, and the fact that most of his officers and men had served under him for a matter of days, this must be accounted one of Rupert's most brilliant exploits. Meldrum, who had lost all his arms and ammunition as well as a certain reputation for invulnerability, furiously blamed his defeat on the amateurism and disobedience of his local officers. But in fact Parliament's failure to deal conclusively with

---

* However, captured officers of the Irish army, like George Monck at Nantwich, were not exchanged for their opposite numbers, as was usual, but imprisoned on a charge of treason, though it does not appear that any of them were brought to trial.

Newark in 1643 had given the garrison time to make it virtually invulnerable. It lay partly on an island formed by a bifurcation of the River Trent, and it was now protected by huge and elaborate earthworks planned on Continental lines. Such works had a short natural life – though in fact many of Newark's can still be traced on the ground, notably the star-shaped fort known as the 'Queen's Sconce' – but before the invention of the shell they could soak up almost any amount of artillery fire. Later that year the Earl of Manchester declined to tackle it with his full field army, and it subsequently resisted a six-month siege by the Scots, only surrendering voluntarily on the King's orders in 1646.

At this stage the Scots were advancing slowly but steadily south, and the new Army of the Eastern Association was advancing into Lincolnshire; on the face of it Rupert would have done well to remain in the North. But this would be to assume a degree of central planning which was entirely lacking, and in any case his Leicestershire men had enlisted only for this one expedition, and he himself was needed further south. He returned at once to Shrewsbury.

In the South, in fact, the royalist cause was foundering. In March Charles tried to strengthen Hopton's new army by sending him another 800 horse and 1,200 foot from Oxford, but with them he also sent his Commander-in-Chief, the Earl of Forth – 'loyal, ancient, brave and bibulous, vastly experienced and seriously gouty'.* Perhaps because of this division of command, perhaps because of a lack of confidence and drive on Hopton's part evident ever since he had been injured in the ammunition explosion at Lansdown, they were comprehensively defeated by Waller on 29 March at Cheriton, just south of Alresford and eight miles east of Winchester – sweet revenge for Roundway Down. Waller was soon having his usual difficulty with the London regiments, which, having won a victory, wanted to return home, but this was not at once obvious. Charles could only recall the remnants of Hopton's army to Oxford and abandon the whole area south of the Thames.

As for Maurice's Western army, this had emerged from winter quarters in March merely to resume the siege of Lyme (now Lyme Regis). This was manfully defended by Colonel Robert Blake, who was to go on to play a similar role at Taunton, before emerging in the 1650s as

---

* He had just been created Earl of Brentford in the English peerage, but he will continue to be described as 'Forth'.

one of England's greatest admirals, but why the royalists should have attached such importance to this tiny fishing port, which took only the smallest ships and was of no strategic importance, is not clear. Moreover, despite overwhelming numbers the royalists could make little headway against the militant townspeople, and all-out assaults mounted on 28 April and 6 May were repulsed with heavy losses. A parliamentary naval squadron hung off the harbour mouth to supply the defenders, who may in fact have had more field guns than the besiegers.

The royalists could not afford this kind of wastage. Both sides had had to resort openly to conscription the previous autumn, but neither found the results very promising. In particular the Oxford army was not making good its losses, including those incurred by Hopton and Forth at Cheriton. The royalist MPs summoned to Oxford in January 1644 to form an unofficial 'Oxford Parliament' had some sharp comments to make. They criticised the high proportion of officers to men in the royal army (in some brigades as high as 1:5), and called for a new campaign of conscription to bring the proportion of foot to horse up to the approved Continental level of 2:1. But this campaign was an abject failure; by now the Oxfordshire area and the central Midlands were denuded of potential fighting men; and when Charles called a rendezvous at Aldbourne Chase, north of Oxford, on 10 April, the army was found to number less than 10,000 – a little more than 5,000 foot and 4,000 horse. It was doubtful if it could tackle either Essex's army or Waller's, and certainly not both together. Oxford itself was clearly in peril.

Charles at once sent for Rupert from Shrewsbury, but his arrival coincided with disastrous news from Yorkshire. Thomas Fairfax, returning in triumph from Nantwich, had summoned further contingents from the Hull garrison and from the West Riding towns, and had been joined by Meldrum with the Nottinghamshire regiments surviving from the débâcle at Newark. On 11 April they suddenly stormed Belasyse's main base at Selby, with complete success; Belasyse himself was captured, with sixty-eight royalist officers and 1,600 men; the rest were killed, or dispersed in a demoralised rout. Selby was the key to the whole northern campaign; Fairfax and his father could now move north to York, denuded of troops by Belasyse, and Lord Newcastle had to abandon his delaying campaign against the Scots and rush south. He arrived at York on 18 April with 6,000 foot and 5,000 horse. He sent the horse, which would only be an embarrassment in a siege, south to

Newark, where they were fortuitously reunited with their old commander, George Goring, who had just been released in exchange for
the Earl of Lothian. Leven now put on much greater speed, and joined
the Fairfaxes and their Northern army at Tadcaster on the 20th.
Meanwhile on 6 May the Committee for Both Kingdoms, directing the
war effort from London, had ordered the Earl of Manchester to join
them with the Army of the Eastern Association. He arrived on 4 June,
and the 'Great and Close Siege of York' began.

Charles was now so alarmed by the deteriorating situation that on
17 April he sent the Queen, who was over six months pregnant, to
Exeter, whence she could easily escape to the Continent. (Their last
child, the Princess Henriette-Anne, later Duchess of Orleans, was born
at Exeter on 16 June.) It was agreed that Rupert must do his best to
save York, and he left for Shrewsbury on 5 May, to recruit yet another
striking force; but this time he took with him his own brigade of cavalry,
leaving the King himself in a perilous situation. He advised him to
deploy his shrunken army in and between the ring of fortresses which
encircled Oxford, at Wallingford, Reading, Abingdon and Banbury.
However, within two weeks of his departure Charles was advised by
the Earl of Forth that he could not afford to hold onto Reading, which
was always of doubtful value unless he contemplated an attack on
London; it was accordingly evacuated on 19 May and re-occupied by
Essex. However Essex, heavily reinforced and unexpectedly aggressive,
then pressed on to seize Abingdon, while Waller swung round to the
south of Oxford and crossed the Thames at Newbridge to the west. His
army was still rather unstable, but on 9 May the Committee of Both
Kingdoms ordered another 4,200 men from the London trained bands
to march out 'unto Sir William Waller, wherever he may be'. Early in
June the Committee also began to recruit a third army under Richard
Browne, raised on the counties of Buckinghamshire, Berkshire and
Oxfordshire, and supplemented by another 4,000 London auxiliary
troops.

It was time for the King to leave, and he did so with some panache.
He sent out a small force to 'make a grimace' at Abingdon, which
momentarily drew Waller away and left a gap through which he sped
'with 3,000 horse, each with a musketeer mounted behind him, eight
pieces of cannon and thirty coaches, but little baggage'; he left his
pikemen and his heavy guns behind. Travelling light and fast, he easily
outdistanced Essex and Waller, reaching Worcester in safety on 6 June.
His tactics were probably dictated by the fact that this was turning out

to be an exceedingly wet summer. Lord Thomas Grey at Leicester lamented on 9 June that 'the ways were never so deep at Christmas in comparison as they are now'; on the 8th at York the Earl of Manchester was complaining that the 'tempestuous rainy weather' had flooded his mines; and on the 10th Waller remarked that the weather was 'so foul that the infantry and artillery could not march'.

At this stage, too, the parliamentary chain of command began to come apart. The Committee for Both Kingdoms had been set up in January to co-ordinate the joint war effort; it consisted of five peers and ten MPs, with three Scots representatives, and it met every day at three o'clock at Derby House, including Sundays. Reading its business-like minutes from day to day, and the stream of orders it issued to commanders, high and low, in all parts of the kingdom, it is impossible not to marvel at its drive, its efficiency and above all its good sense. The royalists had nothing like it. Nevertheless, though one of its main functions was the direction of the armies in the field this was just what it could not do. By the time it was informed of any given situation, had discussed it and sent down its orders the situation had usually changed. All the generals regarded it with some scepticism, and Essex in particular resented it as an encroachment on his authority, flouting its orders whenever he could.

At this juncture none of the generals shared the Committee's obsession with Oxford. It was now protected by a complex system of earthworks and ditches, linked to the rivers Thames and Cherwell, and could be reduced only by a long, formal siege. Moreover, sentiment apart, it was no longer the royalists' most important base; in April they had begun to transfer the small-arms factories, the ordnance factories and the powder mills established there in 1643 to Bristol, which was less exposed to attack from London, which could draw on the iron industry of Gloucestershire and which was a significant port. In any case, the reduction of Oxford would involve a degree of co-operation between Essex and Waller for which neither was prepared.

In fact, when Essex conferred with Waller at Stow-on-the-Wold on 6 June he argued that now Rupert had gone north Waller was well able to deal with the King's field army; he himself would advance into the West. His excuse was that the Committee for Both Kingdoms had ordered them to relieve Lyme, though in fact the Committee had intended nothing more than the despatch of a strong detachment, perhaps from Waller's army. His real reason, apart from a desire to distance himself from Waller, was that he had allowed himself to be persuaded by the Westerners on his staff, particularly Lord Robartes, that his appearance in Devon and Cornwall would bring those counties out in Parliament's favour and destroy one of the King's main pillars of support. He may also have doubted whether the long-suffering Midlands could support three armies, his, Waller's and the King's, in this singularly wet summer. Waller's objections were brushed aside; he was in no position to argue with the Lord General. Essex set off at once.

By the time the Committee for Both Kingdoms awoke to the situation it was too late. On 12 June they ordered Essex to return and lay siege to Oxford while Waller, with the assistance of the Gloucester garrison under Edward Massey, saw to the King. But this only threw Essex into one of his famous huffs. 'If you think fit to set him [Waller] at liberty, and confine me,' he wrote, 'be pleased to make him general, and me the major general of some brigade.' He had had enough of plodding up and down the Thames valley. He added, ironically in view of what was to come: 'That army which hath the greatest strength of foot will be most able, by God's blessing, to reduce the West, and I believe that I have the most resolute foot in Christendom.' He relieved Lyme on 15 June, Prince Maurice retreating before him, and pressed on into the West, hugging the south coast as far as he could, so that Warwick's ships could supply him from the sea; in this respect the expedition was an unusually sophisticated exercise in combined operations. On 25 June the Committee for Both Kingdoms referred the problem back to Parliament, and they decided that they could only endorse the Lord General's strategy, dubious as it was. The royalists were astonished and exultant. Digby told Rupert that the King's condition was 'very hazardous still, yet comparatively with the former may be thought comfortable'. 'The Earl', he said, 'is certainly possessed with such a frenzy as nothing can cure, but that ruin he is certainly destined unto.'

Waller, too, firmly declined to tackle Oxford. He told the Committee on 7 June:

> We resolve to follow the King wherever an army can march. Our reasons are, we believe the war can never end if the King be in any part of the land and not at the Parliament, for break his army never so often, his person will raise another; all the histories of England will manifest that sufficiently.

In fact, with the scratch troops at his disposal Waller could not keep up with the King at all. Charles swept down to Woodstock on 21 June, picked up the rest of his army from Oxford, which gave him a total of

5,500 foot and 4,000 horse, and struck east towards Buckingham. Panic ensued: Charles was heading straight for the undefended Eastern Association, the great milch cow of the parliamentary cause. The Committee told Waller, 'The preservation of that Association is of very great consequence, for if that be spoiled the Earl of Manchester's army will be dissolved for want of pay, besides . . . the enriching and recruiting of the enemy in those counties, which have hitherto been unplundered'; and in a flood of urgent despatches it began stripping the local garrisons of troops to supplement Waller's army: 1,500 foot and 520 horse from Warwick, Kenilworth, Northampton, Newport Pagnell and Cambridge. Richard Browne's 'third force' had been stood down, but he was now sent out to Barnet with 1,000 men from the City regiments and 3,000 scraped up from Essex and Hertfordshire, though unfortunately they answered the call with the utmost reluctance and arrived in a state of near mutiny.

However, from Buckingham Charles turned back once more to Banbury, allowing Waller to catch up with him. He was anxious for the Queen's safety in the West and troubled by the crisis in the North, but before he could march in either direction he must deal with Waller. On 28 June the two armies spent the whole day manoeuvring round Banbury, like wrestlers seeking a hold. But Waller was hard to beat at this game; evening found him established on Crouch Hill, a slight eminence south-west of the town, and he could not be lured down. So next morning Charles struck camp and marched away north along the River Cherwell, Waller keeping roughly parallel to him and alongside him on the west bank, the two armies only a mile or so apart, and in clear view of one another much of the time.

Just before eleven Waller climbed a slight hill to get a better view, and noticed the interesting fact that a gap had opened in the royalists' line of march. The rearguard under Henry Wilmot was just approaching Cropredy Bridge, while the vanguard, with the King and the Earl of Forth, was a good mile and a half further on. With his usual readiness to improvise, he at once threw Lieutenant-General John Middleton over Cropredy Bridge with two regiments of horse (Haselrigg's 'Lobsters' and that of the Dutch professional Jonas van Druske), a few foot companies and eleven guns, while he himself galloped back with another detachment to ford the river at Slats Mill, hoping to surround and destroy the rearguard.

It was a brilliant scheme, but it went badly wrong. At Slats Mill Waller was repulsed and never made it over; at Cropredy Bridge the fighting was more even, but Charles soon realised something was wrong, swung his vanguard round, and sent his own lifeguard back to Wilmot's aid. Wilmot was then able to drive the enemy back across the bridge with heavy casualties, leaving their guns behind, and with them Waller's much prized artillery colonel, the Scotsman James Wemyss, who had been Charles's master-gunner before the war. Waller took the loss of his guns very badly, and the whole episode undermined his self-confidence. In his memoirs he wrote: 'I strained myself in missing my aim, and my failing was my punishment.'

Neither side would risk another encounter, and after a day of sporadic artillery exchanges Charles, hearing that Browne was bringing up another 4,500 men, decided to retire to Evesham, arriving on 3 July. But he need not have worried; by the time Waller and Browne met at Towcester on the 2nd both their armies were on the point of disintegration. They moved on to Northampton, where on the 4th it was bravely resolved 'that Sir William should horse all his foot and follow the King into the North'. The necessary horses, rather surprisingly, were forthcoming, but the men were 'in great discontent by reason of hard marches, with want of provisions and lodging', and the London regiments were raising their usual cry of 'Home! Home!'. This is not really surprising, since Waller calculated that they had marched more than 200 miles since he had parted with Essex four weeks before. By the 7th 2,000 of them had deserted. Meanwhile Browne's men had attacked and injured him in a scuffle, and refused point-blank to march any further; 'Such men are fit only for the gallows here and hell hereafter', said Waller, but a court martial was out of the question. Waller was disgusted when Browne decamped on the 8th to attack Greenland House, a comparatively unimportant royalist outpost near Henley, but it was the only way he could pull his men together; it offered them the prospect of plunder and it was in the general direction of home. Waller hung on, doing his best to shadow the King with his horse and dragoons, but his infantry would not 'stir one foot further, except it be towards home'. The Committee for Both Kingdoms now accepted a *fait accompli*, and ordered his Essex and Hertfordshire contingents home, ostensibly for the harvest; he now gave up altogether and returned to London in mid-July.

By this time the King had finally decided to follow the Earl of Essex into the West. News of the battle of Marston Moor was beginning to come through, making it pointless to turn north.

\*      \*      \*

Rupert, it will be remembered, had left Oxford on 5 May, taking with him only his own cavalry brigade (p. 96 above). At Shrewsbury he collected another 2,000 horse and 6,000 foot, including the Irish contingent he had taken to Newark two months before, under Henry Tillier. On 16 May he took them on to Lancashire in search of further recruits. Men flocked to his banner, as they always did, and the news of his coming threw the local enemy commanders into a panic. Stockport surrendered on the 25th after a token resistance, and he pressed on to Bolton, where the defenders were suicidal enough to hang another royalist prisoner from the walls before his eyes; he stormed the town, and this time put it to the sack in true Continental fashion, with the loss of 1,600 civilian lives. Then he marched on to Bury, rounding up more recruits as he went, and on 30 May Goring joined him from Newark with the Marquess of Newcastle's horse, 5,000 in all, plus 500 foot. Why Rupert then struck west and laid siege to Liverpool on 5 June is not at all clear; it was as strongly fortified as any town in England – and, though it might be said to pose a threat to his rear, that would scarcely matter if he was successful in Yorkshire. He ignored Manchester, which was the nerve centre of parliamentary resistance in this region. As it was, Liverpool capitulated after four days, but only after a prolonged artillery bombardment which left him dangerously short of gunpowder.

He then continued north to Lathom House near Ormskirk, a royalist outpost resolutely defended by the Countess of Derby, the French-woman Charlotte de la Trémoille. The siege of Lathom, which had been proceeding intermittently since April 1643, when Lord Derby had retired to the Isle of Man, illustrates the futility of this kind of warfare. The place was of no strategic importance, lying as it did well to the west of the main road north to Scotland via Carlisle (the modern M6), but it was a symbolic thorn in the flesh of the powerful Manchester Committee under Alexander Rigby, who resented the survival of any royalist outpost in *their* county. Yet it was extremely difficult to take; the walls of the massive medieval keep were resistant to any but the heaviest artillery, and since it lay in a declivity it was difficult to depress the gun barrels sufficiently to align them on the target without the shot rolling forward. If the gunners descended into the declivity, they came under almost point-blank musket fire from the walls. Fairfax came to inspect it in February 1644, fresh from his victory at Nantwich, but it was not amenable to his usual storming tactics, and after a courtly exchange with the Countess he was glad to be on his way. In March

Rigby began to dig proper siege trenches, but his guns, the largest a 24-pounder demi-cannon, still made no impression on the walls, and on 4 April he brought up a huge mortar, firing an 80-pound stone ball. But because of its high trajectory it had to be stationed too near the castle for safety, and on the night of 10 April (unfortunately after a four-day prayer meeting by the besiegers calling upon divine help) the Countess's men sallied forth, overturned it and crammed it with rubbish. On the night of the 26th they captured it and triumphantly dragged it into the castle. Next day Rigby drew his other guns back out of range, and from then on it is difficult to say which of the two sides was on the defensive. Learning of Rupert's coming, he retired altogether on 26 May.

Rupert, always a stern realist, and a male chauvinist to boot, saw no point in maintaining these isolated outposts; they were no help to the royalist cause in general, they were a waste of manpower and a focus for trouble. He ordered the Countess to join her husband in the Isle of Man and replaced her with one of his professional captains, Edmund Rostow, who eventually surrendered the castle on generous terms in September 1645. (He was even more ruthless with Lady Beeston, besieged in Bridgnorth Castle, Shropshire. He had raised the siege in March, and afterwards dined with her in state. But at the end of the meal he told her to pack her bags and leave next morning, so that his engineers could blow the castle up.)

Lathom dealt with, he was ready for York – or was he? He had been in no hurry up to now, and some time in the first week of June he sent his uncle a letter which unfortunately has not survived. In it it seems that he represented his acute shortage of powder and suggested an alternative plan, perhaps a strike into Scotland which would oblige Leven to abandon the invasion of England. It reached Charles at Worcester, where he faced a bleak future; he had left a third of his army at Oxford, and he was no match for Essex and Waller, who were coming up fast, not to mention Richard Browne in the background. Thus he wrote back on 14 June in a mood of utter despondency:

> If York be lost, I shall esteem my crown little less, unless [I am] supported by your sudden march to me, and a miraculous conquest in the south, before the effects of the northern power can be found here. But if York be relieved, and you beat the rebels' armies of both kingdoms which were before it, but otherwise not, I may possibly make a shift upon the defensive to spin out time until you come to assist me. Wherefore I command and

conjure you, by the duty and affection which I know you bear me, that, all new enterprises laid aside, you immediately march according to your first intention, with all your force, to the relief of York. But if that be either lost or [they] have freed themselves from the besiegers, or that for want of powder you cannot undertake that work, that you immediately march with your whole strength directly to Worcester, to assist me and my army, without which, or your having relieved York by beating the Scots, all the successes you can afterwards have most infallibly will be useless to me.

This famous letter has exercised the minds of historians ever since. Rupert construed it as an unequivocal order to fight the allied armies round York, whatever the cost; as such, he carried it on his person to his dying day. But was it? True, Charles says, 'If York be lost I shall esteem my crown little less,' but later in the letter he assumes that this might happen. Clearly the Prince had suggested 'new enterprises', which Charles is quick to veto; but he then gives him two alternatives, which he sets out twice in different words: either he relieves York and beats the allied armies (and the one would almost certainly involve the other), or he returns south to join the Oxford field army at Worcester. The first is the preferred strategy, but Charles accepts that it might be impossible, if only because of shortage of powder. Certainly the letter reflects a passing mood; within the next day or two Charles must have learned that Essex was on his way to the West, and with that threat removed he was to prove more than a match for Waller and his mutinous army.

Moreover, even if this *was* an unequivocal order to fight, it was not unrealistic, and Charles did not know that the Eastern Association army had now been ordered into Yorkshire. Even so, the fact that Rupert lost the subsequent battle did not make this a suicide mission. He had 7,000 top-quality horse and at least 7,000 foot, with the prospect of further recruits; at York he could pick up another 5,000 crack infantry from Newcastle's army. The allied army *en masse* was much larger, but it was a mélange of different nationalities, regional allegiances, aptitudes and experience, and it had no less than four commanders, if we count the Fairfaxes, father and son, as two. Leven's Scots were of poor quality, and the Eastern Association infantry had only recently been recruited, and had never been tested in a major battle.

Certainly the news that Rupert had turned east threw the allies into confusion. He struck high across the Pennines; on 24 June he was at Clitheroe, on the 25th at Gisborne, the 26th Skipton and on the 29th

Denton. On the 30th he reached Knaresborough, less than twenty miles west of York. The reaction of the rebel commanders is significant. Understandably, they at once abandoned the siege of York; they had no wish to be pinned against the fortifications like Meldrum at Newark; but despite their numerical superiority of at least 28,000 men to Rupert's maximum of 20,000 they were in no mood for a pitched battle   at least, not until Meldrum brought up reinforcements from Nottinghamshire. In fact, they withdrew in the direction of Tadcaster and Leeds, at sixty degrees to Rupert's presumed line of march from Knaresborough, and took up their position on the ridge at Long Marston, whence they could observe the city from a safe distance. However Rupert, instead of heading east from Knaresborough, marched due north to Boroughbridge on the Great North Road, then swung west before turning south on the present road from Thirsk, entering York from the north.

On 1 July the allied armies stood all day on the ridge of Marston Moor while the generals dithered. York was quiet. Leven, the ranking general, was all for caution; he was certainly supported by Lord Fairfax, and probably by the Earl of Manchester too. The younger commanders, Thomas Fairfax, Oliver Cromwell and David Leslie, wanted to fight – or at least, so they said afterwards. However, Leven's advice prevailed, and early next morning, 2 July, they broke camp and moved off down the Tadcaster road, leaving a cavalry detachment under Cromwell and Thomas Fairfax behind on the ridge to keep an eye on York. Their tactics were scarcely those of confident men.

That day, 1 July, was also taken up with deep discussions inside York, mainly between Rupert and James King, Lord Eythin, Newcastle's Scots infantry commander. Obviously there was a strong clash of personalities here, and Eythin was not slow to remind the Prince of their last meeting, at Lemgo in 1638: 'Sir,' he said, 'your forwardness lost us the day in Germany, where you yourself was taken prisoner.' He was against fighting now that the siege had been raised without bloodshed, and Newcastle was inclined to agree with him, but when Rupert pleaded the King's direct orders there was no more to be said. It was agreed that they seek a battle next day, 2 July; Rupert would lead out the horse as early as he could, and Eythin would follow with the foot.

Rupert's cavalry began to debouch from York about ten o'clock next day, and they were sighted by Cromwell and Fairfax from the Marston ridge. They at once sent word to Leven. The last thing Leven wanted was to fight a running battle with Rupert in open country, and he promptly reversed the allied armies, which must have taken some doing, because his vanguard was nearly at Tadcaster. By two o'clock he had them back on the ridge. There he drew them up in an extremely complex order of battle, with the three armies intermingled and inter-locked – perhaps to prevent any one of them from withdrawing *en bloc*.

By two o'clock Rupert's cavalry were also in position facing the ridge. Newcastle himself had arrived between ten and twelve with his own lifeguard, but there was no sign of Eythin until four, perhaps even five o'clock, and then he brought up only 4,000 men, out of about 5,000 available. Many explanations have been offered; it was said, for instance, that the men had stopped to loot the abandoned par-liamentary siege lines, or (even less likely) that they had temporarily mutinied for lack of pay; some of Eythin's many critics said that he was reluctant to fight his fellow Scotsmen, though he had shown no such reluctance on the retreat south. In the last analysis it seems that he had no confidence in Rupert and was just being 'bloody-minded'; he certainly arrived on the scene in no very good mood, and when the Prince showed him a plan of battle drawn up by Bernard de Gomme he sourly remarked, 'By God, Sir, it is very fine on the paper, but there is no such thing in the field.' However, on one thing they were agreed: that it was too late to initiate a major battle that day. A desultory exchange of artillery fire had been going on all afternoon, with little apparent damage to either side, but about five o'clock it died away. Some of the allied troops 'fell to singing psalms'. Newcastle retired to his coach, and Rupert took supper; in fact, when the battle began 'he was set upon the earth at meat a pretty distance from his troops, and many of the horsemen were dismounted and laid upon the ground'. (This was not as negligent as it sounds; these were reserve regiments.)

Watching from the hilltop, Leven had noticed the stir occasioned by Eythin's arrival, then a certain relaxation of tension in the royalist camp. He at once sent round orders to his various brigades, and about six o'clock, or perhaps even later, his huge army began to roll down the hill. It was a bold decision, for which he has never been given suitable credit.

The foot in the centre were soon heavily engaged, neither making much headway. On his right wing Rupert had placed Byron's Cheshire and Lancashire horse in a strong defensive position, with a ditch in front and hedges on the flanks manned by musketeers, and had forbidden him to move. Unfortunately, as soon as Byron saw the Eastern Association

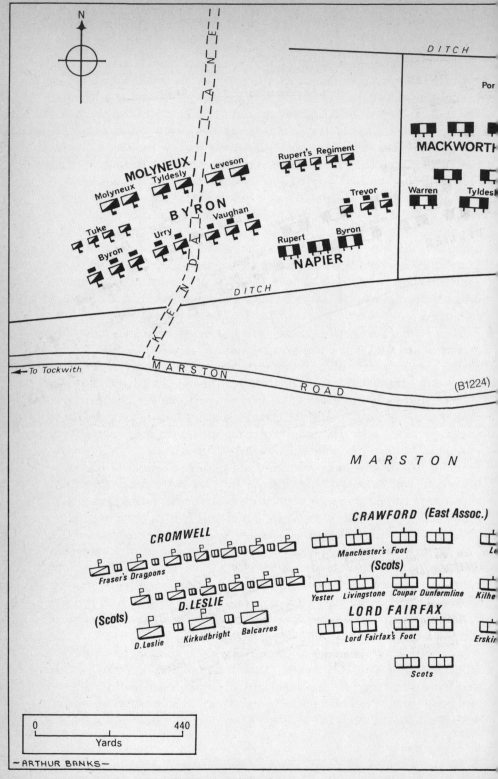

**MARSTON MOOR: THE ARMIES DEPLOYED**

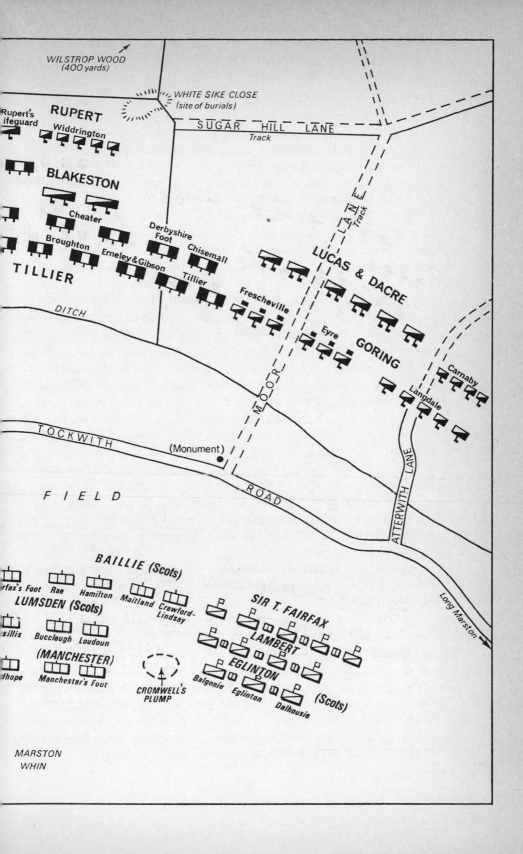

horse, led by Cromwell, bearing down on him he foolishly emerged from cover and was swept clean away. However, at this stage Cromwell was wounded in the head and retired, perhaps concussed, leaving David Leslie's Scots regiments to face the reserve which Rupert now threw in – probably his crack horse from the Oxford army. The struggle was fierce, and it seems that at one stage Lawrence Crawford, the Eastern Association infantry general, had to move over and take command. Cromwell's absence at the height of the battle caused much adverse comment later, particularly from the Scots, but when he did return he found the situation more or less stabilised, with the royalist horse nowhere to be seen and his men trying to break down the enemy infantry adjacent to them.

But on the allied right wing it was another story altogether. Here Thomas Fairfax, leading the charge, came to grief in a maze of hedges and ditches; Goring, at the head of the Northern horse, stood his ground. Fairfax and his troop ploughed through, only to find that Goring's counter-charge had swept away the rest of his regiments, and the regiments under John Lambert which formed the second line, and even a reserve brigade of Scots under the Earl of Eglington. Goring hurtled on in true Rupertian fashion until he reached the Scots baggage train well to the rear, though Sir Charles Lucas rallied his own regiment and began to hack away at the Scots infantry on the right of the allied line nearest to him. At this stage Newcastle threw in the last royalist cavalry reserve under Sir William Blakiston against the allied centre, which was held by Lord Fairfax's Yorkshire foot, with the Scots forming the second and third lines. Blakiston smashed through all three lines and charged clear to the top of the hill, almost overrunning the allied command headquarters.

It was at this stage that Leven and Lord Fairfax – with smoke obscuring much of the field and the light fading, with no certain news of their left wing and the right apparently broken, with their baggage train plundered, with their infantry in the centre overwhelmed and enemy troopers hard upon them – concluded that the day was lost. They both fled, taking with them contingents from their respective armies; Leven got as far as Wetherby, fourteen miles away, and it was said that Fairfax never drew rein till he reached Leeds. Neither returned for a good forty-eight hours. (The more phlegmatic Manchester probably stayed on, though the next we hear of him is in the early hours of the following morning, touring the battlefield to succour the wounded.) On the other hand, Rupert seems to have left the field early too, and nothing is heard of Lord Eythin from start to finish; Newcastle appears to have been in sole charge.

But at this stage all was transformed. Fairfax, ordering his men to throw away their distinguishing badges, had led them round the back of the royalist army to the left wing, where he found Cromwell sporting a bandaged head but in charge of a virtually intact cavalry brigade. They led their men round the back again, looking for Goring's horse, triumphantly returning from the plunder of the baggage train. Goring found himself charging through hedges and over ditches as Fairfax had, and he was even more comprehensively routed. This disposed of the last of the royalist horse, for Sir Charles Lucas's attack on the Scots infantry brigade commanded by Sir William Baillie had only demonstrated the invulnerability of well-drilled pikemen against cavalry. Lucas's own horse was impaled on a pike, and he was dragged under and captured; few of his troopers fared better, many worse, and the survivors simply fled.

By this time night had fallen, but a harvest moon gave enough light to doom the abandoned royalist infantry. Few of them asked for quarter, and the last to go were Sir William Lambton's whitecoats, and Sir William with them. It was a scene of brutal carnage. Cromwell ordered in three regiments of Scots dragoons, but:

> By mere valour for one whole hour [they] kept the troops of horse from entering amongst them by push of pike; when the horse did enter they would have no quarter, but fought it out till there was not thirty of them living, whose hap it was to be beaten down upon the ground. As the troopers came near them though they could not rise from their wounds, yet [they] were so desperate as to get a sword or a pike or piece of them, and to gore the troopers' horses as they came over them or passed them by.

In the end 'every man fell in the same order and rank wherein he had fought'. It was heroic, perhaps, but it was not war. Neither side had the facilities to handle prisoners of war, and if these men had surrendered they would simply have been disarmed, and released a few weeks later. Their destruction, at a time when infantry were at a premium in the South, was an even greater disaster than the loss of the battle.

But the battle of Marston Moor was not necessarily a decisive defeat. It had been the bloodiest battle of the Civil Wars. It is estimated that over 6,000 men were killed, two-thirds of them royalists, with an unusually high proportion of officers. Another hundred officers, and 1,500 men, were captured. But the next day Rupert rounded up about

3,000 horse, including most of Goring's Northern horse, and 2,000 more arrived from North Yorkshire under Sir William Clavering; there were still between a thousand and two thousand infantry who had never left York. Moreover, the Scots army was about to retire north, to reduce Carlisle and Newcastle; it did not return until the following year. The Earl of Manchester was hastily recalled to the South; the counties of the Eastern Association were under threat, and with Waller's army falling apart, and Essex's marching farther and farther into the West, he was needed to deal with the King. In other words, the royalists might have to surrender York, but the North was not lost.

However, Newcastle would have nothing of it; nor, of course would Eythin. They both departed for Scarborough and exile next day, though it may be significant that they eventually sailed in different ships. Newcastle's refusal to go to Oxford – 'I will not endure the laughter of the Court', he said – is understandable. He had bankrupted himself in the royal cause, and his vast estates in Nottinghamshire and Northumberland were under enemy occupation. But his attitude seems to have communicated itself to Rupert, who simply left for Lancashire with his remaining cavalry on 4 July, two days after the battle. The King showed more resolution, and the war in the South was now swinging in his favour; he insisted on regarding Newcastle's resignation as provisional, and appointed Goring temporary Commander-in-Chief North. However, Goring simply trailed after Rupert into Lancashire, with the Northern horse. York surrendered on the 16th, and its governor, Sir Thomas Glemham, departed with the garrison for Carlisle, where he held out until July 1645, tying down a large part of the Scots army. Leven forced the surrender of Newcastle on 22 October, but by that time the campaigning season was over.

The rest of the month Rupert wandered up and down Lancashire to no apparent purpose, when he would have been better employed in the South. On 9 July he was at Ingleton, the 10th Hornby, the 12th Garstang, the 14th Preston, the 17th Garstang again; then to Kirkby Lonsdale on the 18th, back to Garstang on the 20th, Preston on the 21st. Such enemy forces as there were gave him a wide berth; on the other hand he avoided their headquarters at Manchester. On 21 July he paid a brief visit to Lathom House, next day he was at Liverpool, but then he cut straight down to Chester and on south to Shrewsbury, taking Goring with him. The Northern horse opted to stay behind under Sir Marmaduke Langdale, but on 25 August they were beaten in a scuffle at Ormskirk by the redoubtable Sir John

Meldrum, who had brought a small army over from Nottinghamshire, and they headed south to rejoin Rupert.

Meldrum went on to Liverpool with the German engineer Rosworm, from Manchester; they took its surrender on 1 November. Meldrum, like Rupert, thought such places were more trouble than they were worth. In fact, he was rather appalled to find that the defences of Liverpool were as strong as any he had seen in Europe, and he told the Committee for Both Kingdoms:

> I cannot forbear that accustomed freedom I have taken to acquaint your lordships with what, in my apprehension, I conceive may be both dangerous and unprofitable to this state, which is to keep up forts and garrisons which may foment rather than finish a war. France, Italy and the Low Countries have found by experience during these three hundred years that losses are entailed by places being fortified, while the subjects of the Isle of Britain, through absence thereof, have lived in more tranquillity. If Gainsborough had not been razed by my order, the enemy might have found a nest to have hatched much mischief at this time. Reading might have produced the same effects if the fortifications had not been demolished. If there be a garrison kept at Liverpool there must be at least three hundred men, which will make the jealousies and emulations amongst these [local] gentlemen endless and chargeable.

The Committee agreed, the local parliamentarians did not, with the result that a year later Liverpool still had a garrison of six hundred, though it took no further part in the war.

Meanwhile, if the King had lost the North, by the end of July Parliament was in danger of losing the South. Its main field army, under the Earl of Essex, reached Tavistock on the 26th, but on the same day the King marched into Exeter, less than thirty miles behind. There he found his youngest child, the six-weeks-old Henriette-Anne, in the charge of Lady Dalkeith; her mother had fled to France three weeks before. Essex was demanding that Waller be sent after him to harass the King, unaware that Waller's army was on the point of collapse. He now forsook Plymouth, which could have resisted a siege almost indefinitely, and could be supplied by sea, and pressed on into Cornwall. But the idea that his coming would rouse latent support for Parliament proved a delusion, and at Bodmin he turned south towards the Lostwithiel peninsula and the port of Fowey, looking for naval assistance. The Committee for Both Kingdoms was still trying to whip up a relief force, but it could only send out Lieutenant-General Middleton

with 2,000 horse and dragoons; too little, too late. Waller was sent back
to join the remnants of his army at Abingdon, but as usual the London
regiments would not move 'one foot further, except it be home'. Early
in September he was back at his old base at Farnham; Parliament
sent him another 1,400 men, but he remarked that they had 'brought
their mouths with them', and he had pay and provisions for only three
weeks. Eventually he did set out with a scratch force of 2,000 foot
and less than 1,000 horse, but by then he could only rendezvous with
Middleton at Taunton and retreat east again with the remains of
Essex's horse.

At Exeter Charles was joined by the Western army under Maurice,
bringing his numbers up to about 16,000. Essex, having left garrisons
dotted all over Devon, was now reduced to 10,000. But the King
had his own troubles. He discovered that Henry Wilmot, Lieutenant-
General of Horse in Rupert's absence, had put out feelers to Essex for
a truce, to be followed by a negotiated peace, which would be imposed
by force if necessary on the leaders on both sides. Rupert was informed,
and he sent Goring to join the King. He arrived on 7 August at
Boconnoc, three miles from Lostwithiel. Next day Charles suddenly
ordered his provost-marshal to arrest Wilmot at the head of his brigade
and sent him under strict guard to Exeter, his place being taken by
Goring. The result was a near-mutiny; the King had to ride round the
regiments in person and reassure the officers. All the same, he received
a petition from the 'Old Horse', the elite brigade which Wilmot had
led to victory at Roundway Down and Cropredy Bridge, expressing
their 'great amazement almost to distraction', and requesting 'some
light from your Majesty concerning this business'. Lord Digby wrote
irritably, 'This is the most mutinous army that ever I saw, not only
horse but foot', and it was fortunate that they were in the middle of a
highly successful campaign, not returning from a defeat. There was a
good reason for Wilmot's disgrace, if one assumed that the war must
be fought to a finish, as did the King and Digby. Professional officers
like Wilmot were beginning to have doubts, and these were soon to be
shared by commanders on the other side; the Earl of Manchester
obviously, perhaps Essex himself. Rupert was to join them the following
year, but for the moment he acquiesced, having no liking for his second-
in-command. All the same, Charles had to compromise; he abandoned
the idea of court-martialling Wilmot, who was allowed to leave for
France, where in exile he became a trusted adviser of the young
Charles II.

Meanwhile Essex was still penned up near the bottom of the Fowey peninsula. On the night of 31 August he ordered his cavalry to break out under his Dutch Commissary-General, Behre, which they did; they reached Plymouth with the loss of a hundred men, and joined Middleton and Waller at Taunton. Next day Essex slipped away in a fishing coble, leaving Philip Skippon to make the best terms he could for the infantry. He explained, 'I thought it fit to look to myself, it being a greater terror to me to be a slave to their contempts than a thousand deaths.' But a royalist news-sheet pertinently enquired why his men had voted 'to live and die with the Earl of Essex, since the Earl hath declared that he will not live and die with them'. In fact, the men were simply disarmed and allowed to march home, having given their word that they would not fight again until they reached Portsmouth, where they arrived a fortnight later. Charles's leniency allowed these experienced troops, most of them veterans of Edgehill and Newbury, to survive intact; they comprised the core of the New Model Army infantry in 1645.

It was a failure so spectacular as to be numbing, and Essex's hectoring letter of self-exculpation, blaming everyone else, and especially Waller, was tacitly accepted by the House of Commons, though Sir Arthur Haselrigg burst into irreverent laughter. The only logical step was to dismiss the Lord General out of hand, but no one was ready for that, and it was agreed to recruit and re-equip his army as soon as possible. But it was certain that Waller would no longer serve under him, and unlikely that Manchester would either. In fact, there was an epidemic of disputes among Parliament's general officers. Hans Behre was bitterly unpopular with the Scots officers in Essex's army, an issue made public by the exchange of printed statements and counter-statements. Essex refused to dismiss him, but he solved the problem himself by resigning as soon as he returned from the West and retiring to Holland. He was succeeded by his leading critic, Sir William Balfour. As for Waller, apart from his disagreements with Essex he had been quarrelling with Richard Browne most of the summer, and the Committee for Both Kingdoms called in vain for an end to such 'distractions' between 'men of worth and honour'. More seriously, in the aftermath of Marston Moor a violent dispute had broken out over who deserved most credit for the victory, the English or the Scots, which found its natural focus in the mounting antipathy between Cromwell and Lawrence Crawford.

Cromwell had always been bitterly opposed to the Scots alliance; he was contemptuous of their military ability, and feared that if they did make a showing in the war they would use it as a lever to impose on the English their own brand of intolerant Presbyterianism, as foreshadowed in the Solemn League and Covenant – a solution towards which a majority of Lords and Commons was now turning as the only remedy for the religious anarchy into which England seemed to be falling. He took the Solemn League and Covenant at the last possible moment, and his cup was filled to overflowing in February 1644, when the Scotsman Crawford appeared out of the blue and was appointed Major-General of Foot to the Eastern Association, superseding him as second-in-command. Crawford was twelve years younger than Cromwell, but he had been a professional soldier all his adult life; he had served for eleven years in the Danish and Swedish armies, three more in the personal guard of Charles Lewis, Elector Palatine, and three more under Ormonde in Ireland. On the Cessation in 1643 he had refused to serve the King and had fled to Scotland, then England, where Parliament received him with open arms. An uncompromising Presbyterian, he soon won the confidence of the Earl of Manchester, who was of like mind, and took up the persistent complaints that Cromwell was deliberately filling his cavalry regiments with working-class men infected with Anabaptism and suchlike sectarian deviations. He did nothing to discourage the accusations of cowardice and dereliction of duty which the Scots levelled against Cromwell after Marston Moor, and may even have endorsed them behind his back. On 10 September the Committee for Both Kingdoms felt obliged to write to Manchester, Waller, Skippon, Behre, Middleton, Crawford and Cromwell, with a copy to Essex, exhorting them 'to lay aside all disputes of their rights and privileges, and to join heartily in the present service'. But two days later Manchester left his army at Huntingdon and posted down to London to ask the Committee, amongst other things, to mediate between Crawford and Cromwell.

Manchester had been slow to move south after the surrender of York; he hung around Lincoln the rest of July and most of August, but he declined to mount an attack on Newark. He had some excuse; he reported that casualties, sickness and desertion had reduced his army to 6,000 men, and their pay was £30,000 in arrears. Such men as he had were 'under great indispositions and infections'. When it seemed that the King might make another feint at East Anglia, in late July, he warned the Committee:

The Association by which we were raised and should be paid will have just cause to withdraw or slacken their hands from our further recruiting or maintenance, and seek for some other body or head to protect them, and the same only to be maintained by them.

Whatever this rather oracular warning meant, it could not be ignored. More than ever the Eastern Association was central to Parliament's war effort. In theory Parliament had access to ample supplies of cash. In February 1643 it had introduced the weekly assessment, for £44,235, levied on the whole country – by the same method as ship money, ironically enough.* It was regularly renewed, and was made monthly in 1645. In March 1643 another ordinance provided for the sequestration of royalists' estates, the income thereof being diverted to 'public uses', and in July a 'New Impost', or excise, was imposed on alcoholic drinks and imported luxury goods.

However, all this was in the realm of theory. None of these taxes, obviously enough, could be levied in areas outside Parliament's control, though in public it continued to pretend that they could. A more realistic guide is the counties listed in an ordinance of 31 October 1643 for the support of those widowed, orphaned or maimed in the service of Parliament; that is, Berkshire, Buckinghamshire, Bedfordshire, Cambridgeshire, Essex, Hertfordshire, Huntingdonshire, Hampshire, Kent, Middlesex, Northamptonshire, Norfolk, Surrey, Suffolk, Sussex and, of course, London. If we take these counties alone, then the income from the weekly assessment drops from £44,235 to £21,272 10s, less than half, and even then this was the absolute maximum, rarely achieved if ever. As for the excise, this was hit by the disruption of trade and active public hostility. Moreover, there were constant complaints from London that the income from the assessment, the excise and sequestered estates was being diverted to local uses, and it proved very difficult to impose these novel taxes on 'reconquered' counties like Lincolnshire and Yorkshire. In these circumstances the sheltered wealth of the Eastern Association, apart from west Wales the only area not so far damaged by the war, became increasingly desirable, and increasingly useful.

The Army of the Association had been raised the previous winter at its own expense, naturally (p. 76 above); an ordinance of 20 September

---

* That is, the lump sum was divided amongst the counties roughly in proportion to their assumed population and wealth, and each county committee had to raise its share by whatever means possible.

1643 levied an extra weekly assessment on the Associated Counties, in addition to their usual assessment; thus Essex's assessment of £1,125 was doubled, Huntingdon had to pay £250 a week on top of £200, and so on down the line. On 22 October the Association was also ordered to contribute £21,000 to a general forced loan to finance the Scots invasion; Essex's share was £5,000. But this was not the end. On 1 December, with four more weeks of the additional special assessment to run, the Association, plus Northamptonshire, was asked to finance the establishment of a new base at Newport Pagnell in Buckinghamshire, which was represented as an essential outlying shield for East Anglia. A lump sum was demanded to raise and equip the garrison; Essex's share was £125, Huntingdon's £45, and so on; and for their maintenance a monthly levy was to continue indefinitely, equal to the lump sum. So, in this one month, December 1643, the taxpayers of Essex had to find £4,500 ordinary assessment, £4,500 special assessment for the army and £250 for Newport Pagnell, not to mention another £300, being the county's share of a special levy imposed on 31 October for six months for the support of war widows, orphans and invalids. Moreover, on 1 January 1644 the special assessment had to be renewed for four months at a higher rate: in Essex £1,687 10s as against £1,125, in Huntingdon £330 as against £250, and so on *pro rata*. On 1 May it was renewed for another four months. Shortly afterwards the army for which the Associated Counties were paying so heavily was ordered north, leaving them unprotected, and on 3 July, when it seemed that Charles I was going to advance into East Anglia, Parliament had the effrontery to order them to raise an emergency defence force, self-financed of course, to repel, as they put it, 'the invasion and fury of the Irish rebels, popish and ill-affected persons who seek the ruin and destruction of the whole kingdom'. Fortunately, Charles turned back towards the West, and this defence force was apparently never raised, but it is against this background that we must view the Earl of Manchester's operations that autumn.

Thus, despite a stream of orders and entreaties from London, he did not leave Lincoln until 4 September, and then only for Huntingdon. There on the 8th news reached him of the débâcle at Lostwithiel. On the 12th he went to London in person to plead his case, and the Committee for Both Kingdoms scraped together what money it could to meet his troops' arrears of pay, and sent him 1,800 new conscripts. He then resumed his march south, but he made slow progress. On 22 September he reached Watford, on the 29th Reading, but here he stuck, brushing aside categorical orders to join Waller in Dorset so as to intercept the King on his return. Cromwell and most of his other field officers argued against him, but he was almost certainly right. The King was returning in triumph from a signal victory; to confront him with what was for the moment Parliament's only effective army, and that under-strength, would be to court disaster. Better to wait, he argued, until Essex's army was re-formed; then Essex and Waller could take up their positions at Reading and Abingdon, keeping up the pressure on Oxford, while he himself withdrew to St Albans, north of London, whence he could outflank an attack on the Associated Counties, which was still on the cards.

In fact Charles was slow to forsake the West; he had his own supply, recruitment and command problems. He also had to leave a garrison at Plymouth and siege detachments at Taunton and Lyme, which he had no time to reduce. Eventually he left Plymouth on 10 September with an army of 10,000; he reached Chard in Somerset on the 23rd, Sherborne in Dorset on 2 October, where Rupert awaited him.

They had been apart for nearly six months, and in the Prince's absence his enemy Lord Digby had made the most of his chances. But if Wilmot's disgrace two months before had been a triumph for Digby, it had also strengthened Rupert's position on the Council of War, and once he was back in his uncle's presence he soon reasserted his authority. It was now agreed that he should supersede the veteran Earl of Forth as Commander-in-Chief at the earliest opportunity, though not yet. For the present he returned to Shrewsbury. Nor did the King call on the forces Rupert was holding at Shrewsbury, consisting of his own cavalry brigade, the Northern horse under Langdale, and 2,000 foot newly recruited by Charles Gerard in South Wales – and this despite the fact that at least a thousand men had by now deserted Charles's army; presumably men of the old Western army reluctant to leave their home area again. Nevertheless, it was decided that Rupert and Gerard should make a diversion, which in fact came to nothing, while the King pressed on to relieve Basing House before retiring to winter quarters. Both sides seem to have put a disproportionate valuation on Basing, but it was a modest enough aim, considering the enemy's palpable disarray.

So Charles continued east, reaching Salisbury on 15 October. Waller fell back on Andover, and Manchester grudgingly advanced to Basingstoke, where Waller joined him on the 18th. Manchester now sent for four London trained-band regiments to supplement his infantry, and

Essex's horse soon arrived under Sir William Balfour, and his re-equipped foot under Skippon. Since Essex would take orders from no other general, and no other general would now take orders from him, the Committee for Both Kingdoms had appointed a War Council consisting of Essex, Manchester, Waller and their senior field officers, which was to reach decisions by majority vote, though even then it could be overruled by the Committee in London. Fortunately for all concerned, Essex now fell seriously ill, and was bed-ridden at Reading for the rest of the campaigning season.

When the King came up he realised that he could do little for Basing House at that moment, hedged in as it was by three enemy armies. But he fancied his chances at Donnington Castle, near Newbury, about sixteen miles north-west, and so confident was he that he sent away nine hundred horse to raise the siege of Banbury, though this reduced him to about 8,000 men, against at least 17,500. However, he took up a formidably strong position just north of Newbury: to the south was the town itself, strongly garrisoned; to the north stood Donnington Castle, a tall, heavy medieval castle whose height gave its guns considerable range and force; to the east was Shaw House, a semi-fortified manor house protected on three sides by prehistoric earthworks; and to the west was Speen Hill, on which Prince Maurice planted his guns. The whole area was hedged and not well suited to cavalry.

He had to be dealt with somehow, and the parliamentary armies came up from the east on 26 October. After sizing up the situation the Council of War came up with an extraordinary plan. They decided to send about two-thirds of the combined armies – Essex's horse and foot, the London trained bands and Waller's and Cromwell's horse – round to the north in a thirteen-mile arc so as to attack Speen Hill from the west. Then at a prearranged signal Manchester would hurl the remaining infantry against Shaw House, squeezing the royal army from two sides.

Waller set off before midnight, but he bivouacked on the way and did not arrive until about 3 p.m., leaving him two hours of daylight at the most. He attacked Speen Hill and after some heavy fighting captured it, forcing Maurice back on Speen village. Balfour's horse charged on the right wing and drove the royalist cavalry back on the village too, but on the left wing Cromwell was too slow, and a sudden charge by Goring's horse drove him back. This gave Prince Maurice's horse, on the other wing, a breathing space; they rallied, and the parliamentary infantry were temporarily marooned in the village. (Second Newbury was emphatically not one of those 'mercies' on which Cromwell loved to dwell in later years.) As for Manchester, he hesitated to launch his prearranged attack, despite Lawrence Crawford's urging. Why he hesitated is not clear; he may have missed the agreed signal from Waller, but from the general din to the west it was obvious that the royalists were engaged in that quarter. As it was, it was not until 4 p.m. that he ordered a two-pronged attack on Shaw House, and then it was repulsed with heavy losses.

The fighting died away at dusk, but clearly the King's army could not linger. Charles left his artillery in Donnington Castle and slipped quietly away to the north through the small gap between the castle and Shaw House, none of the enemy commanders having thought to post a watch. A few miles north he left with a small escort to meet Rupert again at Bath while the rest of the army headed for Oxford and home. Next morning Waller, Cromwell and Haselrigg took horse and chased them for thirty miles, but despite repeated messages Manchester refused to send his infantry after them, and they returned for an angry meeting of the Council of War. Waller and Haselrigg wanted to pursue the King to Bath, and bring him and Rupert to battle, but Manchester turned on Haselrigg: 'Thou art a bloody fellow', he said. 'God send us peace, for God does never prosper us in our victories to make them clear victories.' He agreed to storm Donnington Castle, but his men were repulsed with further heavy losses. The combined armies then moved eleven miles to the north, in the direction of Oxford, then eleven miles back, ending up near Newbury again. No one knew what to do.

But the King did. On 30 October he and Rupert left Bath with about 3,000 horse and foot, and ordered the Northern horse to meet them at Burford, just north of Oxford. There they called out most of the Oxford garrison, bringing their total numbers up to about 15,000. The King also took the occasion to announce, on 6 November, that the Earl of Forth had resigned and was to be replaced by Rupert, as arranged at Sherborne four weeks before. There is no suggestion that Forth resented this; he was over seventy, he was a martyr to gout, and he had been wounded at Newbury; he had also been given the honour, unusual for a Scotsman, of an English peerage, as Earl of Brentford.

Next day, 7 November, Charles marched straight for Donnington to retrieve his guns, and on the 9th his army came to rest near the field of First Newbury in 1643, west of the town. He wheeled his guns out of the castle, waited for an hour or two in case Manchester wanted to give battle, then retired in triumph, drums beating and banners waving, without a shot fired.

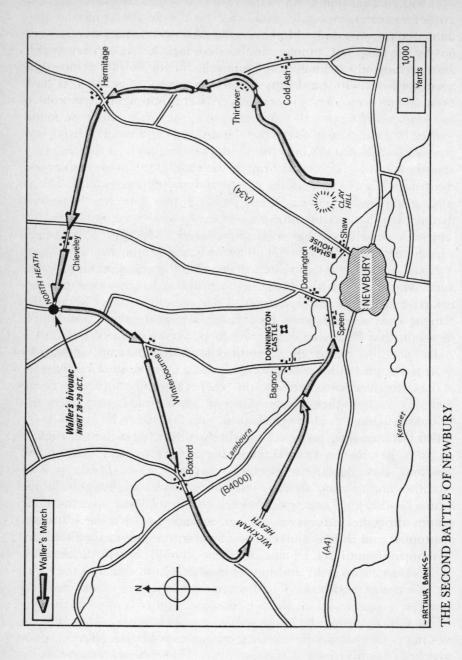

THE SECOND BATTLE OF NEWBURY

—ARTHUR BANKS—

It was an astonishing end to the year's campaign. However, the two armies were now roughly equal, for men were deserting the parliamentary armies daily. Moreover, the men who remained were worn out by the long, wet summer, and so were their horses – 'Very unable for marching or watching,' said Cromwell, 'having now for so long time been tired out with hard duty in such extremity of weather as hath been seldom seen.' The general officers were thoroughly demoralised too, and when Cromwell demanded that they give battle he found himself in a minority of one in the Council of War. Even Haselrigg was now against it; if the King beat them, he said, they had no back-up army nearer than Newcastle. Manchester took up this point and carried it further: 'If we beat the King ninety and nine times,' he said, 'yet he is King still, and so will his posterity be after him; but if the King beat us once we shall all be hanged, and our posterity made slaves.' To which Cromwell gave his celebrated answer: 'My lord, if this be so, why did we take up arms at first? This is against fighting ever hereafter.'

Apart from its epigrammatic succinctness, there was nothing new in what Manchester said; Haselrigg had said as much a few minutes before, and Waller had remarked a few months earlier, 'Break [the King's] army never so often, his person will raise another.' But there is no doubt that Cromwell's was the 'official view' held at Westminster. In fact on 13 November the Committee for Both Kingdoms decided 'to write to the Earl of Manchester and the other commanders taking note of the late dishonour in suffering the relief of Donnington; also to desire them not to go to their winter quarters as long as the enemy is in the field, and to have a care to prevent the relief of Basing'.

But this brought a positive howl of protest from Manchester, backed up by Waller, Balfour and Skippon (though not Cromwell). Both horse and foot, they said, were seriously weakened, in quality as well as quantity, and sickness was rife. They were not strong enough to storm Basing, and a long siege, with winter setting in, would destroy their armies altogether. Moreover, the surrounding area was now drained of supplies and in real danger of famine. In conclusion they told the Committee roundly: 'If any inconvenience should come to the State by not keeping such castles and houses from relief, we conceive the error lies in the first undertaking such sieges, and the loose prosecuting of them.'

The Committee could only acquiesce. Manchester stayed put at Newbury; the King threw fresh men and supplies into Basing, then marched jauntily back to Oxford on 23 November. To the Long

Parliament it must have seemed that its armies were collapsing on every front. Massey reported a wave of desertions at Gloucester, Browne at Abingdon, this time horse as well as foot. Even the Windsor garrison had mutinied, raising fears of a royalist plot, and three hundred London militia auxiliaries had to be sent out to deal with them. Manchester marched his three tattered armies back to Reading for the winter, then he and the other principals left for London and the inevitable post-mortem.

# 7

# THE LAST
# CAMPAIGN

Both sides were now on the point of collapse,
though Parliament seemed more conscious
of this than the King. Charles was unde-
rstandably buoyed up by his outstanding personal success in the campaign of 1644, by the pathetic incompetence of the enemy generals,
and by the failure of the Scots to play the major role expected of them.
With the removal of Wilmot and the Earl of Forth it seemed that he
had also solved his command problems, though these were minor
compared with Parliament's, and he looked forward to the next campaign with some optimism.

However, he had one serious weakness: shortage of infantry. In
fact, both sides were finding it difficult to recruit fresh pikemen and
musketeers, and it was a longstanding problem. It seems that there was
no serious shortage of cavalry right to the end: their pay was higher
(when pay was issued), their battle casualties were lighter, they had
their own transport, and at the end of a day's march they could roam
far and wide in search of food and shelter. Cavalry troopers were
also drawn from a slightly higher social class, of yeomanry or even
freeholders, which is why Cromwell was criticised so sharply for enrol-
ling 'mere mechanics' in his regiments.

The infantry were another matter. The men recruited on both sides
in 1642 and early 1643 were most of them highly motivated for one

reason or another, but when battle casualties began to erode their numbers they proved difficult to replace. Thus from the autumn of 1643 both sides began to resort to conscription, but they found it did not serve. They called in almost identical terms for able-bodied and well-motivated men, but what they got were the off-scourings of society. Even the High Constable of Norfolk, recruiting for the Eastern Association army, unblushingly told his deputies, 'Have an especial care to take idle serving men and such other able persons as live dissolutely or idly without employment.' Such men continued to live dissolutely and idly in the army, and deserted at the first opportunity. The levies from Suffolk in 1643 frightened even Cromwell. 'They are so mutinous', he said, 'that I may justly fear they would cut my throat.' In September 1643 the Essex trained bands had to be called out to protect the public against one such group of conscripts, though they were not yet armed. This is why Parliament increasingly turned to the London trained bands, though with mixed results; when they were brought to battle, as at Edgehill, First Newbury and Cheriton, they performed excellently, but they would not put up with the routine slog of campaigning, especially under Waller, who never inspired the same loyalty in his troops as Essex did. Moreover, many of these militiamen could ill be spared at home. When they stood down the Essex trained bands in July 1644 the Committee for Both Kingdoms remarked:

> We know they are men of trade and employment, and cannot well be absent from their occasions, by attendance on which they are enabled to pay those great levies which issue from that county among the rest of the Association. Besides, they are men of that quality and course of life as cannot well bear the difficulties of a soldier's life.

This was to become an increasing preoccupation in 1645, as we shall see; once the surplus elements in working-class society had been used up the government found itself recruiting taxpayers.

Waller thought that the King was better able to raise recruits, and so did other parliamentary leaders; Edward Massey remarked in July 1644, 'The more his Majesty's armies show themselves abroad and the farther they march, the stronger they grow.' However, there is no evidence for this, and by 1644 Charles was finding it increasingly difficult to make good the losses incurred by the veteran infantry of the Oxford field army, and his inability to supply Hopton's new Southern army with sufficient infantry led to its defeat at Cheriton (p. 94 above). As we have seen, the Oxford Parliament commented on the disproportion of cavalry to infantry in the royal army, and early in 1644 it ordered the conscription of another 6,000 men. But this produced less than six hundred, none of them of the best quality; in April the Earl of Forth commented that out of 334 men conscripted in Berkshire only 121 had reached him, and 51 of these had promptly deserted. After the King's successful campaign in the West that summer an ambitious scheme was floated for a new Western army, but it came to nothing, and when the Prince of Wales arrived at Bristol in March 1645 the authorities were hard put to it to raise a regiment of lifeguards for his personal protection.

This makes nonsense of any theory of popular involvement in the cause, on either side, certainly amongst the lower classes. The reservoir of working-class support enjoyed by both sides in 1642 was soon drained and could not be refilled. Another pointer is the ease with which prisoners of war were recruited by their captors. Fairfax drew heavily on this source, and regarded ex-royalists as being amongst his best troops; when a captured royalist officer commented on this, he told him: 'I found you had made them good soldiers; I have made them good men.' At first the King enjoyed similar success; in October 1642, when he took Banbury, the whole garrison changed sides; so did the garrison of Cirencester the following February, and about a thousand of the Bristol garrison in July. But instances of this in 1644 are rare, and if any attempt was made to recruit Essex's infantry after their surrender at Lostwithiel it failed; they were present almost to a man at Second Newbury.

There is some suggestion that this was because Parliament was better able to pay its troops. For instance, in July 1644 Massey reported that the previous winter he had taken more than a thousand royalist deserters into the Gloucester garrison, only to lose them again for lack of pay; indeed, according to him Gloucestershire was full of such freebooting gangs, ready to serve any commander on either side able to pay them.

Unfortunately, pay is a complex problem; it is obscured by the wholesale destruction of royalist financial records at the end of the war, and the much fuller evidence left by the Long Parliament has never been properly analysed and assessed. Certainly in the beginning both sides undertook to pay their troops; the going rate varied very little, and was usually 6s a week for infantrymen, 12s 6d for dragoons and 17s 6d for cavalry troopers, though the two last were expected to feed their horses out of this. However, it seems that the King soon abandoned the effort to pay his cavalry, and it is questionable whether he paid his infantry at all regularly after the first winter of the war. In November 1643 he was promising to pay new foot soldiers 4s a week, the other 2s being placed to their credit, but it is doubtful if he could keep this up for long. We know that Hopton and Grenville's Western army was never paid in any regular way, and apparently enlisted on those terms; they were provided with food and clothes, which were usually docked from a soldier's pay, occasional financial windfalls were shared out amongst them, and they were allowed a certain amount of controlled looting. By 1644 we may guess that this was the standard pattern. The King levied 'contributions' on the counties under his control, usually at a higher rate than the parliamentary assessment, but much of this was devoted to the day-to-day maintenance of the forces in the area, and any spare money was appropriated for war supplies in general. He also tried to impose an excise, again at a higher rate than Parliament's, on the ports he controlled, notably Bristol, but it was not a success. All in all, he lacked the smooth-running machinery provided by Parliament's county committees, and the central bureaucracy associated with the Committee for Advance of Money at Goldsmiths' Hall.

On the other hand, Parliament's insistence that all tax proceeds be brought up to London and redistributed from the centre was on the face of it sophisticated and enlightened, but it did not work well in practice and in the post-war crisis of 1647 had to be abandoned altogether for a time. Moreover, though its income was most probably larger than the King's, there were more calls on it. In 1642 and 1643 it continued to send occasional refreshers to Ireland, and in 1644 it undertook a heavy financial commitment to the Scots army in England which it had difficulty fulfilling. It was even more difficult to fulfil its promise to maintain the Scots army in Ulster; in fact it could not, but it made sporadic efforts to do so, and this was another occasional drain on its resources. Partly as a result, in January 1644 it decreed that army officers drawing 10s a day or more were to 'respite' half their salary, those drawing less, one-third: a kind of 'post-war credit' only redeemed by those who stayed on into 1649 and 1650, and then usually in debentures on Irish land. As for the troops, it seems that by 1644 Parliament had quietly given up any pretence of paying those in garrisons, and the pay of the remainder was falling heavily into arrears. In that calendar year the cavalry of the Eastern Association was paid for only 126 days out of 366, Essex's cavalry for 91, Waller's for 77. The Eastern Association infantry were paid for 35 or 37 weeks out of the 52, Essex's for only 13 to 15. (We have no figures for Waller's infantry.) However, mutinies on this score were postponed until after the war; such mutinies as occurred in 1644 were amongst the London trained-band or auxiliary regiments, who were not paid anyway. Others simply deserted, and though this was the subject of constant complaint on the part of the parliamentary generals the royalists were worse affected. Between 26 July and 30 September 1644 Prince Maurice's Western army shrank from 4,600 to 2,000, and as a result he posted provost-marshals on the border between Devon and Cornwall to intercept deserters, but to no avail. In the campaign of 1645 both armies were seriously short of infantry, even the New Model.

Nevertheless, right to the end the King was able to feed, clothe, equip and arm his men well enough, and this is on the face of it surprising when we consider the fact that the pre-war small-arms industry was concentrated on London, the gunpowder industry on Surrey and Sussex, the ordnance industry on Sussex and Kent, and the main cloth-making centres on East Anglia and the West Riding of Yorkshire. However, for his ordnance the King set up mills and foundries in Worcestershire, for small arms he established factories at Oxford and later at Bristol, for uniforms tailors were pressed into service over a wide radius from Oxford. But for small arms, ammunition and gunpowder he also relied heavily on imports from abroad, at first through Newcastle, then through Bristol, Weymouth and other west-coast ports. The parliamentary navy could never impose anything like a tight blockade; in this connexion it is suggestive that out of eight major shipments of troops from Ireland to England in the winter of 1643–4 only one was intercepted. In fact, royalist gunrunners were much more at risk from Dunkirk privateers, and their shipments to the West Country continued well into 1645. They were paid in part from the profits of the Cornish tin mines, vested in the Queen – though she had to keep up the interest payments on the Crown jewels, which she had pawned in Holland in 1642 – and otherwise the King's credit held good almost to the end; his Continental suppliers apparently assumed that he must eventually win, or achieve a compromise settlement which would enable him to pay his debts. As for the cloth industry, its ability to supply huge quantities of 'uniforms' at short notice is astonishing. With the resources of East Anglia behind it, it is understandable that Parliament was able to reclothe the New Model Army in a matter of a few weeks in the spring of 1645; it is not so easy to understand how Hopton and Prince Maurice could refit the whole of their Western army with new uniforms and shoes over about six weeks in September and October 1644.

Shoes are a major conundrum in themselves. Troopers and dragoons wore knee- or thigh-length boots, which they apparently provided for themselves, but the infantry wore ordinary shoes, which to judge from illustrations were no more substantial than modern 'casuals'. Even allowing for the fact that few seventeenth-century roads were metalled, they must have worn out very quickly and been in constant need of repair. Yet in all the detailed accounts we have of the personnel of army baggage trains and other ancillary staff there is no mention of cobblers or cordwainers, and the need to replace shoes is rarely mentioned either. There is a suggestion in one document that Essex ordered his army to rendezvous at Northampton in September 1642 so that he could shoe them there. Otherwise, in May 1645, after the New Model Army had made a round trip of two hundred miles, from Windsor down to Dorset and back, Fairfax protested that the soldiers' shoes were worn through and must be replaced, and in January 1646, on his western campaign, he was held up at Tiverton while he waited for fresh shoes and stockings to arrive from London. Also, when Cromwell marched from South Wales to Yorkshire in August 1648 he deliberately went via Leicester, where he picked up 1,500 pairs of shoes sent over from Northampton and 1,500 pairs of stockings from Coventry. That is all; but this must represent the tip of a large iceberg.

However, apart from men, the only commodity which was frequently in short supply was gunpowder. Both sides did their best to interfere with its production by their opponents; when he withdrew his forces from Surrey in November 1642 Charles ordered that the powder mills at Chilworth, near Guildford, be razed to the ground and the dams broken; they were not reopened until 1644. On the other hand, the mills established at Lydney, Gloucestershire, by the Queen's Secretary, Sir John Wintour, were constantly threatened by Massey from Gloucester, and eventually taken over. However, the main problem was how to ensure a regular supply of one of gunpowder's main constituents, saltpetre, or potassium nitrate. This was only available as a by-product of bird-droppings or human urine, and its collection was often difficult, always controversial. Before the war it had been a royal monopoly, and the activities of the government 'saltpetre men', who had the right to enter any man's premises and dig at will in his henhouses, dovecotes and privies, were deeply resented.* The Long Parliament moved to

---

* In 1628 they even applied for authority to excavate the floors of churches, because 'the women piss in their seats, which causes excellent saltpetre'. (I owe this reference to Professor David Cressey.)

abolish these pests in 1641, then rather shamefacedly had to re-enlist them in October 1643. Even then, domestic supplies were insufficient to meet the unprecedented needs of civil war, and though Parliament chauvinistically asserted that 'foreign saltpetre is not equal in goodness with that of our own country, and foreign gunpowder far worse conditioned and less forcible', by 1644 it was having to import large quantities of both. Also, though the evidence is fragmentary, we know that in 1644 and early 1645 the King was importing large quantities of powder, sometimes a thousand barrels at a time, into the West Country, usually from France.

Even so, examples of acute shortages are not hard to come by. Just before Roundway Down Hopton had to confiscate all the bedcords he could find in Devizes and boil them in resin to make match – usually made of flax soaked in saltpetre – for his musketeers. In September 1644 Sir Samuel Luke complained that he had only twenty barrels of powder at Newport Pagnell, and no match at all; the Committee for Both Kingdoms gave one of his officers a pass to the Tower, but he found the magazines empty. In February 1646 Parliament issued a warning that 'the great expense [expenditure] of gunpowder occasioned by the present wars hath well near consumed the old store, and doth exhaust the magazines so fast that without a larger supply the navy, forts and land armies cannot be furnished'. Shortage of powder may have caused the King to break off the first battle of Newbury in 1643, and he and Rupert were desperately short of powder again the following June, though it seems to have had no effect on their subsequent military operations, in the North or in the Midlands and the West. But neither side was ever anxious to advertise its wants and it may well be that such shortages had a concealed influence on more military operations than we know; it may even have stifled others in the planning stage.

There was one further problem in the winter of 1644–5 which both sides intermittently recognised as being serious, but which neither was willing to tackle. For two years now the Midlands counties, plus Wiltshire and Somerset to the west, Cheshire and Lancashire to the north, had suffered from periodic incursions by rival armies, and the extortions practised by local garrisons. Crops had been trampled down, or devoured by cavalry horses, labourers who could ill be spared had volunteered or been conscripted, and penal levies had been imposed, often by both sides in the same area. For instance, in the winter of 1642–3 the town of Chippenham in Wiltshire had to pay three 'contributions' to the parliamentarians and two to the royalists, with a further fine of £200 imposed by the royalists for dealing with the parliamentarians. Such cases were not uncommon.

Worst of all was the cost of quartering soldiers. When there was cash available they or their officers paid on the spot for their board and lodging and fodder for their horses; all the armies had standard rates, the New Model's were 8d a day for troopers, 7d for dragoons, 6d for foot soldiers. However, when no money was available, and by 1644 it usually was not, the troops resorted to 'free quarter'. This was not actually 'free'; the officer or NCO in charge gave the householder a ticket or receipt which in theory could be redeemed later, but it is not clear how this was done or when. We know from the records that many vouchers issued by the Army of the Eastern Association were eventually redeemed, but with regard to Essex's and Waller's armies the situation is not so clear. As for royalist vouchers, unless they could be cashed fairly soon with some local commander, they presumably stood as one of the many debts of Charles I which were never repaid, even after 1660. And the sums involved could be quite considerable; at the end of the first Civil War the rural district of Yellow, near Bath, was owed £1,202 10s 8d. In many areas yeomen, labourers and some tenant farmers and minor gentry were now so angry at the depredations of the armies on both sides, whether 'legalised' by free quarter or not, that they began to form vigilante associations of 'Clubmen', whose aim was to harass the troops as best they could in the hope of driving them off their territory or even stopping them from entering it. They began to form in Shropshire, Worcestershire and Herefordshire between January and March 1645, where they gave Massey's new Western Association army a great deal of trouble, and in May and June the movement spread to Wiltshire, Dorset and Somerset, in part a reaction against the indiscipline of Goring's troops.

Parliament was apparently indifferent to the Clubmen, but it could not ignore the possibility of a taxpayers' strike in areas which were nominally under its control. In February 1645 the Lords were outraged to learn that Waller's troops had looted the mansion of one of their number, the Earl of Northumberland, at Petworth, Sussex, and the following week the Commons sent Waller a petition from the gentry of Surrey,

> Representing the great sufferings of that county, especially the western part, by the long free quartering of soldiers under your command amongst them, who, notwithstanding former orders for their removal before this time, do yet continue there, and commit many insufferable outrages both

upon men's persons and estates. We therefore earnestly desire you to command those forces speedily to remove to other quarters out of that county, that it may no longer be disabled to pay the taxes which are now required of them.

Fairfax, too, was warned away from Surrey in very similar terms that April, and on 3 June the Committee for Both Kingdoms wrote sharply to Edward Massey, recently appointed commander of the Western Association:

We have received very great complaints from the country of the intolerable miscarriages of your troopers under Major Buller, whereby great disservice is done to the Parliament by the robbing, spoiling and plundering of the people, they also giving extreme offence by their swearing, drinking and all kinds of debaucheries. Inflict exemplary punishment upon such notorious misdemeanants, and let a better discipline be maintained, they being now looked upon as the greatest enemy in those places where they come.

If the war were not brought to an end quickly, there was a real danger that the patience of the people at large would snap.

Parliament certainly wanted a quick end to the war, but it still had no idea how to set about it. The peace terms it presented to the King in November 1644, which were then discussed by commissioners from both sides for much of the winter at Uxbridge, offered no solution; in fact, they were much harsher than those offered at Oxford in the first winter of the war. The list of proscribed royalists was much longer, for instance, and Charles was now required to take the Solemn League and Covenant and preside over the establishment of Presbyterian church government.

Cromwell had his own ideas about this, and about the conduct of the war. As soon as he took his seat again in the Commons on 25 November he and Waller launched an attack on Manchester's conduct of the Newbury campaign. However, this provoked the House of Lords into supporting the Scots' demand for Cromwell's dismissal, and on 9 December he climbed down. He had no wish, he said, to dwell on the 'oversights' of any one commander; he himself had been guilty of oversights in his time. But it was important at this stage of the war that the politicians divest themselves of military command; their enemies and even some of their friends were now saying:

That the members of both Houses had got great places and commands, and the sword into their hands, and what by interest of Parliament, and. what by power in the Army, will perpetually continue themselves in grandeur, and not permit the war speedily to end, lest their own power should determine with it.

His ally Zouch Tate then rose on cue to present a Self-Denying Ordinance, barring members of either House from civil or military office until the war's end. Cromwell at once supported it, though on the face of it it would have terminated his military career. The Commons agreed, and at the same time accepted a further proposal for the creation of a new, mercenary, 'go-anywhere', 'go-anytime' army, the 'New Model'.

The Lords predictably rejected the Self-Denying Ordinance early in the new year, but on 15 February 1645 they agreed to raise a new army of 22,000 men: 6,600 horse, in eleven regiments; one 1,000-strong dragoon regiment; and twelve regiments of foot (14,400 men), the whole to be kept 'in constant pay' by a special additional levy of £53,500 a month. As before, the Eastern Association counties footed the greater part of the bill; their share of the £53,500 was £29,567, and they were asked to provide more than half the conscripts needed: 4,450 out of 8,460. After strenuous debates, with the Lords still putting forward the claims of Essex and Manchester, it was agreed that its new commander should be Sir Thomas Fairfax, one of the few field commanders of any distinction who was not an MP, and who was safely distanced from the broils of the previous autumn in the South. After some further argument it was decided to drop the pretence, maintained with previous armies, that it was intended for 'the protection of his Majesty's person'; nevertheless, its ostensible purpose was still 'the defence of the King and Parliament, the true Protestant religion, and the laws and liberties of the kingdom'.

Since the new army would absorb Essex's and Manchester's armies, with the remains of Waller's, there was little point in the Lords' continued resistance; even so, it was not until 3 April that they passed a second Self-Denying Ordinance, which simply obliged members to lay down their commands, without forbidding them to resume them later. Essex and Manchester laid down their commissions at once (Essex after a long, whining speech), and so did Lord Fairfax, though as a Scots peer he was not technically required to do so. His place as Commander of the Northern Association was taken first by his deputy, John Lambert, then by Sydenham Poyntz, who, though he had just returned

from service in the Imperial army in Germany, was a firm Presbyterian.
Lambert then went south to join the New Model. The Northern
Association army remained in being, as did Massey's army in
Gloucestershire, reconstituted as the Army of the Western Association.

It is not clear whether Cromwell resigned his own commission or
not. It was an open secret that Fairfax badly wanted him as his
Lieutenant-General of Horse, but his prompt recommissioning, though
permitted by the ordinance, would set an awkward precedent, and his
controversial role at Westminster made him something of an embarrassment. The Lords blamed him for the deliberate humiliation of Essex
and Manchester and he was anathema to the Scots, whom Parliament
was reluctant to offend at a time when they were trying to persuade
them to play a more active part in the next campaign. With Sir Henry
Vane he was emerging as the leader of the Independents in the House
of Commons, whose stand on religious toleration put them at odds with
the majority Presbyterian party under Denzil Holles. Moreover, there
were still persistent complaints, now vigorously taken up by the Earl
of Manchester, that he was of a radical, 'levelling' temper, and had
deliberately infiltrated working-class officers into the Eastern Association army.

This is highly debatable. Certainly Cromwell was on record as saying
that he wanted strenuous, committed fighting men, irrespective of social
rank, but he preferred gentlemen if he could find them. In a celebrated
letter to the Suffolk County Committee in 1643 he told them: 'I had
rather have a plain, russet-coated captain that knows what he fights
for, and loves what he knows, than that which you call a "gentleman"
and is nothing more.' But he added – and this sentence is too often
omitted – 'I honour a gentleman that is so indeed.' In fact the fortunes
and opportunities of war brought many working-class men to the top,
and they were not unknown in the royalist armies. A regiment raised
by Lord Loughborough in Leicestershire in 1644 had amongst its
captains a former tailor, a waiter and a miller, and Thomas Hooper,
a former shoe-maker who had served as an NCO in the Low Countries,
was even commissioned as a colonel of dragoons in the Oxford army in
1643. On the other hand, out of thirty-seven officers of colonel's rank
or above in the New Model Army, twenty-one were commoners from
good families, nine were related to the nobility, and only seven were
not gentlemen by birth.

Moreover, Cromwell could scarcely be spared at this juncture. Parliament's armies were falling apart and the Scots still refused to stir,

though in February 1645 Parliament imposed an additional assessment of £120,000 a month 'to the intent that our brethren of Scotland may receive the greater encouragement to march southward'. Meanwhile Goring was on the rampage in the West; he left Oxford in mid-December with about 5,000 horse and 2,000 foot and executed a wide sweep through Dorset and back. He took Salisbury on 4 January, then swung south to Southampton and back to Aldershot; on the 28th he captured Waller's old base at Farnham. Returning to Dorset, he met with his first check at Weymouth, but he then resumed the siege of Taunton, which was now Parliament's only outpost still in the West. But Parliament was at a loss to deal with him because it was still plagued by recurrent mutinies. There was a serious mutiny at Henley in February, and when the government tried to transfer some of Essex's old cavalry to Waller they mutinied too at Leatherhead: 'We will rather go', they said, 'under any the Lord General should appoint than Sir William Waller, with all the money in England.' Waller had clearly forfeited the confidence of the troops to a disastrous degree, but even Cromwell's own regiment of horse mutinied briefly in January, declaring that they were 'against fighting in any cause whatsoever', and had to be 'refreshed' by an advance of pay. However, Goring had to be stopped, and on 13 February the Committee for Both Kingdoms sent Waller to deal with him with what troops he could scrape together, accompanied by Cromwell and a detachment of Eastern Association cavalry. But they sent a rather extraordinary letter direct to Waller's regimental officers:

> Sir William Waller has received commands to march into the West on very important service, which admits of no delay. We are appointed by the House of Commons to enjoin you to give all ready obedience to such directions, orders and commands as you may receive from him, for performance of which obedience they will require a strict account.

This was enough to avert any incipient mutiny, and in fact this last campaign of Waller's was not his least distinguished, though he found it deeply frustrating. With the forces at his command he could only shadow-box with Goring up and down Dorset, but this was a game in which Goring excelled too, and he twice 'beat up' Cromwell's cavalry in their quarters, at Dorchester on 29 March and Shaftesbury on 3 April, without retribution. After that Goring was recalled to the siege of Taunton, and Waller returned to London to lay down his command for the last time. In his memoirs he left this impression of Cromwell:

He at this time had never shown extraordinary parts, nor do I think that he did himself believe that he had them; for although he was blunt he did not bear himself with pride or disdain. As an officer he was obedient, and did never dispute my orders nor argue upon them.*

The war was still poised on a knife edge. With the old armies breaking up and the new one still being formed the Eastern Association horse were Parliament's only effective weapon, and as soon as he returned Cromwell had to be sent out again to make a number of sweeps across the Midlands, so as to prevent the King debouching from Oxford too soon. Nothing could be expected from the Scots either, at least for the time being. The previous July, 1644, the Marquess of Montrose had left the royal Court and departed for Scotland with a commission as the King's Lieutenant-General north of the Border; at Blair Atholl in Perthshire he was joined by 2,000 tough professional soldiers from Ireland led by Alasdair MacColla, intent on regaining his hereditary lands in Argyll. Added to the Highland volunteers who flocked to his banner, they made him more than a match for the scratch local forces hurriedly raised to deal with him. He marched first on Perth, defeated Lord Elcho at Tippermuir on 1 September, and pressed on to Aberdeen, which he stormed and sacked. Then in December he took advantage of a spell of mild weather to march right across country to Inveraray and ravage the lands of Clan Campbell, whose chief, the Marquess of Argyll, was effectively head of the Scottish government. Leven now had to send back a detachment from his army in England, led by Sir William Baillie, but even he found Montrose elusive and virtually unstoppable. After a remarkable march over the desolate heights of Lochaber in the depths of winter he swooped down on Inverlochy, at the southern end of the Great Glen, and destroyed Argyll's clan army. This was on 2 February.

Montrose's astonishing winter campaign drew the attention of the English royalists back to the North, and none more so than the Northern horse. Now that Goring had succeeded Wilmot as Lieutenant-General of the King's army, this elite force, composed almost entirely of gentry or the sons of gentry, had been handed back to its austere and revered

---

* The two men did not meet again until 1657, when Waller, as a prominent member of the outlawed Presbyterian party, was haled before the Lord Protector himself. By this time Cromwell affected not to know him: 'He did examine me as a stranger,' says Waller, 'not as one whom he had aforetime known and obeyed; yet he was not discourteous.'

commander, Sir Marmaduke Langdale of Holme-upon-Spalding Moor, 'a lean, mortified man', known as 'the Ghost'. Even his eldest son, 'being a father of many children' and 'a man of high spirit', regarded him 'with a childish awe'. He and his men increasingly chafed at their exile in the South after Marston Moor, and early in 1645 they sent a petition to the King, deprecating his apparent decision to abandon the North, and pointing to the sufferings of the royalists there, particularly the defenders of Pontefract, which had been holding out for nearly six months against a determined siege, organised latterly by Thomas Fairfax. They pointed out that:

> Many of our soldiers are already wasted, and do daily moulder away, and that the main of our present strength consists of officers, gentlemen of quality and their attendants, unmeet for those duties which are expected and required, and that the loss of any of them is not small, but involves in it such multitudes as may, by their power and respect, be raised, if they once approach their own habitations.

This elitist attitude was resented by the rest of the army, which is probably why there was a tendency later that year to blame the Northern horse for the disaster of Naseby. However, there was no point in keeping them at Oxford all winter in this mood, and there was a lot to be said for harassing an already harassed enemy by random raids; Goring had just departed for the West on one such raid, and now Langdale was given permission to attempt the relief of Pontefract. This led to one of the most exciting feats of arms in the whole war, and the least-noticed.

Langdale left Banbury on 23 February with about 2,000 men, and they rode so fast that they outstripped the news of their coming, though waves of alarm swept across the counties on their flanks. On the 24th they fought a sharp action near Northampton, the next day they routed a cavalry force of about 2,000 under Colonel Rossiter at Market Harborough, and the day after that they reached Newark, where they took on another two hundred horse and two hundred foot from the garrison. Thereafter they moved more slowly, but all the same their sudden appearance on 1 March at Wentbridge, only five miles from Pontefract, took the besiegers by surprise. John Lambert, who had now taken over from Fairfax, had about 4,000 horse and 2,500 foot, but he was trapped between Langdale's troopers and the exultant defenders, who sallied from the town in force. Driven back on the passage of the River Don at Ferrybridge, he was utterly routed, losing 300 men killed and 800 taken prisoner, together with all his guns. Yorkshire was wide open; but Langdale could not call on any infantry reinforcements, without which his force was a mere raiding party, nor was there any sign of the 'multitudes' who were supposed to rise at his coming. Nor could his men be spared much longer; they were an important component of the King's main field army. So, having torn down the siege works and provisioned the town, they turned south again to join the King's last campaign, and theirs. The siege was resumed on 25 March.

In fact, there are some hints that the idea of a full-scale campaign in the North in 1645 was seriously discussed at Oxford that winter, and Rupert himself was in favour of it. But on 22 February Shrewsbury suddenly fell to a surprise attack, with a strong hint of treachery. Shrewsbury had been the royalists' first successful rallying point in 1642 and Rupert's headquarters for much of 1644, and it was a vital link in the chain of communications between Oxford or Bristol and North Wales and the North West generally. Its loss was a mortal blow to the royalist cause.

It was also symptomatic of a more general anaemia; in the third winter of the war support for the King was silently, steadily draining away. Shrewsbury had defected because the leading townspeople and merchants, oppressed by heavy royalist taxation ever since 1642, were desperate to resume their trade in wool with London. Parliament had decided the previous September to allow royalist 'delinquents' to compound for their offence and resume their sequestered estates on payment of a graduated fine, and they were beating a path to Goldsmiths' Hall in ever increasing numbers. The attitude of the Oxford Parliament in its last session, from November 1644 to March 1645, betrays an acute war weariness. They loudly complained of the depredations of royalist troops in the Midlands and the West, they urged the King to seek a compromise settlement with the Westminster Parliament, and they bitterly criticised Digby's policy of war to the death. Charles prorogued them in anger, describing them as 'a mongrel parliament', 'base and mutinous', and he ordered all their records to be destroyed. Realising that his prime recruiting grounds in Wales and the Marches were drying up, he now made a desperate attempt to reanimate the West by sending the fifteen-year-old Prince of Wales to Bristol with a court and council of his own, but in terms of rallying local support the move was a failure, and it removed from Oxford councillors like Edward Hyde, the future Earl of Clarendon, who had acted as a brake on Digby.

Nevertheless, if the royalists had their problems Parliament's were apparently much worse, and they had no fear of the 'New Noddle',* still less of its young commander. Indeed, the appointment of this thirty-three-year-old Yorkshireman to command an army which was effectively Parliament's last hope was on the face of it very strange. He had been strongly endorsed by Cromwell, and many contemporaries saw him as a screen for that worthy's ruthless intrigues, a mere figurehead. Some historians have fallen into the same trap. But there is no doubt that until the day he retired in 1650 Fairfax's authority over the army was absolute and unquestioned, in peace as in war, and questioned least of all by Cromwell, who was thirteen years his senior but stood in considerable awe of him.

Indeed, 'Black Tom Fairfax' was a remarkable man. Slightly built, self-effacing, non-committal as he was, his absolute self-command, his deep integrity, made him a superb leader of men, though he treated his troops, if needs be, with the same ruthlessness as he did the enemy's. He was not a man for diversionary manoeuvres in battle or for set sieges; he preferred a head-on assault or a storm, whatever the cost in human life, as he showed at Langport and Bridgwater in the western campaign of 1645. The long-drawn-out siege of Colchester in 1648 irked him unendurably. On the other hand he was the first general on either side who succeeded in stopping plunder, largely by the expedient of hanging offenders on the spot; but in return he demanded that Parliament supply his men adequately and pay them regularly, a demand which was on the whole met, at least until the end of the war. His word was always law in the army, the final decisions his. Bulstrode Whitelocke, who saw him at work, says:

> The General was a person of as meek and humble a carriage as ever I saw in great employments, and but of few words in discourse or council; yet when his judgment and reason were satisfied he was unalterable.... I have observed him at councils of war that he hath said little, but hath ordered things expressly contrary to the judgment of all his council.

Thus in July 1645, after a week's agonised debate, he ordered the storm of Bridgwater against the unanimous advice of his Council of War.

So, Parliament had hit upon a commander of genius, but what of his army? There was no shortage of horse or dragoons; in fact, many of Waller's men were 'reduced' – that is, demobilised – even his own

---

\* The term 'New Model' was a nickname; its official title was always 'The Army of Parliament under the command of Sir Thomas Fairfax'.

lifeguard, and so were the personnel of his artillery train at Farnham, though it took months to pay them off. Some of his officers and Essex's found employment under Massey in the Western Association, but at least 140 had to resign. Two hundred and forty infantry officers were also made redundant, because their regiments were seriously under strength, and because the New Model was to have larger regiments; the five regiments taken over from Essex and Waller were remustered as three. After a sharp struggle at Westminster Fairfax was left free to nominate his own officers, subject to parliamentary approval, which meant that Lawrence Crawford, for one, left for the Western Association. He was killed at the siege of Hereford later that year. Serious trouble was expected from Essex's veteran infantry, who had hitherto refused to serve under any other general, but their old commander Skippon mustered them at Reading on 6 April and 'delivered a speech with such grave emphasis, martial courage and prudent sweetness as gave general satisfaction and full content to all'; so much so that even Essex's lifeguard re-enlisted with a will, and many NCOs, and even some officers, remustered as privates. To men like this the army had become a profession, a way of life.

At the same time the need to re-equip this army produced a remarkable industrial surge, which needs to be fully investigated and properly assessed. The evidence is unfortunately far from complete, but the records we have show that in March, April and May orders in their hundreds for muskets, swords and pistols, saddles and bandoliers, shoes, shirts and tunics, were issued daily from the Ordnance Office in the Tower; orders to be fulfilled in most cases in two or three weeks. Small arms were to be of exact and uniform gauge, in accordance with specifications which could be consulted at the Tower; the infantry's coats were to be of red woollen cloth and pre-shrunk, which remained the uniform of the British army for the next two centuries or more. It is striking that the manufacturing industry was able to meet this sudden demand with such speed and efficiency, and it demonstrates what a stimulus to industry the war was.

However, shortage of infantry was an abiding problem. Essex's former army only yielded 3,048 foot soldiers, Manchester's 3,578 and Waller's a paltry 600, and to bring the total up to an establishment of 14,400 the rest had to be conscripted. Added to the fact that many of those who voluntarily remustered were undoubtedly attracted by the promise of 'constant pay', this makes nonsense of the claim, then and later, that this was an elite force of highly motivated and dedicated men. It was a professional army through and through. On 19 March Parliament ordered the conscription of 8,640 men, more than half the projected infantry establishment, from the counties of the Eastern Association plus Kent, Surrey, Sussex and London, but they met with mixed success. The French Ambassador saw men being virtually kidnapped on the streets of London by daylight, and they were then sent upriver to Maidenhead by boat, lest they escape on the way. Elsewhere an ordinance of 24 April imposed the death penalty on those conscripts who did not report for duty within six days, but it was unenforceable. The Kent contingent broke loose, barricaded themselves in a mansion near Wrotham, and had to be winkled out and escorted to Windsor by the trained bands; but once there they simply deserted and returned home. When Fairfax took the field that spring he was at least 4,000 men short, perhaps more, and it seems that the deficit was never made up; on the contrary, his numbers continued to be reduced by desertion as well as battle casualties throughout the subsequent campaign. After Naseby he demanded and got the power to conscript replacements on the road as best he could.

As for Cromwell, his position was still ambiguous; so much so that some historians question whether he was now in Parliament's employ at all. However, the second half of April found him and his cavalry brigade still patrolling the country north of Oxford, amongst other things confiscating all the draught horses they could in the hope of immobilising the King's artillery train. On the way they routed a small royalist contingent under the Earl of Northampton, some of whom took refuge in a fortified manor house at Bletchingley. Cromwell demanded its surrender, but he was palpably bluffing; without guns or infantry he had no hope of taking it. But the young governor, Colonel Francis Windebank, fearing for the safety of his newly wedded wife, promptly asked for terms, only to be court-martialled and shot on his return to Oxford. The war was turning very nasty indeed.

By now the New Model was ready, but with the previous year's events in mind Parliament decreed that it must be subject at all times to control by the Committee for Both Kingdoms, which could find nothing better to do with it than send it to the relief of Taunton, which had become something of an obsession on both sides. Fairfax duly marched from Windsor on 30 April, and by 7 May he had reached Blandford in Dorset. However, as soon as his back was turned Charles and Rupert left Oxford, heading north-west; they recalled Goring from Somerset, and when they met at Stow-on-the-Wold on 8 May they mustered 11,600 men: 6,300 horse and 5,300 foot. Rupert, perhaps swayed by Langdale, and certainly impressed by Montrose's headlong victories in Scotland, wanted to head north. They could retake Shrewsbury on the way, relieve Carlisle and Pontefract and regain Lancashire and Yorkshire, which were now thinly guarded. Charles, too, seemed to incline that way, but Goring argued that they should pursue Fairfax into the West, a strategy which had been resoundingly successful the previous year, and he stood out for his views.

The result was a fatal compromise: Goring departed for the West with 3,000 horse to harass Fairfax, leaving the King with a mere 8,600. On the face of it it was a lunatic decision, but everyone seriously underestimated the New Model Army, even its employers. Thomas May, the official historian of the Long Parliament, reminds us that this was 'an army seeming no way glorious either in the dignity of commanders or antiquity of soldiers'; in fact, 'never did hardly any army go forth to war with less confidence of their own side, or more contempt of their enemies'.

However, by now the Committee for Both Kingdoms had taken alarm. What if Charles now struck north and doubled the size of his army by recruiting in Lancashire and Cheshire, as Rupert had done the year before? Worse still, what if he invaded the Eastern Association counties? They ordered Fairfax to halt at Blandford, send on a brigade to relieve Taunton – which it successfully did on 11 May – and return with the rest of the army to lay siege to Oxford, which they hoped would pin Charles in the Midlands; meanwhile Cromwell was sent back to organise the defence of the Isle of Ely. They were shaken still further by news of another shattering victory by Montrose, at Auldearn near Inverness on 9 May, which caused Leven to pull his army back into Westmorland, ready to return to Scotland. Fairfax was ordered to detach 2,500 horse under his Dutch Commissary-General, Vermuyden, and send them to Yorkshire to frustrate any attempt to relieve Pontefract. (These two petty outposts, Taunton and Pontefract, had now reduced the army's strength by at least 4,000 foot and 4,300 horse.) Meanwhile the siege of Oxford proceeded slowly; it was not a task to Fairfax's liking, and the city could not be formally invested, anyway, until his siege train arrived from Windsor on 19 May.

Oxford was now of little practical value to either side, but its symbolic importance was undeniable, and Charles was reluctant to leave it to its fate. Rupert agreed, but argued that the best way to relieve it was to threaten some major parliamentary outpost, and what better than the Puritan manufacturing town of Leicester, near to hand? Leicester was duly stormed and sacked on 31 May. The shock was profound, especially since the first reports spoke of a wholesale massacre of the garrison, though in fact only about 200 defenders were killed in a fiercely contested action, and 1,200 taken prisoner. The Committee for Both Kingdoms at once pulled out all its Midlands garrisons as far east as Burleigh House in Lincolnshire, and the City of London sent Parliament a peremptory letter demanding that it give Fairfax complete freedom of action. On 5 June the Committee ordered him to abandon the siege of Oxford and march north-east to Newport Pagnell, on the assumption that the King would now head for East Anglia, but on the 9th they capitulated, and simply ordered him to bring Charles to battle when and where he could. He asked by return that Cromwell be appointed his Lieutenant-General of Horse, and they complied without further argument.

It is very difficult to assess the strength of the New Model Army at this stage, but it was certainly not up to the huge establishment so confidently voted by Parliament that winter. As we have seen, Fairfax set off in April with about 10,000 infantry, instead of 14,400, though they would still have been divided into twelve regiments, of about 830 men each, instead of 1,200. He had detached four of those regiments, 3,320 men, for the relief of Taunton, and it seems they did not return, certainly not in time for the battle of Naseby. Which left him with a notional 6,680. It is not clear that the men withdrawn from the Midlands garrisons ever reached him, but if they did they would have numbered hundreds, not thousands, and they probably did little more than replace his losses by desertion. His cavalry, though, must have been near its establishment strength of 6,600, minus 1,800–2,000 sent to Taunton; Vermuyden, recalled after the fall of Leicester, rejoined the army on the eve of Naseby. Cromwell, too, appeared on the eve of Naseby, presumably bringing some men with him from Cambridge.

As for Charles, he had incurred some losses at Leicester, and after the sack some of his men had deserted with their loot, though no doubt the royalists exaggerated these factors in the subsequent post-mortem. Clarendon puts his numbers at 3,300 foot and 4,100 horse, but Clarendon was not there, and it looks as though his figures should simply be reversed; if Goring had taken 3,000 horse with him to the West, this should have left the King with 3,300, about half of them consisting of the Northern horse, who were more restless than ever, 'and could hardly be kept from disbanding, or returning home in disorder'. It appears that he had 5,300 foot at Stow-on-the-Wold, and his casualties at Leicester, and the need to leave a garrison there, could plausibly have reduced this figure to 4,100. This whole exercise reveals the difficulty of establishing exact figures for Civil War armies, but it seems that Fairfax now had twice as many cavalry as Charles and 40 per cent more infantry. Whether Charles knew this is another matter; his scouting and intelligence system was poor. By this time Fairfax realised that Charles was not intent on invading East Anglia; from Leicester he had retired south-west into Warwickshire, and there Fairfax's scouts found him on 12 June, encamped on Burrow Hill near Daventry. 'The King was a-hunting,' we are told, 'the soldiers in no order, and their horses all at grass.' The armies were then only two miles apart.

The King at once struck camp and retreated towards Market Harborough, but, finding that he was steadily pursued, he agreed with Rupert that it would be less weakening and demoralising to stand and fight. So, on the morning of 14 June the two armies were drawn up just north of the village of Naseby, two miles south of Market Harborough. After a certain amount of preliminary manoeuvring each army ended up on a slight eminence, the ground between them offering few obstacles to the use of cavalry. In many ways it was an ideal battleground.

Shortly after ten o'clock the royalist foot began to advance, and Fairfax's soon after. Despite their inferiority in numbers, the royalists had much the better of the initial encounter; Skippon was seriously wounded, which affected his men's morale, and the front line began to give way. At the same time Rupert led a charge against the left wing of the New Model cavalry, commanded by the young Henry Ireton. Returning the previous day from the North, Vermuyden had insisted on resigning and returning straight to Holland, 'for personal reasons'.* Cromwell then urged the appointment of Ireton as Commissary-General over the heads of many colonels his senior in age and experience. It was a blatant piece of nepotism; Ireton was one of his favourite protégés, and was to marry his daughter Bridget later that year.

Predictably, Ireton's brigade was simply swept away, but Rupert's troopers, many of them on their fourth campaign, had still not learned to draw rein at the moment of victory and turn against the enemy infantry. As it was, Rupert himself led them thundering across the

---

* Like Hans Behre, Vermuyden was a foreigner who had risen to high command in a major Civil War army while remaining (to us) virtually anonymous. He may have been related to the famous Dutch drainage expert Sir Cornelius Vermuyden, but this cannot be proved, and we do not even know his Christian name, only the initial 'H'.

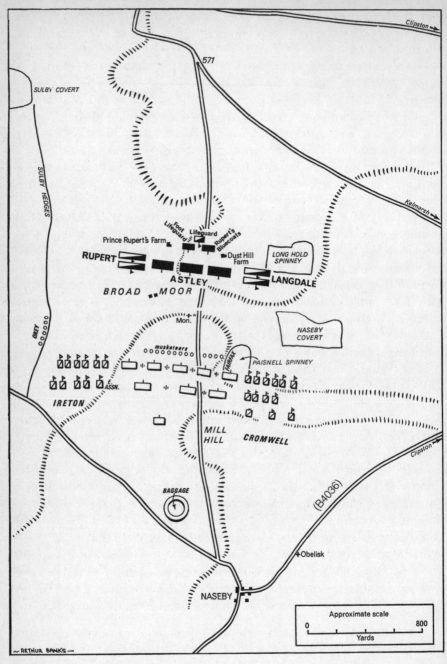

THE BATTLE OF NASEBY

Right: John Pym. A miniature by Samuel Cooper.

Below: Thomas Wentworth, 1st Earl of Strafford. Detail from a painting *c.* 1640 by Van Dyck.

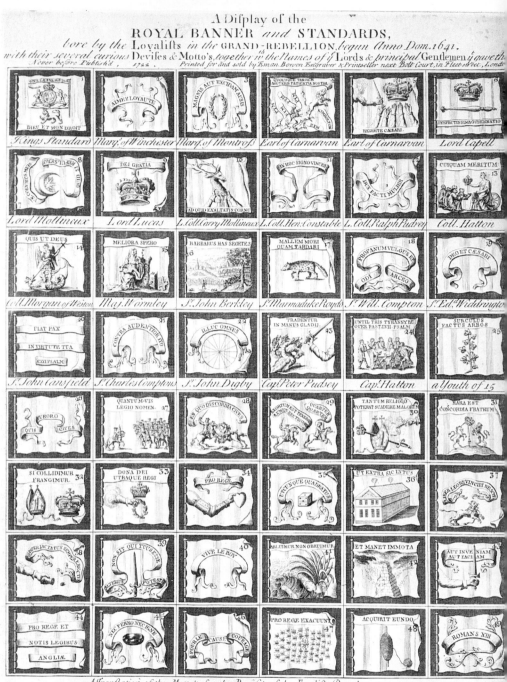

Royalist battle standards. A selection of banners and standards engraved in 1722 from a seventeenth-century MS. (Note the banner at the bottom right, referring the enemy to Romans 13: 'Let every soul be subject to the higher powers, for there is no power but of God'.)

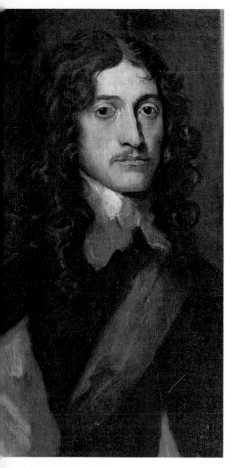

Above: Prince Rupert in 1645. An unfinished portrait by William Dobson.

Right: William Cavendish, 1st Earl, Marquess (later Duke) of Newcastle, by Van Dyck.

Right: George, Lord Goring.
Detail from a painting by Van
Dyck.

Below: Sir Marmaduke
Langdale. An eighteenth-
century engraving from an
original portrait.

Below right: Sir Ralph Hopton
by an unknown artist, c. 1637.

Above: James Butler, 12th Earl, 1st Marquess and 1st Duke of Ormonde. A portrait after Lely.

Left: Sir Edward Hyde, later Earl of Clarendon. A portrait after A. Hanneman, *c.* 1648–55.

Though the armour and uniforms are slightly different, these contemporary pictures of European armies and warfare give us some idea of what the Civil Wars looked like. (From Jacques Callot's *Les Misères et les malheurs de la guerre*, 1633.)

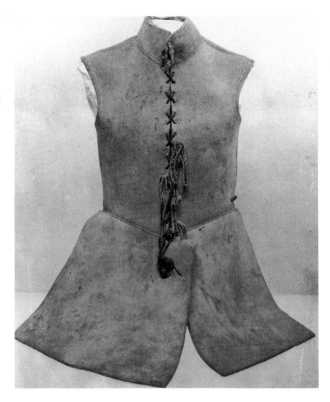

Above: a contemporary (Continental) musketeer with his match alight in his left hand. (Notice his flimsy shoes and leggings.)

Right: a steel 'pot, breast and back' typical of those worn by cavalry troopers or dragoons in the 1640s.

Above right: the infantryman's famous 'buff coat', capable of turning a sword or pike thrust, and even withstanding a musket ball at over a hundred yards' distance.

Above: Robert Devereux, Earl of Essex. An engraving by Hollar, 1643.

Left: Archibald Campbell, 8th Earl and 1st Marquess of Argyll ('the glae-eyed marquess'). A portrait by David Scougall.

Right: Sir Thomas Fairfax, 1645.

Below: Sir William Waller, by Lely, *c.* 1647.

Below right: Edward Montagu, 2nd Earl of Manchester, by Lely, *c.* 1643.

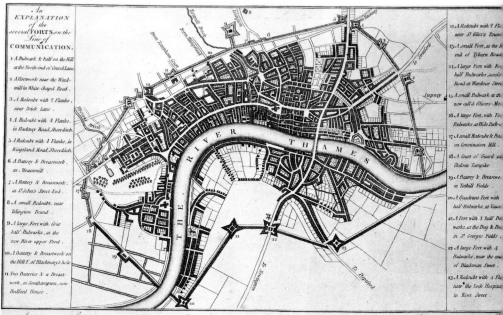

A PLAN of the City and Environs of LONDON, as Fortified by Order of PARLIAMENT, in the Years 1642 & 1643.

London: Published as the Act directs by Alexr Hogg at the Kings Arms No 16 Paternoster Row.

Above: a plan of the elaborat 'Lines of Communication' erected round London early i 1643, and demolished four years later.

Left: an aerial photograph of the Queen's Sconce outside Newark, a rare survivor of th elaborate and often effective earthworks thrown up round many English towns during t Civil Wars.

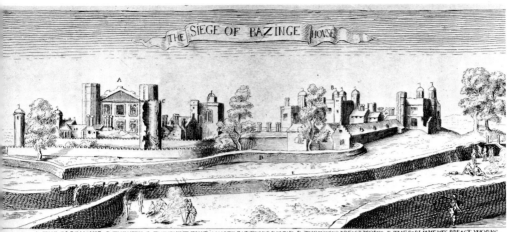

A. THE OLDE HOVSE. B. THE NEW. C. THE TOWER THAT IS HALFE BATTERED DOWNE. D. THE KINGES BREAST WORKS. E. THE PARLIAMENTS BREAST WORKS.

above: the siege of Basing House in its final stages, in 1645, when the principal tower had been battered to pieces by Dalbier and it was closely invested by the parliamentary forces.

right: contemporary illustrations of heavy artillery, demonstrating the huge transport problems it posed.

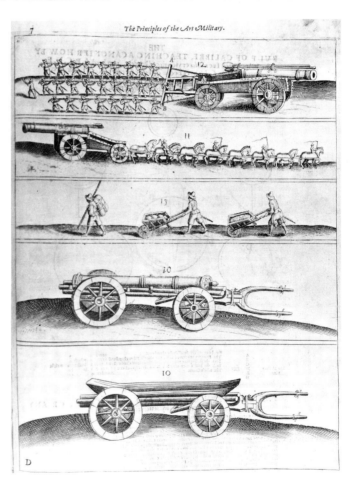

The Principles of the Art Military.

Above: Putney Church, Surre[y] the scene of the famous debat[e] between the Levellers and the Army generals in October–November 1647. An eighteenth-century engraving

Left: Fairfax and the Council [of] the Army, 1647, from a contemporary woodcut. (The presence of the men standing [to] Fairfax's left suggests that thi[s] was the General Council, including representatives fro[m] the regiments.)

Right: Charles I at his trial in 1649. A portrait by Edward Bower.

Below: a contemporary engraving of the execution of Charles I on 30 January 1649.

The EXECUTION of KING CHARLES the FIRST, before the Banqueting House Whitehall, January 30. 1648-9.

Right: Oliver Cromwell. The famous unfinished miniature by Samuel Cooper, *c.* 1650. (Legend has it that he told Cooper to paint him just as he was, 'warts and all'.)

Below: Bridget Ireton, Cromwell's eldest daughter.

Below right: Henry Ireton. Copy, by George Perfect Harding, of Samuel Cooper's original miniature of 1649.

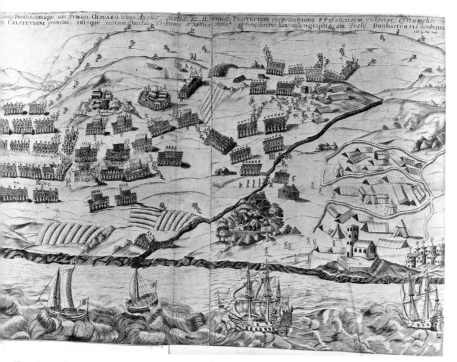

Dunbar. A contemporary print, commissioned by Parliament in 1651, exaggerates the David and Goliath nature of the battle, with Cromwell's army, seeming much tinier that it was, penned up on the centre right, between the hills and the sea.

Lambert. A portrait after Robert Walker, 50–5.

George Monck. An unfinished sketch by Samuel Cooper.

Right: Oliver Cromwell. A tiny illustration from the initial letter of a charter issued by the Lord Protector to the city of Chester in 1658. He is dressed in regal robes and is showing his age.

Below: Charles II in the early 1660s. Detail from a portrait by the school of Lely.

countryside until they reached Fairfax's baggage train far in the rear; they then wasted time in a fruitless exchange of fire with the baggage guard. In fact, it is difficult to understand why Charles let his commanding general lead a cavalry charge at all, something Rupert's brother Maurice could have done just as well, instead of directing the battle from the centre rear, alongside him. As it was, by the time the Prince returned the battle was all but over.

Meanwhile Ireton had recouped the situation. In effect, he did the job Rupert ought to have been doing, in reverse. As soon as the royalist horse disappeared into the distance he rallied his men and launched an attack on the royalist infantry brigade nearest to him. True, he met with little success, and he himself was disabled by a pike thrust, unhorsed and temporarily captured; but at least he had distracted the enemy at a critical moment, and on Parliament's right wing the situation was now very different. Here Cromwell attacked with overwhelming force, and scattered the Northern horse like chaff. There was probably little they could have done to counter the first shock, but they at once fled the field as fast as they could, some ending up as far away as Newark – conduct which Langdale found it very difficult to explain or excuse. And at this juncture Cromwell demonstrated his superiority to Rupert and most other royalist cavalry generals; he sent two regiments to speed the fleeing enemy on their way, and turned the rest of his brigade against the royalist foot, calling in Okey's thousand-strong dragoon regiment as well, which had been lining the hedges on the flank of the battlefield.

The King, bereft of Rupert's advice, or that of any other senior officer, was uncertain what to do; but he had with him a small reserve of about nine hundred horse and three hundred foot, and he now moved forward as if to lead them into the fray. But one of his attendant courtiers, the Scots Earl of Carnwath, seized his bridle with an oath (so blasphemous or obscene that no one set it down on paper), and said, 'Will you go upon your death in an instant?' He was arguably right, but his sudden intervention was disastrous; he startled the King's charger, which wheeled away to the right, and the reserve followed suit. With Charles still undecided they all retreated towards the rear in some disorder.

This left the royalist infantry virtually alone on the field. They fought well; these were the seasoned professionals of the 'Old Foot', based on Oxford since 1642 or 1643 and the veterans of many battles; but simply because they were professionals they were not the men to throw away their lives needlessly. They knew when they were beaten and when it was honourable to accept the fact, and once their ranks were broken most of them laid down their arms. Only one regiment, perhaps Rupert's lifeguard, held out, and Fairfax himself had to deal with them:

> They standing with incomparable courage and resolution, although we attempted them in the flanks, front and rear, until such time as the General called up his own regiment of foot (the Lieutenant General being likewise hastening of them), which immediately fell in with them with butt end of muskets (the General charging them at the same time with horse) and so broke them.

About this time Rupert at last returned, but with his men tired and his horses broken-winded, and hopelessly outnumbered as he now was, he could only gallop away with the King towards Leicester. Fairfax sent a couple of regiments after them, with a threat to court-martial any man who stopped for loot.

Loot there was in plenty: the Queen's colours, the Duke of York's, Rupert's and Maurice's, and those of every foot regiment on the field, and all the King's guns, ammunition, stores and baggage, right down to his coach, where copies were found of his correspondence with the Queen and the Irish rebels, gloatingly published by Parliament a few weeks later as *The King's Cabinet Open'd*, to the great detriment of his reputation. Surveying the scene next day, one Puritan wrote:

> I saw the field so bestrewed with the carcasses of men and horses as was most sad to behold, because subjects under one government, but most happy in this because they were most of them professed enemies of God and his Son. The field was about a mile wide when the battle was fought. The bodies lay slain about four miles in length, the most thick on the hill where the King stood. I cannot think there were less than four hundred men slain there, and truly I think not many more, and three hundred horses.

Indeed, comparatively few men were killed – about a thousand in all, contemporaries thought – but about 4,500 royalists were taken prisoner, including five hundred officers. A large proportion of these men were veteran infantry, irreplaceable at this stage of the war, and Parliament did not make the same mistake as the King after Lostwithiel. The prisoners were all marched to London, to decorate a kind of Roman triumph; then about one-third were induced to 'volunteer' for Ireland, others were recruited for service in Europe by the Spanish and French ambassadors, and the rest remained in gaol for at least another year. After Naseby the process was really one of mopping up, though both sides were slow to realise it. As one historian remarks, 'It was more than the end of an army; it was, for all practical purposes, the end of a reign.'

On the news of Naseby many royalist fortresses which had been holding out for months began to topple one by one. Carlisle went down at last on 2 July, its garrison reduced to the last extremities of starvation, Pontefract followed on the 21st, and Scarborough next day; by the end of the year eighteen garrisons had surrendered without being challenged by a major field army. That indomitable Scots freebooter Sir John Meldrum had sworn to take Scarborough or lay his bones there. In the course of the siege he miraculously survived an accidental 200-foot fall from the cliffs, his voluminous cloak acting as a parachute; he even survived a shot 'in the cods', only to succumb to another shot, 'in the guts', about a fortnight before the castle fell.

As for the King, he retired with the remnants of his army into South Wales, to the Marquess of Worcester's seat at Raglan Castle. Including those who had returned after the battle, or rallied to him since, he still had about 4,000 horse and 2,500 foot – his losses in cavalry had been comparatively slight – but he remained curiously passive. His secretary, Sir Edward Walker, wrote: 'There his Majesty stayed three weeks, and as if the genius of the place had conspired with our fates, we were there all lulled to sleep with sports and entertainments; as if no crown had been at stake, or in any danger to be lost.'

By this time Leven was at last moving south again with the Scots army, and by 20 June he had got as far as Mansfield in Nottinghamshire, dashing any last hopes of a royalist revival in the North East. Charles's obvious plan was to join Goring in the West, where their combined armies could well have equalled the New Model. But he left it far too late. After Naseby Fairfax's next step was to retake Leicester, which he did without too much difficulty on 18 June. (Charles typically accused Lord Loughborough, the garrison commander, of treachery, though he had done nothing to help him.) Fairfax then turned back to the West to deal once and for all with Goring, reaching Taunton after a forced march of seventeen miles a day for five days. On his way he was confronted by large groups of Clubmen, first near Salisbury, then near Dorchester. He had long parleys with their leaders, and they eventually let him pass without bloodshed; they were impressed by the evident discipline he was imposing on his men, and he seemed likely to advance their main aim, which was to bring the war to a speedy end. In' contrast Goring's troops, on their return in May, had positively run amok, and the Somerset Clubmen were glad to give Fairfax any help they could.

At Taunton Fairfax learned that Goring had retired and taken up his position on the banks of the River Yeo. He promptly turned his position, forcing him further back, towards Langport, but by a clever diversion Goring induced him to send 4,000 men back to guard Taunton against possible attack, reducing the odds against him somewhat. He now had about 7,000 men, Fairfax not much more than 10,000; the latter had complained to Parliament on 26 June that he had less than half his proper establishment of foot (that is, less than 7,200), and the farther he marched into the West the higher the incidence of desertion. He also complained that his cavalry losses at Naseby had not been made good, and many of his troopers were still unhorsed. Certainly he was not blessed with an overwhelming superiority in numbers.

To cover his retreat on Bridgwater, the next fortified town, Goring on 10 July took up a strong defensive position just outside Langport. His army was posted at the top of a steep slope, the only access to which was down a narrow lane, across a ford which would barely take four horses abreast, then up the hill again. Here Fairfax displayed the ruthlessness which was part of his character, and his men the élan they felt after Naseby. Overwhelming artillery fire silenced Goring's two guns on the hilltop, while picked volunteers crossed the ford on foot and weeded out the marksmen posted on the lower slopes opposite. Then three troops of horse led by Major Christopher Bethel, followed by another two under John Desborough, charged full tilt down the lane four abreast, across the ford without drawing rein, and right up the hill and on to Goring's position at the top. After a furious scrimmage there the royalist army gave way.

Military historians are quick to point out that Langport was· not technically a defeat; Goring effected a strategic withdrawal, leaving a strong garrison posted at Bridgwater. But it was a severe moral blow, and it enhanced the reputation for invincibility which the New Model Army was beginning to acquire. Certainly Fairfax always regarded it as his finest victory. Moreover, as Goring retreated west from Bridgwater his army began to fall apart; discouraged by the hostility of the local people, who had suffered cruelly from their ravages over the past month or so, his men were deserting in droves. Here Fairfax's strict discipline stood him in good stead, as did his insistence on a steady supply of money and equipment from London.

Fairfax's next task was to reduce Bridgwater; this, with Langport, Taunton and Lyme, would complete a chain of fortresses from coast to coast and bottle Goring up in Devon and Cornwall, to be dealt with at leisure. But even he quailed at the strong walls, the elaborate forts, the sea moat, which made Bridgwater one of the strongest fortified towns in England. However, he had no time for a siege, which could last months, and after an agonised debate he overruled his Council of War and ordered an all-out assault on the night of 22 July, setting fire to the town first and throwing a makeshift bridge over the moat. The citadel surrendered next day, but the town was devastated, and took a generation to recover, and according to Fairfax it was one of the few decisions which weighed on his conscience in later years. However, other towns took note of the fact that in his present mood he was unstoppable; a contingent sent up to Bath took its surrender on the first summons, and Sherborne Castle, Dorset, capitulated after two days' token resistance. Fairfax then detached Cromwell to deal with the Dorset Clubmen, who had been interrupting his supply line from London. Cromwell found them assembled 2,000 strong on Hambledon Hill, a Stone Age earthwork near Shaftesbury. He was reluctant to attack what he plausibly regarded as simple-minded peasants infiltrated by royalist *agents-provocateurs*; but in the end he had to storm the hill, with Desborough again in the van. The way was now clear for an assault on Bristol, the last important town in royalist hands; for even Charles admitted that Oxford was of little practical importance, and though the Scots had bypassed Newark they had now laid siege to Hereford. Rupert was in command at Bristol, and assured his uncle that he could hold out for at least four months.

Charles left Bristol to the Prince; he was understandably reluctant to take refuge in any fortified town with no means of escape. Otherwise, however, his best course of action, given the prevailing confusion, was not apparent. He finally left the safety of Raglan Castle in late July to canvass for volunteers in South Wales, but that prime royalist recruiting ground was now exhausted, and when he set out from Cardiff on 5 August for his last campaign he had added only about 2,500 men to his tiny army. His only possible route was north, for though his last bastions in Lancashire and Yorkshire had fallen or were about to fall Montrose was still winning stunning victories in Scotland – his latest was over Sir William Baillie, at Alford, west of Aberdeen, on 2 July.

However, for all his victories in the field Montrose was not conquering and holding territory, nor threatening the stability of the Covenanting government, and by this time even the reckless and ebullient Digby was beginning to lose hope. On 27 August he admitted to one of his friends:

> There is such a universal weariness of the war, despair of the possibility for the King to recover, and so much of private interest grown from thence upon everybody, that I protest to God I do not know four persons living beside myself and you that have not already given clear demonstrations that they will purchase their own and, as they flatter themselves, the kingdom's quiet at any price to the King, to the Church [and] to the faithfullest of his party.

Charles marched north-east into Yorkshire, as far as Doncaster, where he arrived on 11 August. But Sydenham Poyntz, commander of the Northern Association, had just completed the reduction of Scarborough and was marching south to meet him; behind him was Leven's 4,000-strong cavalry under David Leslie, detached from the siege of Hereford. Charles hastily retreated south to Huntingdon, but he ventured no further into the Associated Counties, though there was little to stop him; instead he continued south to Oxford, arriving on the 28th. There news reached him that Montrose had routed the Covenanters more decisively than ever before, at Kilsyth on 15 August, and had occupied Glasgow. The immediate result was that David Leslie's horse threatened to mutiny unless he led them back into Scotland, and Leven, his army seriously depleted, had to raise the siege of Hereford on 1 September. Charles left Oxford in haste on 30 August and took possession of Hereford, but no further volunteers were forthcoming to swell his army, now exhausted by forced marches, and he retired once more to the comfort, the unreal serenity, of Raglan Castle.

There he received the appalling news of the surrender of Bristol. Optimistic though Rupert was beforehand, once Fairfax began to invest the city on 4 September he found himself in the same position as Nathaniel Fiennes two years before. The fortifications were magnificent, but he only had 1,500 men to man them; they could not cover the whole perimeter, and if they foregathered to repulse one attack they left themselves wide open to another in their rear. So it was on 10 September, when Fairfax launched simultaneous attacks on the eastern and southern sectors. Thomas Rainsborough's foot broke through on the east, followed by the horse, and after a two-hour battle they captured one of the town's main forts, at Prior's Hill. Rupert could have retreated on the citadel, street by street, but this would have meant the utter destruction of the second city in England, and it would have been a useless gesture. No relief force could be expected: none existed. He surrendered on generous terms.

It was the action of a professional soldier and a political realist, but he had undertaken to hold Bristol for four months, taking them into the winter, and as Charles sharply reminded him, he had not held it for four days. To the King his conduct smacked of treachery, and he probably remembered a letter Rupert had sent to the Duke of Richmond a few weeks before, after Langport, avowedly intended for his eyes, in which he said, 'His Majesty hath now no way left to preserve his posterity, kingdom and nobility but by a treaty. I believe it a more prudent way to retain something, than to lose all.' His natural flamboyance, even in a crisis, made the affair all the more irritating, and the news-sheets described his exit from the city thus: 'The Prince was clad in scarlet, very richly laid in silver lace, mounted upon a very gallant black barbary horse; the General and the Prince rode together, the General giving the Prince the right hand all the way.' Charles incontinently dismissed him and sent him a pass to go abroad, ordering him not to approach his person. Parliament's comment was to restore Nathaniel Fiennes to the Commons seat he had forfeited in 1643.

However, Charles had to do something; he could not lurk at Raglan until Fairfax came to seek him out. He left Raglan again on 18 September, intending to march north through Lancashire and Cumberland and join Montrose at Glasgow. On the way he relieved Chester, where Sir John (now Lord) Byron was still holding out. From Chester he sent Langdale with the Northern horse to meet Poyntz, who had marched the Northern Association army across from Yorkshire. (The Northern horse, about three thousand strong, was now the only regular cavalry he had left.) He himself remained in Chester with his infantry. Langdale gave battle at Rowton Heath on 24 September – the last formal battle of the war – but after a series of misunderstandings he was squeezed between Poyntz's army and the city walls. Charles retreated on Denbigh, with Poyntz in hot pursuit, but he managed to elude him and double back across country to Newark, arriving on 4 October. He clung to the illusion that Goring might still break out of the West to join him, but news now arrived that Montrose's fairy-tale campaign had ended in disaster. Deserted by Alasdair MacColla and the Irish, who had never been much concerned with the broader issues of the Civil War, he struck south through the Borders in an attempt to reach England, only to be trapped by David Leslie at Philiphaugh near Melrose on 13 September and utterly routed. Nevertheless, Montrose was still at large, and the magic of his name might still raise another army; Leven had taken up his station on the River Tees accordingly. It was too dangerous for the King himself to strike north, but as a last desperate venture he ordered Digby to take the remainder of the Northern horse and make for Scotland, if necessary up the west coast.

The last ride of the Northern horse from Newark is a poignant epilogue to the story of the first Civil War. Pontefract, that symbolic rallying-point, had fallen three months before, on 19 July. They themselves, after Naseby and Rowton Heath, were reduced to not much more than a thousand men. On 15 October they brushed aside a small enemy force which tried to bar their way at Ferrybridge, scene of former glories, but before the day was out they were overtaken at Sherburn-in-Elmet by a Colonel Copley with 1,500 men. Langdale told them:

> Gentlemen, you are all gallant men, and have done bravely, but there are some that seek to scandalise your gallantry for the loss of Naseby field. But I hope you will redeem your reputation, and still maintain that gallant report which you ever had. I am sure you have done such business as never has been done in any war with such a number.

But it was not to be. Langdale himself miraculously survived four point-blank pistol shots, but his men were so thoroughly beaten that barely three hundred escaped, and what had started as a gallant ride, like their relief of Pontefract in February, turned into a desperate flight – first to Skipton, then to Bolton-in-Swaledale and across the Pennines into Cumberland. They picked up a few adherents as they rode through Yorkshire, bringing their numbers up to about six hundred, but an enemy force of four or five hundred men under Sir John Brown was in hot pursuit, and David Leslie was sending 1,100 men south from Glasgow under Jonas van Druske to meet them.* Local royalists guided the forlorn band over the treacherous Portmoake Sands and up the coast towards Carlisle, taking full advantage of the tidal streams to frustrate pursuit. However, Brown ran them down in the fading light of an October afternoon, the 24th, on Carlisle Sands, with the tide coming in. So hazardous were the conditions that Brown left his colours

---

* The Dutchman van Druske had been one of Waller's colonels in 1644. Presumably he had been excluded from the New Model and had remustered under Leslie: an example of the mobility of such mercenaries, and their ready acceptance.

behind before he ventured out onto the sands, but he won an easy victory; three hundred of his opponents were killed, many of them driven into the sea and drowned, and another two hundred were captured, with their colours. A handful fled back into Yorkshire, where we lose them; to all intents and purposes the proud Northern horse, raised in the autumn of 1642, were gone. Langdale and Digby escaped in a 'cock-boat' to the Isle of Man.

Fairfax meanwhile was ploughing back into the West, ignoring the onset of winter and determined to crush the last royalist resistance there. There were strong rumours that now the Thirty Years' War was in its last phase France was going to send Charles military assistance at last, and foreign troops could now only land in Cornwall. However, on the way he detached Cromwell and sent him all the way back to deal with Winchester and Basing House, the only royalist outposts in the South. Winchester Castle surrendered on 3 October, three days after Cromwell brought his guns to bear on it, but Basing was still a difficult nut to crack, though it had been under siege since 20 August by the Dutch engineer Jan Dalbier, who had brought down the corner tower by methodical artillery fire. Cromwell arrived on 8 October with much heavier guns, including at least one cannon royal of the kind used by Meldrum against Scarborough, and perhaps the same one, brought round by sea, and two demi-culverins (27-pounders), perhaps borrowed from the Navy at Portsmouth. Now that there was no risk of enemy cavalry raids, and little competition for spare draught horses, such guns could be moved around the country much more easily. They soon tore massive breaches in the walls, and on the 14th Cromwell took Basing House by storm, a victory marred by the slaughter of many of its Catholic defenders, an atrocity Fairfax would never have permitted. It took Dalbier another six months to reduce Donnington Castle, that controversial element in the campaign of 1644, but with the fall of Basing another chapter of Civil War history closed.

By the time Cromwell rejoined Fairfax at the end of October he had taken Tiverton and quartered the army round Exeter. Heavy rains made him disinclined to move for the time being. However, the royalist cause in the West was now crumbling of its own accord. Much of Devon and Cornwall had been swept bare by the royalist forces, but if there had been any chance of propelling them back towards the Midlands the local people might have been induced to provide more supplies; as it was, there was no point in helping to prolong a hopeless struggle so near at hand. The local commander, Sir Richard Grenville, younger brother of the late Sir Bevil but something of a desperado, declined to obey Goring's orders, and treated the people, even on his home ground, with a savagery and a disrespect for the law which he had apparently learned in Ireland, where he had campaigned in 1642–3. In November Goring himself resigned and left for France, pleading illness and the effect of old war wounds.

However, by 6 January 1646 the New Model was on the move again, despite bitter frost and snow, and on the 19th they stormed Dartmouth. The Prince of Wales, now at Tavistock, sent for Hopton out of retirement to take over from Goring, though he was no better able to control Grenville. As Clarendon said, it was an unenviable assignment, 'to take charge of those horse whom only their friends feared, and their enemies laughed at; being only terrible in plunder, and resolute in running away'. Nevertheless, Hopton scraped together about 2,000 foot and 3,000 horse, with which he made a stand at Torrington. Fairfax ordered a storm on the night of 16 February, and after some confused street fighting, which cost him a couple of hundred men, he put the royalists to flight. Anything remotely resembling an army could not be recruited again, and on 2 March the Prince and his retinue sailed for the Scilly Isles and eventually Jersey. On the 12th Hopton accepted generous terms from Fairfax. Exeter capitulated on 9 April, leaving only Pendennis Castle holding out in the West.

Charles was still at Oxford, where he had taken up his winter quarters the previous October, though not before he had had a last quarrel with Rupert. Though forbidden to approach the King, the Prince had arrived at Newark in September with his brother and several of their colonels and demanded a hearing before a Council of War. The Council exonerated him for the surrender of Bristol, but Charles refused to reinstate him; indeed, he removed his friend Will Legge from the governorship of Oxford and replaced him with Sir Thomas Glemham, the hero of York and Carlisle. Rupert, Maurice and their followers rode off down the Great North Road, requesting a safe conduct from Parliament on the way. It was granted.

At Oxford that troubled winter all was intrigue. Cardinal Mazarin, Richelieu's successor as the virtual ruler of France, was now alarmed at the situation in England, and the Queen had high hopes that he would finance an expedition led by the Duke of Lorraine with 10,000 mercenary troops, but it all came to nothing. So did another appeal to the Pope. Charles, himself, through the French Ambassador to England,

Montreuil, was engaged in clandestine negotiations with the Scots. He was now ready to yield, or at least bend, on the key question of the establishment of Presbyterianism in England, but apart from anything else the Scots' feeble military performance over the past year had left them without much leverage at Westminster.

His only prospect of military aid seemed to be from Ireland. There the war was still deadlocked. Though the Cessation of 1643 had technically expired after a year, the bulk of Ormonde's army had been sent to England, and he could only remain on the defensive. The Confederate leaders, however, still hoping for a generous settlement from Charles, held their hand. In the North the Scots army under Monro seized Belfast in May 1644 and made a wide sweep through Sligo, but early in 1645 half of them were recalled to Scotland to help deal with Montrose, and Monro had little choice but to stay put. As long ago as the autumn of 1644 Charles had conceived the idea of calling upon the rebel Confederation to supply him with 10,000 Irish Catholic troops, a piece of imprudence which alarmed even Digby, especially since in return the Confederates demanded full toleration for Roman Catholics, recognition of and financial provision for the Catholic priesthood, and an independent Irish Parliament. These demands lay on the table, and were stepped up even higher on the arrival in Ireland of a papal nuncio, Giovanni Battista Rinuccini, in October 1645. Ormonde dismissed all this as unthinkable; not so the Earl of Glamorgan, a light-headed and unrealistic Welsh Catholic whom Charles now sent over as his personal envoy. Fortunately he was overruled by Digby, who providentially arrived in Dublin from the Isle of Man in December, after his adventures with the Northern horse. After a great deal of hard bargaining it was decided, on 30 March 1646, that Ormonde would sign the political articles in the treaty, but that the religious articles must be left for Charles's personal decision. The Confederates were ready with their troops, but by this time Chester had fallen, and so had any other likely ports in Devon and South Wales; moreover, infantry could not well be landed in hostile country without cavalry support. Charles admitted sadly that he now had 'no horse nor ports in our power to secure them', and the treaty lapsed – perhaps fortunately for his reputation.

All he had now, apart from a shrunken Oxford garrison and another at Newark closely besieged by the Scots, were 3,000 men brought together in Worcestershire by old Lord Astley, and early in March he ordered them to join him at Oxford. Astley reached Stow-on-the-Wold on the 21st, but there he was trapped by units from the Gloucester garrison, with a force of cavalry under Sir William Brereton. A few royalist horse got away to Oxford, but the remainder, with Astley and his second-in-command Sir Charles Lucas, had to surrender. As he sat on a drum afterwards chatting with some of his captors Astley uttered his famous remark, 'You have done your work, boys, and you may go play, unless you will fall out among yourselves.'

Fairfax, returning from the West, was now moving in on Oxford. Charles offered to return to Westminster to negotiate a peace settlement, but Parliament refused unless he would give specific guarantees beforehand. He was still in touch with the Scots through Montreuil, and this was his only hope now. On 27 April he slipped out of Oxford in disguise, with only two companions. He rode fast for Cambridgeshire, where he paid a brief visit to the hermetic Anglican community at Little Gidding, an episode commemorated in T. S. Eliot's *Four Quartets*:

> It would be the same at the end of the journey,
> If you came at night like a broken king . . .
> And any action
> Is a step to the block, to the fire, down the sea's throat
> Or to an illegible stone.

Then he rode straight to Newark, where he surrendered to the Scots army. At their request he ordered the garrison commander, Lord Belasyse, to surrender, which he did on 8 May, and the Scots at once struck camp and marched north, taking their King with them. They had reached Newcastle before Parliament learned the astounding news. Sir Thomas Glemham was prepared to defend Oxford to the last dog and the last rat, as he had Carlisle, but he was overruled by the Privy Council, who forced him to capitulate on 24 June.

In this twilight of the royal cause tiny groups of desperate men still rode hither and thither across the land, emerging from the shadows only to re-enter them almost at once. Some of them went to ground in remote castles which were one by one reduced, though in many cases we do not know by whom or when. Fairfax tackled the outlying fortresses surrounding Oxford – Boarstall House on 10 June, Faringdon Castle on 24 June and Wallingford on 27 July – and a detachment from his army secured Worcester on 22 July. On 19 August Pendennis Castle surrendered in the far West; two days later Charles's old refuge, Raglan Castle. Other Welsh castles still held out; Conway until 18 November, Holt in Denbighshire and Harlech in Merioneth well into the new year. In fact, Harlech enjoys the distinction of being the last royalist outpost to surrender, on 16 March 1647, but by that time its garrison were forgotten men, defending a forgotten cause.

In November 1646 Fairfax unostentatiously returned to London and slipped into his house in Queen Street, shunning publicity. But on the 14th he had to receive a formal deputation from both Houses. Ironically, it fell to the Earl of Manchester, as Speaker *pro tempore*, to convey the Lords' congratulations; Essex, perhaps fortunately, had died the previous September. Speaker Lenthall for the Commons was careful to point out that the General had only been the instrument of Almighty God, but he went on to say:

> It was the custom of the Ancient Romans, after a glorious and successful prince, to derive his name to posterity in memory of his virtues, as after that great prince Julius Caesar his successors retained the name of Caesars, as Augustus Caesar, Tiberius Caesar, &c. Thus hereafter all famous and victorious succeeding generals in this kingdom (if the time shall prove so unfortunate) will desire the addition of the name of 'Fairfax'.

A hint Cromwell did not take.

# 8

# PEACE OR NO PEACE

The King's surrender ushered in a period of unparalleled confusion. It is in the nature of civil wars that they rarely end in a legal and binding treaty, and in 1646, given Parliament's insistence that it had all along been fighting to preserve the King's government, there was even some doubt whether a war as such had taken place at all, which was to have serious implications, especially for those on the winning side.

For one thing, despite his total defeat the King remained the one indispensable factor in the constitutional equation. Scarcely anyone thought in terms of a republic, and even they did not urge it publicly; there was some scattered talk of deposing the King, but this was not practical politics, especially since his eldest son was safely abroad. So Charles had to be persuaded, if possible of his own free will, to accept a new settlement, though this was something he showed no disposition whatsoever to do. It was even more embarrassing, and potentially dangerous, that he was now in the hands of the Scots. The failure of the Scots to pull their weight in the Civil War after Marston Moor had dashed their hopes of wielding a decisive influence on the settlement in all three kingdoms, but possession of the King gave them a second chance.

However, the Scots had had enough. They were nearly bankrupt, and quite as war-weary as the English; Montrose was still loose somewhere in the Highlands, and might come again. They were ready to do a deal provided their darling project of an English Presbyterian Church on Scottish lines was adopted as official policy at Westminster. Here they were pushing at an open door; an increasing number of MPs, whatever their personal religious beliefs, were coming to think that only the imposition of strong, centralised church government could arrest the prevailing anarchy and curb the alarming spread of sectarianism or congregationalism amongst the working classes. Episcopacy was a lost cause, and only Presbyterianism could fill the vacuum. Thus the Newcastle Propositions, drawn up by Parliament and sent to the King on 13 July 1646 with the full approval of the Scots, demanded that he take the Solemn League and Covenant and impose it on all his subjects, and that he move at once to establish a new Presbyterian Church of England, for which Parliament was now laying the statutory foundations. The armed forces, meanwhile, were to remain under Parliament's direct control for ten years, and under its indirect control indefinitely. All his general officers, and his civilian advisers, by name, were excluded from pardon, and whole categories of lesser royalists were to be barred from public life, including, for example, those who had sat in the Oxford Parliament.

It was scarcely to be expected that Charles would agree to such terms outright, but while he havered Parliament succeeded in reaching a financial settlement with the Scots. The Scots presented a bill for £1.8 million, though £500,000 of this was for free quarter in the northern counties over the previous nine months and was at once crossed off. In September 1646 Parliament offered a token £100,000; the Scots held out for £500,000, but eventually compromised on £400,000, to be paid in two instalments. On 30 January 1647, having received the first instalment, the Scots army quietly broke camp and retreated north from Newcastle while contingents from the Northern Association army took up guard around the King; on 11 February they disappeared over the Tweed into Scotland. Comparisons with Judas and his thirty pieces of silver were not wanting, even at the time, and they were remembered with bitterness two years later. However, when Charles left on 3 February under escort for the South he was greeted with subdued acclaim along the way; Fairfax came to meet him at Nottingham with suitable deference, and took him on to Holmby (or Holdenby) House, Northamptonshire, where he remained in 'protective custody'. Now that his capacity to inflict direct harm on anybody was at an end his popularity was rising, and to the politicians, facing a host of problems at Westminster, he was if anything more indispensable than ever.

In fact the Long Parliament's position was desperately weak; it had won the war but it was in serious danger of losing the peace. The counties previously under its control were bled white; those outside, or on the periphery of, its control had been plundered by the royalists, often by the parliamentarians as well, sometimes by the Scots. Trade, internal and external, was slow to recover; much of industry was still geared to war production, especially the iron, leather and cloth industries; and thousands of soldiers, it seemed, were now to be decanted back into civilian life, many of them with poor prospects of employment. On top of all this, the summer of 1646 saw the first of three disastrous harvests in succession, which pushed the price of wheat up from 30s a quarter to 58s in that year, and 65s in 1647, other food prices rising in proportion. Begging, particularly in the towns, was a growing scandal, and at the other extreme many demobilised troopers, taking their horses and pistols back into civilian life, made a new career in highway robbery, which was to prove an endemic problem for the next hundred years or more.

At the same time a London-based group of radicals, soon nicknamed the 'Levellers', were mounting an explicit and insistent critique of Parliament's policy (or non-policy) over a wide field, by means of a strident pamphlet campaign backed up by mass petitioning at Westminster. The Lords' clumsy attempt to stifle them by reintroducing press censorship was unpopular in itself after the complete freedom which had prevailed since 1641, and the frequent incarceration of their leaders, particularly John Lilburne, scarcely interrupted their activities and allowed them to pose with some success as martyrs for truth.

In fact on the face of it there was a great deal of truth in the Levellers' case against the government. They pointed to Parliament's conspicuous lack of war aims; since 1642 its only ostensible aim had been to defeat the King in battle, and now this was done, what next? If the nation's differences with King Charles had called for such a huge sacrifice in money, property and human life, why was Parliament now seeking a compromise settlement along lines already laid down in 1641 and 1642? Surely the time had come to bring in a new constitution, with a more equal distribution of power. Arguing from English history and natural law, they concluded that all men had certain inalienable rights, including the right to participate in government at the appropriate level; therefore they demanded that the distribution of parliamentary seats be revised in accordance with the distribution of population, and that the franchise be extended, perhaps to all adult males, certainly far beyond the present charmed circle of substantial landowners and burghers. If the King and House of Lords had any place in this new constitution, which was doubtful, their powers and privileges must be drastically curtailed.

The Levellers also derided Parliament's total failure to reach a religious settlement after six years' debate, and they rejected its belated conversion to Presbyterianism, which was likely to prove just as oppressive as episcopacy, if not more so. They insisted instead on complete religious toleration, this being another of man's natural rights. In the long term they also called for the complete reform of the legal system, so as to achieve that equality before the law which now existed only in theory; in the short term they demanded the immediate abolition of county committees, sequestration committees, and all other tyrannous administrative bodies which were usurping the functions of the common law courts. More specifically, they called for the immediate abandonment of such 'prerogative' taxes as the assessment and the excise, which they blamed for the decline in agriculture and trade respectively, and demanded that the Long Parliament first present its accounts for public scrutiny, then dissolve itself.

Loss of confidence in the government was also reflected in a nation-wide taxpayers' strike. The latest assessment, imposed for twenty months in February 1645, expired in September 1646; arrears were then running at over 50 per cent, and Parliament dared not renew it until March 1647. It was then imposed on fifty-two counties, as against the previous seventeen, and the overall monthly sum was lowered from £80,000 to £60,000. But by December 1647 *not one penny* had come in; nor had a penny been received from the excise since November 1646. (The strike against the excise, accompanied by sporadic rioting, and rabbling of excise officers, continued into 1649.) The Eastern Association was particularly disaffected; from the beginning it had jibbed at supporting an army no longer its own, and in December 1646 Suffolk sent up a petition calling for the immediate demobilisation of the New Model, followed by Essex in March 1647. On 7 October 1646 Parliament reluctantly voted to keep the New Model for another six months, but it was a luxury it could no longer afford, and thereafter it could send it only random and inadequate instalments of pay, gleaned from the arrears trickling in from the twenty-month assessment of 1645–6. The general officers, however, were kept sweet by *ad hoc* grants, chiefly from the confiscated estates of the leading royalists; Fairfax, for instance, was voted land worth £5,000, mainly from the Duke of Buckingham's estates, Cromwell £2,500 courtesy of the Marquess of Worcester, and so on.*

By February 1647 the soldiers' accumulated arrears of pay amounted to £2.8 million. Even if we discount £800,000 of this as representing the arrears still owed to men demobilised in 1645 and 1646, and pay 'respited' for the duration, the balance was far beyond Parliament's resources. So much was patently obvious, and some kind of compromise would have to be reached. The surplus troops from Essex's and Waller's armies had been demobilised in 1645 with a mere two weeks' pay; the Scots, as we have seen, had had to scale down their demands from £1.8 million to £400,000, despite the leverage given them by their possession of the King; in October 1646 the troops in Massey's Western Association were demobilised with six weeks' pay, though this was only a fraction of their arrears. Massey's men were notoriously restive and mutinous, and Parliament had sent Fairfax down with a brigade of New Model cavalry to supervise the operation, but it had passed off without incident.

So Parliament anticipated no trouble from the well-disciplined New Model, next on the list. The Northern army under Sydenham Poyntz, on paper about two-thirds the size of Fairfax's, could wait. The New Model, quartered as it was in the Midlands, was pressing heavily on the wealthier and more articulate parts of the country; Poyntz's men were only annoying Yorkshire, which had little political clout. Moreover, Poyntz was a hard-line Presbyterian, and he and his men might prove useful in some later emergency. In contrast the religious and political complexion of some of the New Model regiments was already giving cause for concern, and it would do no harm to cut Fairfax and Cromwell down to size now the war was over. Therefore on 18 February 1647 Parliament decreed that the New Model should be reduced to 6,600 horse and dragoons, the remaining horse and all the foot to be disbanded forthwith unless they volunteered for Ireland. Such a force would be adequate for police operations, but without infantry it would not be able to threaten the towns. Early in March Phase II of the

---

* This contrasts with the treatment of generals who were forced to resign under the Self-Denying Ordinance. Waller, whose estates had been in royalist hands most of the war, was almost bankrupt when he retired, but he never received anything like his full arrears; he voluntarily remitted £1,000, accepted furniture from the royal palaces in lieu of another £300, and eventually received another £500 at 12s in the £.

operation was unveiled: the creation of a new army to reconquer Ireland, consisting of 8,400 foot, 1,200 dragoons and 3,000 horse. This would absorb most of the New Model foot,* and the additional horse and dragoons required, above the four hundred surplus from the New Model, were presumably to come from those demobilised from Essex's and Waller's armies in 1645.

It was a neat plan, and Parliament was not deterred by the fact that only a handful of Massey's troops had volunteered for Ireland the previous October. Ireland had necessarily been neglected since 1642, but now there was no excuse for ignoring it any longer. Despite a prodigious amount of diplomatic intrigue against a background of sporadic banditry, the situation there was curiously static. Ormonde was still almost helpless, but the Confederates could not get their act together, distracted and divided as they were by the hardline tactics of Nuncio Rinuccini and Charles I's endless prevarications, which accentuated the difficulty of holding together the Old Irish and the Old English. The climax came in March 1646, when the Supreme Council at Kilkenny signed a peace treaty with Ormonde which offered the rebels a general pardon and made some political concessions but left the position of the Catholic Church in Ireland floating. Rinuccini at once denounced this 'Ormonde Peace', and even imprisoned the delegates who had signed it. But the subsequent ructions only sabotaged the Confederates' one conclusive victory in the whole war. On 5 June 1646 Owen Roe O'Neill routed Monro's Scottish army at Benburb, but instead of advancing into Ulster he had to retire south once more, to go to the aid of the Nuncio. In the centre and south the situation was further complicated by the rivalry, part political, part personal, between O'Neill and his fellow veteran Thomas Preston, commanding the Confederate 'army' in Leinster. As a result a concerted attack on Dublin in November went off at half cock. The Nuncio now released the imprisoned members of the Supreme Council, but he summoned a General Assembly of the Confederation in January 1647 which on his advice rejected the 'Ormonde Peace'.

But by this time Ormonde, seeing no prospect of help from the King, had opened negotiations with Parliament; Charles hesitated to approve this *démarche*, but he did not forbid it. Parliament had precious little to

---

* Most historians posit a surplus of about 6,000, but this is on the assumption that the army had reached its establishment of 14,400, which as we have seen it never did. Fairfax had at the very most 10,000 foot at this stage, probably much less.

spare, but it was Ormonde who pointed out that they had to hand one of the best professional soldiers of his generation, with solid experience in Ireland. George Monck had been captured at Nantwich in January 1644, and like other 'Irish' officers he had not been exchanged, but clapped in the Tower on a charge of treason. He now agreed to take the Covenant and return to Ireland, and in February 1647 he was sent with a token force to Cork, together with his friend and distant relative, Philip Lord Lisle, who was named as Lord Lieutenant. But Inchiquin and the other Protestant notables in Munster declined to acknowledge this paper viceroy, and he and Monck returned with their tails between their legs. However, negotiations continued, and on 7 June another Irish veteran, Michael Jones, landed at Dublin with 2,000 men and a group of parliamentary commissioners, to whom Ormonde surrendered his powers as Lieutenant-General; on the 28th he left for France. Jones at once sallied forth to meet another Confederate attack, and routed it decisively at Dungan's Hill near Trim on 8 August. However, it was now evident that he would have to wait for some time for reinforcements from England.

In truth, if Parliament really wanted to raise a new army for Ireland, as it said it did, its way of going about it was stupendously maladroit. Early in March 1647, it went ahead and ordered the demobilisation of the New Model infantry without so much as a week's arrears. At the same time it provoked the senior officers by reducing them all, except Fairfax, to the rank of colonel. Cromwell began negotiations with the Elector Palatine to take a couple of regiments over to Germany.

However, these 'grandees', who had spent most of the winter in London, out of touch with the Army, were suddenly overtaken by a spontaneous revolt amongst their own troops which rapidly spread to the junior officers; Fairfax's own foot regiment was one of the most mutinous. The process by which the soldiers organised themselves is still something of a mystery, but the results were spectacular. A parliamentary delegation sent down to Saffron Walden on 21 March was shouted down at a mass meeting, and presented with a concerted demand from officers and men for the settlement of their arrears, a guarantee of indemnity, and the clarification of their terms of service in Ireland. The officers went on to present a petition to Parliament in similar terms, but they also demanded the prompt settlement of the Church and the confirmation of Magna Carta and the Petition of Right. Cromwell, sitting on the back benches, was as startled as anybody, though few believed him. Those who did not suspect him of fomenting the mutiny for his own ends naturally suspected the Levellers, though it is now clear that the Levellers did not wake up to the significance of what was happening in the Army until the late summer.

So far as arrears were concerned, it is doubtful if the men were so unrealistic as to expect a complete settlement; they would probably have been content with the six weeks' pay awarded to Massey's troops the previous autumn, which would have cost the government about £180,000, with the promise of a final accounting later. But 'indemnity' was another matter. Because of the ambiguous legal status of the Civil War, soldiers and officers had no protection against a barrage of civil suits now being mounted against them, seeking hefty compensation for food, horses and other supplies confiscated, buildings and crops damaged, money exacted, and assaults on the person; suits which were readily entertained by assize judges, justices of the peace and county committees, who were now profoundly anti-military. The result was a complete breakdown of law and order; the troops met this legal persecution with violence, and in the absence of pay resorted to further plunder. Thirty-six of the forty English counties were involved in serious disorder of one kind or another in 1646–7, and in fourteen of them civilian officials were molested, threatened or beaten up. In November 1646 General Poyntz and the Mayor of York were dragged from their beds at gunpoint by mutinous soldiers of the Northern army, who were pacified only with the greatest difficulty and went unpunished. The same men were out again in May 1647; this time they seized the Yorkshire sequestration committee and held them several days, trying to squeeze money out of them. In July 1647 several members of the Leicestershire county committee were 'arrested' by army mutineers, and there were similar incidents in Westmorland, Lancashire and Dorset. At Nantwich in Cheshire a mixed bag of deputy lieutenants, excise commissioners, sequestrators and plain country gentry were herded into a single room and held for several days until army officers could release them, with no food or water or 'accommodation for nature but publicly, like beasts amongst ourselves'.

Such incidents naturally sharpened Parliament's desire for a general demobilisation, but its only policy was one of confrontation. Its reaction to the Saffron Walden petition of 21 March was to pass a declaration registering its 'high dislike' of the men's actions, and warning them that unless they came to heel they would be 'looked upon and proceeded against as enemies of the state'.

In the circumstances this threat was difficult to implement, but

Parliament did its best to encourage desertion from the Army and it tried to embody these deserters in new units. It put forward first Waller, then Massey, then Skippon as commanders of its putative Irish army, only to see them rejected with contempt by officers and men. 'Fairfax and Cromwell and we all go!' they chanted. The Lords were more realistic; on 27 April they voted the Army six weeks' arrears of pay, but by then it was too late. The very next day eight of the more militant cavalry regiments proceeded to elect 'agitators' or 'agents' – we would call them shop stewards – who sent an impassioned appeal to Fairfax, calling upon him to maintain 'the just rights and liberties of the subjects' and to lead them against their new enemies, who, they said, 'like foxes lurk in their dens, and cannot be dealt withal, though discovered, being protected by those who are entrusted with the government of the kingdom'.

Fairfax, that stern disciplinarian, liked none of this, but he now found himself squeezed between Parliament and the Army. Parliament was still inflexible; on the other hand the Army, quartered in a comparatively small area of the Midlands and East Anglia, was beginning to draw together whether he liked it or not, and it was already sending out emissaries to infiltrate the Northern army. Its agents, by some means unknown, were also procuring petitions to Parliament in their favour from Essex, Norfolk, Suffolk, Buckinghamshire, Hertfordshire and Hampshire – all desperate to get rid of the Army at almost any cost. In response Parliament placed the 18,000-strong London militia under new management, and began to negotiate with the Scots for the loan of their army all over again; this time a new, slimmed-down army of 5,000 foot and 1,200 horse commanded by David Leslie. Unfortunately this correspondence was tapped by Army agents sent out to police the Great North Road.

On 25 May Parliament raised the temperature to flashpoint by bullishly announcing that disbandment would begin on 1 June, though it now offered the men eight weeks' arrears. This offer, which might have brought the crisis to an end two or three months before, was now ignored, and confusion reigned as Fairfax struggled to regain control. On 31 May he ordered a general rendezvous of the Army at Newmarket, which was going to happen anyway, and he had to condone the conduct of Cornet Joyce, who took a party of five hundred cavalry drawn from four different regiments to Holmby House on 4 June and brought the King across to Newmarket. Some of Cromwell's friends as well as his enemies saw his hand in this, too, but it is unlikely in the extreme that he would have flouted Fairfax's authority in this way; the Army was now studded with little 'soviets' hatching revolutionary initiatives. However, next day on Kentford Heath, just outside Newmarket, Fairfax brought his full influence to bear; in effect he convinced the Army that the discipline which had won the war could also win the peace. The regimental agitators were persuaded to sign a *Solemn Engagement* in comparatively moderate terms, swearing not to disband until their just demands were met, but confining those just demands to pay and indemnity; beyond this they simply requested Parliament in general terms to expedite a final settlement of church and state. An officer and a man were now elected by each regiment to form a General Council of the Army, together with the general officers.

By now Parliament was having second thoughts. On 21 May it had passed a liberal Indemnity Ordinance, reinforced by another on 7 June, but it was to take time to prove their worth. It also repealed its declaration of 'high dislike'. But this brought it under strong counter-pressure from the Presbyterian government of the City, which was against any concessions. Some reformadoes of the 1644 armies also besieged Westminster, clamouring for the payment of *their* arrears before the pampered rebels of the New Model, and had to be bought off by an immediate cash grant of £10,000. On 10 June the Army began to move slowly south-west towards St Albans, bringing the King with them. Parliament appointed a Committee of Safety, as in 1642, to defend 'the Kingdom, Parliament and the City', and ordered the Lines of Communication to be manned – lines which it had never been necessary to defend against the royalists. But there was no Earl of Essex available now, and neither Waller nor Massey was an adequate substitute; Poyntz was in the hands of his own mutinous troops at Pontefract. The Army halted at St Albans on 14 June and issued a thunderous *Declaration*:

> We were not a mere mercenary army hired to serve any arbitrary power of a state, but called forth and conjured by the several declarations of Parliament to the defence of our own and the people's just rights and liberties. And so we took up arms in judgment and conscience to those ends, and have so continued them, and are resolved … to assert and vindicate the just power and rights of this kingdom in Parliament, for those common ends premised, against arbitrary power, violence and oppression, and against all particular parties or interests whatsoever.

As for the legality of its position in this revolutionary crisis, it appealed to the example of former rebels against arbitrary tyranny, the Dutch in 1572, the Scots in 1638 and the Portuguese in 1640, and it reminded Parliament that 'all authority is fundamentally seated in the office, and but ministerially in the person', neatly turning against it the argument it had used against the King in 1642. It not only called for the immediate satisfaction of its own grievances, but sharply requested Parliament to purge those Members hostile to the Army, proceed with all possible speed to a final settlement, publish its accounts and then arrange for its own dissolution and a new election.

It was not a palatable programme, but it was difficult to evade. Two days later, on the 16th, Parliament sent a month's pay in cash to St Albans, but in return the General Council of the Army demanded the expulsion of eleven named MPs, headed by Waller, Denzil Holles and Sir Philip Stapleton. Receiving no response, the Army then advanced to Uxbridge, whence it could control London's supply lines with the West; on the 25th Parliament rejected the Army's *Declaration* of the 14th as a basis for negotiation, but the eleven Members voluntarily withdrew. The general officers now issued a more conciliatory *Manifesto*, jettisoning for the time being the broader demands of the *Declaration*, and on 29 June the Commons resolved without a division 'that they do own this Army as their Army, and will make provision for their maintenance'. In return Fairfax withdrew, first to Reading, then to Bedford, whence he scattered his militant cavalry regiments across the Midlands, from Northampton as far west as Gloucester. On 5 July a contingent of the Northern army arrived at Bedford, bringing Poyntz with them as a prisoner. Shocked at this treatment of a general officer, Fairfax promptly released him, but on 17 July Parliament recognised a *fait accompli* and placed him in command of all its remaining forces.

But the crisis was not over yet. On 21 July the City broke with Parliament and voted to bring Charles back to London and negotiate with him on the basis of a Presbyterian Church for a trial period of three years (which was largely meaningless) and parliamentary control of the militia for ten. For the next five days both Houses were overawed by tumultuous rioting, of the kind which had unhinged Charles I in 1641; the eleven Members resumed their seats and the Lines of Communication were manned once more, with Massey in charge. Fairfax at once remustered the Army and marched back to St Albans, where he set up his headquarters. He also sent detachments to seize Tilbury and Gravesend, so that if need be he could blockade the Port of London. On 30 July he was joined at St Albans by the Speakers of both Houses, with eight peers and forty-seven MPs; they told him Parliament was no longer a free agent, and placed themselves under his protection.

Fairfax at once advanced further, to Hounslow Heath in Middlesex, where on 3 August he impressed a City delegation with a parade of 20,000 men under perfect discipline. Next day at Hammersmith he received the keys of St Giles's Fort, near Hyde Park Corner, and the Lines of Communication from there south to the river were evacuated. On the 6th he marched into London at the head of 16,000 men, 9,000 foot and 7,000 horse, the men with bays in their hats as for a victory parade. He was ceremonially received by both Houses, though he modestly declined their invitation to sit through the proceedings; then he went on to the City, where he took over as Constable of the Tower. Shown a selection of the Tower records, he called for a copy of Magna Carta, saying reverently, 'This is what we have fought for, and by God's help must maintain.'* He then took up his headquarters at Chelsea, well outside the metropolitan area. The eleven Members were finally expelled (they had already fled, some of them abroad), and on 2 September Parliament ordered that the Lines of Communication be 'slighted and demolished'.

Parliament was far from being tamed, of course, as its continuing attempts to bring the King round to Presbyterianism show (p. 176 below), but it was certainly committed now to appeasing the Army as much as it could. The Indemnity Ordinances of 21 May and 7 June had set up a central committee of fifty-two MPs and twenty-six peers (virtually all the Lords still sitting at Westminster) with sweeping powers to reverse verdicts handed down against soldiers for wartime 'crimes' in the courts of common law, to bring cases pending in those courts before it and conclude them, and to commit plaintiffs and their lawyers who persisted in harassing defendants whom it had taken into its protection. In December sub-committees were set up in each county, also empowered to enforce the ordinances for the relief of disabled soldiers and war widows and orphans, and those facilitating the re-entry of demobilised ex-apprentices into craft guilds. Both the central and local committees were vigilant, active and effective.

The problem of arrears of pay, and for that matter current pay, was

---

* This was not a mere publicity stunt; Fairfax had a genuine care for records. When he took the surrender of Oxford in 1646 he sent a special detachment in ahead to protect the Bodleian Library.

not so easily solved, but Parliament did its best. In September, in an attempt to bring in arrears from the wartime assessments of 1642–4, it set up a new Committee of the Army, with power to imprison defaulting assessors and collectors, though it dared not proceed against the tax-payers themselves. In fact the tax strike which had held up the twenty months' assessment of 1645–6 continued, and the Army could be paid only in dribs and drabs as the arrears were painfully extracted: a month's pay in June 1647, another month's pay in August, which took two months to filter down to the troops, and another in November and December. In December Parliament tried to bring in at least part of the nine months' assessment it had voted for the current year, 1647, by offering to cancel the remaining obligations of any county which had paid six months' tax by 15 January 1648. Not one county qualified for this concession, and in fact the last of this 1647 assessment did not trickle in until 1652. But the troops could see that Parliament was doing its best, and they were well aware of the hostility of the civilian population towards them, which made its best not good enough. So between December 1647 and February 1648 Fairfax was able to demob-ilise 18,000 men, mainly from the Northern army, with only six weeks' arrears of pay and no fuss. For the rest, early in 1648 Parliament decided for the time being to abandon central accounting in favour of more primitive and effective methods. The Committee of the Army began to authorise the payment of regiments directly from the taxes paid by the counties on which they were quartered, the troops being authorised to 'assist' in its collection. It was ironic – and the irony was not lost on contemporaries – that the Long Parliament, having frustrated Charles I's shadowy and unproven plans to establish a Con-tinental despotism, had now instituted such a despotism itself, over-riding the legal system by the imposition of *droit administratif*, and collecting taxes under threat of military force.

Meanwhile the Levellers had belatedly grasped the opportunity provided by a rebellious army, and in the summer and autumn of 1647 their influence on the regiments stationed outside London noticeably increased. As we have seen, it was only natural for the authorities to assume that the mutinous posture of the Army from March 1647 onwards, the election of agitators, their remarkably well-organised subversion of the Northern army, their talk of 'rights and liberties' as if they were inherent in all men, their appeal to Magna Carta and the Petition of Right, were prompted, even orchestrated, by these sophisticated and experienced radicals from London. But in fact throughout 1646 and well into 1647 the Levellers were blankly hostile to the Army, which they blamed for most of the nation's ills – high taxation, continued disorder, the subversion of civilian rights. They tacitly accepted Parliament's plans for a general demobilisation, and the *Large Petition* of March 1647, their most comprehensive policy statement to date, did not mention the Army at all. It was not until May or June, when the authorities in London began a determined campaign to suppress them, that they turned to the Army, realising that whether they liked it or not it was now the key to the whole situation. Even then, their influence on official pronouncements of the Council of the Army, signed by Fairfax, like the *Declaration* of 14 June, was minimal, perhaps non-existent.

Nor is there much sign of Leveller involvement in the *Heads of the Proposals*, drawn up by Henry Ireton, accepted by the Council of the Army on 17 July as an approved scheme for a permanent settlement, and put to the King on the 23rd. True, these *Heads* rejected Presbyterian Church government in favour of a general toleration, but this is something Cromwell and Ireton and many of their officers were already committed to anyway. It also provided for biennial parliaments elected on a new representative system which gave more weight to the counties as against small boroughs, but it did not meet one of the Levellers' key demands, for the extension of the franchise. In so far as it recommended the reform of the legal system, the abolition of tithes, the cancellation of all monopolies in trade or manufacture and the election of JPs at local level it did echo Leveller thinking, but otherwise it was a thoroughly conservative document. The militia was to remain in Parliament's hands for ten years, and so was the appointment of ministers of state, but it tacitly assumed that the House of Lords, the Levellers' *bête noire*, would survive. Its great attraction for Charles was that it reduced the number of proscribed royalists to five (unnamed), and provided for the readmission of the rest, by stages, to public life.

Had Charles accepted this, if only as a working basis for discussion, there is little doubt that Fairfax would have taken him with him to Westminster that August, with incalculable results. As it was he saw his advantage in playing off Parliament and the Army one against the other, and he doubted if the Army had the constitutional authority to sustain these proposals – which was unrealistic, perhaps, but not unreasonable. Discussions continued through September and October at Hampton Court, where he was now lodged, between him, Cromwell and Ireton; they got on surprisingly well together, but at the end of it they were no nearer agreement. Fairfax was indisposed most of the summer, and held aloof. Then on 15 October the Levellers intervened with *The Case of the Army Truly Stated*, a lengthy diatribe signed by five new regimental agitators, later disowned, who had been elected in mysterious circumstances the previous month. It was probably written by the notorious Leveller John Wildman.

*The Case of the Army* drew the attention of the Council of the Army to its public undertakings, notably its *Declaration* of 14 June, and enquired how it proposed to safeguard those rights and liberties which it had so confidently asserted when it could not even obtain its arrears of pay. When and how was it going to force Parliament to put a term to its own existence, and ensure that subsequent parliaments were 'equally' elected, as befitted an assembly which embodied the sovereign authority of the people? In fact, it insinuated, all such questions had been shelved while the grandees, having put the General Council of the Army asleep, negotiated with that discredited and malevolent worthy the King for a compromise settlement which would be more to his advantage than theirs. This was plausible enough to force Fairfax to summon a series of celebrated discussion meetings at Putney Church on 28–9 October and 1–8 November between the agitators of the regiments, the general officers and a number of civilian Levellers down from London. Fairfax himself was prudently absent for the first week, and Cromwell as his second-in-command took the chair; he and Ireton bore the brunt of it.

The underlying purpose of the Putney Debates was to decide how far the *Heads of the Proposals* were consonant with the Army's solemn public undertakings made earlier, but when the delegates met on 28 October the Levellers tabled as a discussion document the *Agreement of the People*, the outline of a radical new constitution based on a unicameral legislature elected annually, which would wield complete executive and legislative power, without King or House of Lords. The only way to impose such a constitution on the present Parliament, or on the nation at large, was by force, and Cromwell and Ireton argued with some success that it went far beyond anything previously contemplated by the Army. The *Agreement* made no mention of the franchise, but the question came up next day, and led to a celebrated and oft-quoted debate on the rights and wrongs of 'one man, one vote'.* Ireton,

---

* In fact it is not clear that the Levellers wanted universal manhood suffrage. They would certainly have excluded 'servants', a category which could cover all wage-earners, and the unemployed.

doggedly defending the conventional view that the vote should be enjoyed only by those who had a stake in society, i.e. property, found himself in a minority of two, with Cromwell, and they had to listen while one of their own colonels, Thomas Rainsborough, told them in plangent words that what the men of the Army had fought for all along was the right to participate in the public life of the nation:

> I think that the poorest he that is in England hath a life to live, as the greatest he; and therefore truly, sir, I think it's clear that every man that is to live under a government ought first by his own consent to put himself under that government; and I do think that the poorest man in England is not at all bound in a strict sense to that government that he hath not had a voice to put himself under.

However, with some difficulty Cromwell managed to adjourn the unruly proceedings to the Monday, 1 November, when the *Agreement of the People* was shelved; the discussion was now focused on the King's 'negative voice', his veto on legislation, which had been omitted from the *Heads of the Proposals*. In the ensuing debates, on the 2nd, 5th and 6th, very sparsely reported, the question whether they should negotiate with the King at all was on the anvil. Fairfax took the chair on Saturday the 6th, and again on Monday the 8th, when it was agreed that the way should be kept open for further negotiations with the King, and that the officers and men present should now disperse to their regiments pending a general rendezvous of the Army, to be held later that month.

The Levellers dispersed docilely enough, planning to use this rendezvous to incite the troops to pledge mass support for the *Agreement*. But Fairfax moved to checkmate them. He ordered the Army to assemble in three sections at three separate rendezvous, on 15, 17 and 18 November, and he issued a formidable *Remonstrance concerning the late Discontents and Distractions in the Army, with his Excellency's Declaration of himself, and Expectation from the Army thereupon, for the future uniting of the Army*. He denounced the Levellers and disowned them entirely; under threat of resignation he demanded that the agitators abide by the decisions of his Council of War (meaning himself), and that each soldier individually pledge obedience to him. In return he undertook to support, as he always had, their claims to arrears of pay, to work for the dissolution of the present Parliament, and to try and ensure 'the freedom and equality of election' to subsequent parliaments, so as 'to render the House of Commons (as near as may be) an equal representative of the people that are to elect'.

The outcome was a staggering personal triumph. The crunch came at the first rendezvous, at Corkbush Field, near Ware, on the 15th. Two regiments turned up which had no business there, Thomas Harrison's regiment of horse and Robert Lilburne's regiment of foot, with Leveller mottoes and green ribbons stuck on their hats. Two officers, a Colonel Eyres and a Major Scott, showed signs of sympathy with this demonstration, but they were promptly arrested and sent away to London, where they were later cashiered. Fairfax then went down into Harrison's regiment and pacified the men in face-to-face argument, but he had to send a few of his officers, perhaps led by Cromwell, perhaps not, into Lilburne's regiment; they tore the mottoes from the hats of those men they could reach and seized the ringleaders and pulled them out to the front, where one of them was shot on the spot for mutiny. They were then forced to tear up the copies of the *Agreement* they had brought with them. The other regiments stood by while this was going on, then dispersed in peace with ringing shouts of 'The King and Sir Thomas!' At the other two rendezvous the troops fell over themselves to pledge their allegiance to the General.

After the high excitement of the Putney Debates, the dénouement at Ware comes as something of a surprise. The answer lies in the nature of this army and its leadership. It was emphatically not an army of 'saints', inspired by a messianic religious purpose, as some contemporaries and many historians would have us believe. Nor were many of the rank and file deeply concerned with matters of state, high politics or human rights. What concerned them were such bread-and-butter matters as pay, indemnity, conditions of service, disablement allowances and widows' pensions. The agitators, like most shop stewards, were somewhat to the left of those they represented, but their radicalism can be exaggerated; as we have seen, the Levellers had to infiltrate five bogus agitators into one of the cavalry regiments in order to float *The Case of the Army Truly Stated*.

Moreover, this very pamphlet betrays the dichotomy between the Levellers' aspirations and the soldiers' needs. The Levellers still fiercely denounced the assessment and the excise and the extension of *droit administratif* through ad hoc committees; in other words, they were proposing to abolish the only tax source from which the troops could hope to obtain their current pay, let alone their arrears, and to suppress the indemnity committees which alone protected them from acute legal harassment, crippling damages, even gaol. Their representatives at Putney might prate of natural rights and manhood suffrage, but faced with a choice between the pursuit of constitutional reform and their own personal security, legal and financial, the men naturally chose the latter.

They were also aware that their enemies were legion, and growing stronger by the day. The Levellers tried to use this as an argument for supporting them, but it rebounded on them. Men of all classes bitterly resented the continuing high taxation and the continuing resort to free quarter; the royalists were regrouping and regaining their confidence; the King had acquired a novel reputation as a man of peace and moderation in face of the unconstitutional extravagances of both Parliament and Army. On 11 November, between the adjournment of the Putney Debates and the first Army rendezvous at Ware, Charles escaped from Hampton Court and disappeared no man knew whither. The nation was thrown into a state of alarm; many, Fairfax among them, thought he had gone north to rally support in Yorkshire and the Border counties and seek the assistance of the Scots. In fact he turned up at Carisbrooke Castle, Isle of Wight, where he was out of the immediate grasp of Parliament or the Army but unable to escape further. But the episode came as a salutary shock. The Army, deprived of its chief bargaining counter, was more isolated than ever. There was a suspicion that the grandees had been guilty of grave negligence, if not worse, but the immediate need was for a resounding demonstration of unity, which they duly provided.

Finally, the resolution of the crisis, at Putney and then at Ware, is a demonstration of Fairfax's personal ascendancy. Entirely trusted and revered by officers and men, almost ostentatiously apolitical, he was the natural focus for the *esprit de corps* which had always been the chief driving force behind the New Model – not radical religion or republican politics. He was in marked contrast to Oliver Cromwell, that emphatically political general, who was already suspected on all sides of grasping at supreme power, briefed and prompted by his idealistic son-in-law, Henry Ireton. But through 1647 and beyond Fairfax's authority was absolute and unquestioned; Cromwell and Ireton merely his senior henchmen. Unfortunately the second Civil War decisively reversed this configuration, at the same time as it bent the alignment of the Army as a whole.

# 9

# THE SECOND
# CIVIL WAR

At the close of the year 1647 there was no end in sight to the constitutional stalemate. By now Charles had rejected the *Heads of the Proposals*, and in late November, after his flight to Carisbrooke, Cromwell and Ireton broke off negotiations with him altogether. Parliament still sought his agreement to a settlement based on state Presbyterianism, and the Army made no attempt to interfere; but their latest proposals, embodied in *Four Bills* presented to him for his assent on 24 December, were almost as stringent as the Newcastle Propositions, and he rejected them out of hand. This was too much, and on 17 January 1648 Parliament passed the *Vote of No Addresses*, not only breaking off all negotiations with him but making it a treasonable offence for anyone to try to resume them.

By now, in fact, it was emerging that the King had double-crossed them. On 24 December, the very day he received the *Four Bills*, he had signed a secret *Engagement* with the Scots Commissioners who had recently come to confer with him at Carisbrooke. Over the past year the Scots had grown increasingly alarmed at the drift of events in England, at the patent inability of Parliament to achieve any kind of settlement, and at the increasing radicalism of the Army, even its high command. Above all they deeply resented the fact that since the negotiations at Newcastle in 1646 they had not been consulted on a settlement which involved their king as well as England's. In a bid for Charles's support they now offered him the best terms so far, which he immediately accepted. He agreed to acknowledge the validity of the Solemn League and Covenant as a voluntary engagement, but it was not to be imposed on him or anyone else. He also agreed to establish Presbyterianism in England for a trial period of three years, after which he and his nominees were to have an equal voice in the final settlement. He also pledged himself to work for the closer union of the two kingdoms, to admit Scotsmen to the English Privy Council and vice-versa, and to visit Scotland as often as he could, and send one of his sons to reside there. There was no mention of the future control of the militia or the fate of the royalists, but Parliament was requested to disband the Army and bring the King back to London to negotiate a detailed peace treaty, with full Scots participation. Failing this, the Scots threatened to bring an army down to England to enforce their will.

To Charles there was nothing dishonourable or treacherous in such an agreement. It was his duty to seek the best settlement he could for the kingship and the kingdom, and the legal standing of the present Scots government was arguably higher than that of the Long Parliament, the remnant of an assembly elected more than seven years ago, on a quite different mandate; it was certainly higher than that of the Army, which had no legal or constitutional standing at all. As for the Scots, watching from a distance, the confrontation between Army and Parliament, and the disputes which racked the Army itself, gave them some cause for optimism. In December 1647 Fairfax followed up his success in re-imposing discipline on the Army by coming to terms with the Levellers; the rank-and-file mutineers still in prison were released, dissident officers under suspension were pardoned, and Rainsborough was even appointed Vice-Admiral of the Fleet – a disastrous decision. But the Levellers' hostility to the 'grandees', particularly Cromwell, was unappeased, and as late as February 1648 Fairfax's own lifeguard regiment was in such a mutinous state that it had to be disbanded.

However, the *Engagement* threw Scotland into confusion. It was very much the brainchild of a small group of influential noblemen led by James, Duke of Hamilton, a personal friend of the King, and John Maitland, Earl of Lauderdale. Neither of them could command general support, and Hamilton was labelled an anglophile. The *Engagement* was at once denounced by the Kirk as a flagrant betrayal of the Covenant, and after some hesitation the Marquess of Argyll took the same stand.

Archibald Campbell, 8th Earl and 1st Marquess of Argyll – he had been promoted in the peerage during Charles's visit to Scotland in 1641 – was the greatest territorial magnate in seventeenth-century Scotland and one of its most able politicians. As hereditary chieftain of Clan Campbell, 'MacCaillum Mor', he could call on huge reserves of manpower as well as the wealth of his vast estates in Argyll, though this had availed him little in the war against Montrose in 1645 and 1646. Red-haired and squinting (men called him 'the glae-eyed marquess'), he was an unprepossessing figure, but contemporaries testify to his great personal charm, and over a long and tortuous career he played the political-cum-religious power game with consummate skill, though in the end it did not save him from the block. Unloved and mistrusted, he could not carry many of his fellow noblemen with him, but he did not need to; his emergence in this crisis as the unofficial protector and spokesman of the Kirk was decisive. The 'Engagers' controlled the Scottish Estates (or Parliament) and the Privy Council, but the Kirk's tremendous social authority, backed by the power of Clan Campbell, decisively impeded the recruitment of men and the collection of the new taxes needed to finance the invasion of England. David Leslie's army, the only trained professional force available, was hopelessly split. As a result it took until July to raise an army at all, and then it was nowhere near the projected figure of 40,000. It was certainly less than 20,000, and perhaps only half that; it had no artillery as yet, it was short of arms and ammunition, and most of the men were raw and untrained. Nevertheless, as early as 11 April the Engagers declared the treaty of 1643 between England and Scotland at an end, and in May they rejected a grovelling offer from the Long Parliament to resume joint negotiations with the King on the basis of the Newcastle Propositions.

Meanwhile the English royalists were on the move. In January the Prince of Wales left Paris and took up his station at Calais, to watch events. The Queen was doing her best to mobilise exiled royalist officers, with some success, and many of them gathered at Edinburgh. On 28 April Sir Marmaduke Langdale secured Berwick without a fight, and began to recruit vigorously in the northern counties, where his name was a rallying-cry in itself; next day Carlisle surrendered to Sir Philip Musgrave. In England the anniversary of Charles's accession on 23 March was marked by widespread riots and demonstrations, particularly in London. Lancashire, Cheshire and North Wales were notably restless, and there were rumours of plots to seize Warwick

Castle, Nottingham and Oxford. Other royalists, like the Duke of Buckingham, the Earl of Holland, Sir Charles Lucas and John, Lord Belasyse, were waiting at the Channel ports.

All the same, the series of scattered uprisings we call the 'Second Civil War' was motivated not so much by positive royalism as by a deep negative resentment directed against the Army and Parliament. In fact the first serious revolt, in South Wales in February, began with a familiar dispute over demobilisation. Colonel John Poyer refused to disband the Pembroke garrison or surrender the castle until his men's arrears were paid; other discontented troops barricaded themselves in Chepstow and Tenby castles, and by the middle of March the whole area was aflame, and substantial numbers of local civilians had joined the revolt. Colonel Thomas Horton, sent down by Fairfax with a couple of thousand men to supervise the demobilisation, was helpless. At the same time the situation in London was deteriorating fast; on 9 April Cromwell had to use his cavalry to disperse a serious royalist riot in the City, killing two, but the rioters were out in force again the following day, and the Lord Mayor had to take refuge in the Tower. They were eventually dispersed again by cavalry.

However, if public opinion was hardening against the Army, so was the Army's attitude towards the King. Those troops not on garrison duty assembled at Windsor on 29 April for a marathon three-day prayer meeting at which they and their officers examined and re-examined their conduct over the past two years. In the end they absolved themselves and their generals from all blame. In the words of one participant:

> Presently we were led and helped to a clear agreement between us, not any
> dissenting, that it was the duty of our day, with the forces we had, to go
> out and fight against those potent enemies which that year in all places
> appeared against us, with an humble confidence in the name of the Lord
> only, that we should destroy them; also enabling us then, after serious
> seeking His face, to come to a very clear and joint resolution on many
> grounds at large then debated amongst us, that it was our duty, if ever the
> Lord brought us back again in peace, to call Charles Stuart, that man of
> blood, to an account for the blood he had shed, and mischief he had done
> to his utmost, against the Lord's cause and people in these poor nations.

Cromwell was there, but not Fairfax, now Lord Fairfax of Cameron on the death of his father the previous month. True, Fairfax was trying to cope with a difficult situation in London, but all the same his absence marks his growing disillusion with the politico-religious preoccupations of many of his officers. Nor would he ever countenance the use of extreme measures against the King. From now on his role was to be almost exclusively military, and on 1 May he ordered Cromwell to leave Windsor for South Wales, taking with him three regiments each of horse and foot, plus two hundred dragoons, which, together with Horton's troops already on the scene, gave him about 8,000 men. On the same day he ordered the Army out of London, handing over responsibility for the maintenance of order to the City militia, commanded once more by Philip Skippon. On the 9th he surrendered the Tower.

Unrest was now spreading fast. On 24 April there was a major riot at Norwich. That same day in London Parliament received a petition from the county of Essex calling for the disbandment of the Army and a personal treaty with the King. It had 30,000 signatures (so it was said), and it was carried to London at the head of a procession 2,000 strong, though in the presence of troops guarding Whitehall and Westminster order was maintained. Next, 12–13 May saw a serious riot at Bury St Edmunds, and the Suffolk trained bands had to be called out. On the 16th the presentation to Parliament of another mass petition from Surrey, similar to that from Essex, led to the most violent rioting for months, difficult to control now the Army had withdrawn; ten people were killed and dozens wounded before order was restored.

Parliament was still agonising over its policy. Some thought Charles might be deemed to have abdicated, so outrageous had his conduct been, but there was no successor available. The Prince of Wales would obviously not usurp his father's throne; Parliament did have custody of his younger brother James, Duke of York, the future James II, now fifteen years old, but on 21 April he escaped from St James's Palace and got clear away to France. Nevertheless, Parliament still flinched from the idea of a republic, and three days later, on the 24th, it voted to maintain the conventional frame of government, of King, Lords and Commons. The resurgence of royalism, and the Army's withdrawal from London, pushed it further to the right, and on 24 May it decided, notwithstanding the Vote of No Addresses, to resume negotiations with Charles on the basis of the *Four Bills*. However, it had to listen to a bitter tirade against the King from the republican Thomas Scott which would have been unthinkable even six months before. 'It was fitter', he said, 'he should be brought to his trial and drawn, hanged and quartered than treated with; he being the only cause of all the bloodshed through the three kingdoms.'

Meanwhile Cromwell reached Chepstow on 11 May by forced marches to find the situation transformed; Horton had unexpectedly routed the insurgents at St Fagans three days before and was now mopping up. Tenby surrendered on the news of Cromwell's arrival, leaving only Pembroke to be reduced, and he was confident of early success. Unfortunately, like many commanders in the 1640s, he underestimated the strength of medieval castles like Pembroke, and he was not helped when the siege train sent after him was accidentally sunk in the Severn. He borrowed some guns from the *Lion* man-of-war, but he soon had to send for some heavier pieces from the Army depot at Wallingford, which he ordered to be sent round overland via Gloucester. In the end he and his troops were pinned down at Pembroke for nearly two months, until 11 July.

And on the very day Cromwell reached Chepstow, 11 May, Kent exploded. This was a peculiar county; it had always been inclined towards royalism, but it was under the direct eye of London, and hemmed in by the counties of Sussex and Surrey which by and large remained loyal to Parliament; thus a series of uncoordinated royalist risings had fizzled out in the summer of 1643. Since then it had been held down by an unusually tyrannical county committee headed by Sir Anthony Weldon; on the other hand it had never suffered directly from the war; no field army had ever crossed its boundaries. It had been notably laggard in supplying troops for Waller in 1643 and 1644, and in 1645, as we have seen, such troops as it could be induced to supply for the New Model had all mutinied and returned home. In this atmosphere a serious riot at Canterbury on Christmas Day 1647, in protest at the Puritan ordinance of 1644 abolishing the festival, acted like a time-bomb. Weldon demanded that the offenders, amongst them several of the leading county gentry, be tried by his county committee under commission of martial law, but this was much too extreme for Parliament in its present mood, and it insisted that they appear before the spring assizes on 10 May.

The result was predictable, if the sequel was not. The Grand Jury threw out the indictments against the rioters amidst wild public rejoicing, and began to canvass signatures to a petition similar to that already submitted to Parliament from Essex, and the county committee's ill-advised attempt to frustrate this led to open rebellion. Outbreaks of disorder at Sittingbourne, Faversham, Rochester and Sandwich had spread by the 26th to Dartford and Deptford. On the 29th an estimated 10,000 rebels assembled on Burham Heath, between Rochester and

Maidstone, and elected as their leader George Goring's father, the Earl of Norwich, who had arrived from France with the Earl of Holland a few weeks earlier to make what mischief they could in the southern counties.* They decided to advance on Blackheath, on the threshold of London, next day. Worse still, news now reached London that ten ships of the fleet had mutinied in the Downs and declared for the King, including the *Constant Reformation*, *Swallow* and *Convertine*, first and second rates. The Navy had deeply resented the removal of its war-time commander, the Earl of Warwick, under the Self-Denying Ordinance; it resented still more the supersession of its Vice-Admiral, William Batten, by the rigorous and humourless Rainsborough, a landlubber to boot. They now sent Rainsborough ashore in an open boat, occupied the ports of Deal, Walmer and Sandwich, and laid siege to Dover. Parliament stopped the rot by hastily reappointing Warwick as Lord Admiral; he secured the remaining nineteen ships of the line and the key base of Portsmouth, through which the royalists might have funnelled reinforcements from France. But no one dared turn these ships against their mutinous comrades.

Fairfax was left to deal with the Kentish rebellion, but his forces, reduced by demobilisation over the past eighteen months, were now seriously over-extended. Cromwell had taken 5,000 men to South Wales; John Lambert had been sent up to Yorkshire to await the Scots with three regiments of horse and one of foot, reinforced in June by another foot regiment and James Sheffield's regiment of horse from Cheshire. (It was assumed that the Scots would take the east-coast route, as in 1639, 1640 and 1644.) There were two regiments at Newcastle, and another two, under Sir Hardress Waller, were guarding the West Country. Another regiment was patrolling North Wales, another was stationed at Gloucester and another at Oxford. The Derby House Committee† refused, with good reason, to leave these centres of royalism unguarded, and it rejected, then and later, all of Fairfax's pleas for reinforcements. He had to do what he could with 7,000 men at most.

He deployed this meagre force, however, with exquisite skill, and they were mostly experienced and hardened veterans, faced by raw

---

* George Goring himself was now commander of the English regiments in the Spanish Army of Flanders. He retired to Spain itself in 1650 to take up another army command, and died there in 1657, six years before his father.

† The Committee for Both Kingdoms had been dissolved in January, and its English members reconstituted as the 'Committee at Derby House'; it seems to have had no other name. It kept a very tight rein on Fairfax, but Cromwell seems to have escaped its control.

civilians, a minority with some intermittent militia training, reinforced by a sprinkling of royalist officers returned from the Continent; they were described as 'cavaliers, citizens, seamen and watermen'. Nor was the Earl of Norwich much of a general.

Fairfax reached Blackheath on 30 May, where he took the surrender of about a thousand rebels who had suddenly decided they were only petitioners after all, and advanced on Gravesend, despatching a regiment under Colonel Gibbons over the Weald to relieve Dover. Before he reached Gravesend he swung south towards Rochester, but learning that the town and castle were staunchly defended he detached another contingent to keep the rebels there in play while he pressed on down towards Maidstone, where the main rebel 'army' under Lord Norwich had assembled. He reached Malling on 1 June and turned east towards Maidstone, taking the rebels by surprise. He drew off some of the defenders by a feint towards Aylesford, crossed the Medway at East Fairleigh virtually unopposed, and ordered an immediate storm. The garrison contested every street, inch by inch, and casualties were heavy on both sides, but by midnight it was all over. Norwich's reserve of 6,000 men had remained supine on Burham Heath, but now it broke up; some retired north to Rochester, others fled to the royalist outposts at Walmer, Deal and Sandwich, some even embarked on the mutinous fleet still hovering off the coast, but about 3,000 of them, with Norwich at their head, marched north-west to Gravesend, hoping to evade Fairfax and even occupy London. Colonel Gibbons relieved Dover on 5 June, and most of the remaining rebels in the eastern half of Kent gathered at Canterbury. But the town was poorly fortified, the rebels' morale was at a low ebb, and the townsmen had no wish to share the fate of their fellows at Maidstone. Fairfax offered lenient terms, including a pardon for all *bona fide* Kentishmen, and on the 9th the town surrendered. Next day the rebel fleet left the Downs and sailed for Holland, where they took on the Prince of Wales as their admiral; they returned in mid-July with four Dutch warships and some Dutch troops. The situation looked ugly, but by now Kent had had enough, and landing parties which went ashore at Sandwich and Deal met with no popular support. The fleet sailed up to Great Yarmouth on 22 July in the hope of provoking a rising in Norfolk, but in vain; nor could they get supplies into Colchester, now under close siege. At this stage Vice-Admiral Batten defected to Parliament, with the *Constant Warwick*, though he had been knighted by the Prince. The remainder made another attempt on the Kent coast, but their landing parties were promptly mopped up by parliamentary detachments under Colonel Rich and Sir Michael Livesey. Walmer surrendered on 14 August, followed by Deal and Sandwich.

Meanwhile Fairfax still had to catch Lord Norwich. The Earl reached Blackheath on 3 June, with Whalley's regiment in hot pursuit. When Skippon, commanding the London militia, closed the gates of the City against him most of his followers melted away, but Norwich himself and a small group of hard-core cavaliers struggled over the Thames next day in small boats. He lingered at Mile End, still hoping to break into the City, but Skippon's militia were now reinforced by the arrival of Whalley's regiment, and Fairfax was not far behind. He could only retreat east into Essex, where the local royalists had staged a rising on the 4th at Chelmsford and captured the county committee; they were soon joined by a number of leading cavaliers, among them Lord Capel, Sir Bernard Gascoigne, Sir George Lisle and Sir Charles Lucas. They retreated, together with Norwich and his Kentishmen, on the fortified town of Colchester, hoping to link up with the royalist fleet via the River Colne. They were harassed all the way by Whalley, and Fairfax, having crossed the Thames at Gravesend, was driving his men on by forced marches, hoping to catch the rebels before they reached Colchester. But by the time his advance guard came up with them on the afternoon of 13 June they were already in the suburbs. Barkstead's regiment stormed on through the suburbs, with reinforcements piling in behind, and the fighting went on until midnight, with a ferocity typical of the second Civil War: 'They [the Ironsides] fell on like madmen, killing and slaying them in a terrible manner, even in the cannon mouths.' When Lucas finally slammed the city gates shut he left about a hundred of his men outside, but the assault had failed, and Fairfax had lost a thousand men he could ill afford, including a hundred officers.

He was now committed to a siege in form, the kind of warfare he least liked, and he had precious few men at his disposal. He had had to leave several contingents behind to pacify Kent, and his losses in the storm had reduced him to 4,160 regular troops, insufficient even to surround the town; and the Derby House Committee – with the Scots expected daily, with Kent still in turmoil and petty risings or rumours of risings in Surrey, Sussex and the West – declined to reinforce him. They were justified when the Earl of Holland, with the young Duke of Buckingham and his brother Lord Francis Villiers, raised the royal standard at Kingston-on-Thames on 4 July, and soon collected five or six hundred followers. These included the Dutch engineer Jan Dalbier, who had served Parliament loyally throughout the first Civil War, especially at the siege of Basing; he was now influenced by his close association in the 1620s with Buckingham's father, the 1st Duke. London was wide open, but Holland could not recruit enough men, and the Derby House Committee sent for Sir Michael Livesey from east Kent, and Colonel Gibbons's regiment from Dover. On 6 July Holland failed in an attempt on Reigate Castle, and by now Livesey had come up; he chased him back towards Kingston, and Francis Villiers was killed in a skirmish at Surbiton. Holland and Buckingham fled north from Kingston via Harrow and St Albans, avoiding London; on the 9th they reached St Neots in Huntingdonshire. In the early hours of the following morning Colonel Scrope, sent by Fairfax with a couple of troops of horse from Colchester, irrupted into the sleeping town. Holland was captured and sent to London, Buckingham escaped in the dark and after some hazardous adventures regained the Continent; Scrope's men hacked Dalbier to death where he lay, as an evident renegade.

Back at Colchester Fairfax had sent for his artillery train on 14 June and four days later for further heavy guns from the Tower; he also began to dig major earthworks, including ten forts with angled bastions, and a ditch and rampart on the western side of the town, towards London. The mouth of the River Colne was blocked off by loyal men-of-war from Harwich. But he could not have sustained the siege or manned the fortifications without the ready assistance of the Essex and Suffolk trained bands. Suffolk provided 3,600 men and Essex 2,000, notwithstanding the fact that the original rising at Chelmsford had been led by a mutinous trained-band regiment.

It was probably to conciliate the county that Fairfax now allowed the merchants and tradesmen of Colchester to hold a weekly fair at Lexdon – as he said, 'a favour without example to a besieged town' – but otherwise the siege was conducted with unusual rigour and even bitterness. Fairfax's men were infuriated by the royalists' supposed use of soft-nosed or dum-dum musket balls, and he persistently refused to allow women and children to leave the town lest it slow down the erosion of the garrison's provisions. When a group of women did slip out his troops stripped them naked and drove them back in. Whole areas of the suburbs were deliberately set on fire and razed to the ground, and at an early stage Fairfax cut the town's water supply, melting down the pipes for bullets and leaving the townsmen dependent on unsafe wells or what they could collect from the skies, though with the continuing rain, day after day, there was no lack of this last. It was one of the worst summers in living memory, worse even than that of 1644, and the earthworks were soon one huge quagmire. One Essex parson recorded in his diary: 'The Lord goeth out against us in the season, which was wonderful wet.... We never had the like in my memory, and that for the greatest part of the summer. Commonly we had one or two floods weekly, or indeed in the meadows there was as it were a continual flood.'

These climatic conditions were common to western Europe, and in the north of England it was the same. The Duke of Hamilton crossed the Border by the west-coast route on 8 July, but he lingered at Carlisle for six days, though he was now something like six months late. Sir Marmaduke Langdale joined him from Berwick with about 3,000 English, mainly from Northumberland and Yorkshire, but the Scots themselves only had about 3,000 horse and 6,000 foot at this stage, and no artillery. David Leslie had stayed behind under pressure from the Kirk, and Hamilton's second-in-command, the Earl of Callander, though he had served as commander of the Scots contingent in the Dutch army, was ignorant of English conditions and had far too much confidence in his own judgment. However, John Middleton and William Baillie, commanding horse and foot respectively, were men of a different kidney, with solid experience in the first Civil War, Baillie with the Earl of Leven and Middleton with Essex and Waller.

The Scots army was certainly smaller than the Engagers had hoped, but it was larger than anything the English government could send against it, and it is difficult to see why Hamilton made such slow progress. However, he seems to have had serious supply problems, and his advance through Cumberland and into north Lancashire was contested every mile of the way by Lambert, who had marched over the Pennines to meet him. On 14 July, however, he reached Penrith, where he was joined by another 6,000 men from Scotland, bringing his numbers up to about 10,000 foot and 4,000 horse. Moreover, Sir George Monro, Robert Monro's nephew, was on his way with over 2,100 battle-hardened infantry from Ulster and 1,200 horse; unfortunately he had some difficulty dodging Parliament's naval patrols in the Irish Sea and he was still some way behind. All the same, Hamilton's numerical superiority was now overwhelming, and his slow progress was not only giving the English time to regroup their forces, it was alienating the local population, many of them potentially royalist. They were terrified by the irruption of this ragged, half-starved horde of barbarians, 'bringing lice and presbytery', and so many women it was feared they would settle for good.

As it was, Pembroke Castle fell at last on 11 July, and Cromwell sent his cavalry hotfoot to join Lambert, with orders to avoid a pitched battle until he arrived. They joined Lambert at Appleby on 27 July, together with a thousand foot and three hundred horse raised by the Lancashire county committee. Lambert then fell back across the Pennines again into Yorkshire, fetching up at Knaresborough on 7 August. He and Cromwell still thought Hamilton would eventually cross over into Yorkshire, if only to join up with the royalists who had seized Pontefract Castle on 1 June; Langdale would obviously press him to do so. If he continued due south instead, they could always cross the Pennines again and fall on his rear, cutting him off from Monro, whose Ulster troops seem to have been the only trained professionals he had. In fact Hamilton was not advancing at all; he reached Kendal on 2 August, and halted there while another week slipped by.

Cromwell himself was coming up with his infantry as fast as he could via Leicester and Nottingham, where he was joined on 3 August by a contingent of auxiliary troops hastily raised in Derbyshire, Nottinghamshire and Leicestershire. He waited at Doncaster until the 8th for fresh supplies of ammunition from London, sent by sea via the port of Hull, but he took the opportunity to drive the local royalists back into Pontefract, and left his Midlands auxiliaries to guard them. He joined Lambert on the 12th at Wetherby.

By now Hamilton had cautiously advanced as far as Hornby in Lancashire, arriving there on 9 August; he then halted for another five days, waiting for Sir George Monro to catch up. Monro himself pressed on ahead to meet Hamilton, Leaving his troops behind him on the road; but after a petty squabble with Lord Callander over precedence it was agreed that he and his men should halt at Kirkby Lonsdale in Westmorland, about ten miles behind, to await the long expected Scots artillery, though in view of the state of the roads this foul summer it could have been of little use. Cromwell's artillery was still lumbering after him from South Wales, but he sent back orders for it to wait at Doncaster.

Cromwell now had at the most 9,000 men, perhaps as few as 8,600, but 6,500 of them (2,500 horse and 4,000 foot) were seasoned veterans from the campaign of 1645. Hamilton had at least 17,000 Scots, plus 3,000 English under Langdale; but the Scots foot were underfed, and exhausted after long marches down mud-bound roads and nights spent in the open, lashed by incessant rain; they were disheartened, too, by the blank hostility of the local people, when they had expected to be greeted as liberators, and they were still short of arms, ammunition and all kinds of basic equipment. Nevertheless, after a long debate at Hornby, Hamilton and Callander decided to march on due south through Lancashire, in the hope of taking Manchester – though it had defied all royalist attempts to take it in the first Civil War – and linking up with a projected rising in Cheshire, led by Lord Byron, which was in fact aborted.

Cromwell had no precise intelligence of Hamilton's movements, but since he had not appeared on the eastern side of the Pennines he could only assume that he was still marching south, towards Preston. On the 12th he decided to strike due west across the Pennines to Preston, hoping either to hit the Scots hard in a surprise flank attack or emerge to the north of them so as to cut them off from Monro's Ulstermen. He set off at once by forced marches; on the 13th he was at Otley, on the 14th Skipton, the 15th Gisburn, and on the 16th his men poured down from the hills onto the plain of Lancashire at Clitheroe, about twenty-five miles north-east of Preston. He bivouacked his army that night in Stonyhurst Park near Whalley, five miles further on.

He found that Hamilton had deployed his army as if inviting a major disaster. Foraging was now such a problem that on Callander's urging he had sent the main body of his horse twenty miles ahead of him, so that on the 16th it was entering Wigan while the foot had scarcely reached Preston. He had deployed Langdale's Englishmen far out on his left flank, and they were only now marching south-west from Settle towards Preston. In fact, if Cromwell had not pressed on to Whalley the two armies would have collided at Clitheroe. Langdale then turned due west so as to reach Preston by a slightly less direct route. According to him he sent word on to Hamilton warning him of Cromwell's arrival, but the Duke discounted it, taking this for an advance guard or even a scouting party.

Next day, the 17th, Cromwell set off in pursuit of Langdale, only to be held up for four hours at Longridge, where the road degenerated into a deep, muddy lane flanked by high hedges, with enclosed fields on either side. Cromwell's cavalry had to force their way down the lane as best they could while the infantry slogged it out, field by field, on the flanks. It was dirty, bloody infighting in the pouring rain, but these were the men of Naseby and Langport who had never tasted defeat, and in the end they bulldozed their way through. The only hiccup came when a squadron of Scots lancers, hastily sent back by Hamilton, charged up the lane and took the Ironsides by surprise.

By now it was past four o'clock, but there was plenty of daylight left and Cromwell pushed on towards Preston. On Callander's urging Hamilton decided to pull his infantry back across the Ribble, though this would leave the survivors of Langdale's contingent marooned. As it was Cromwell came up so fast that Hamilton himself was almost trapped. He had to send his cavalry escort north to join Monro while he scrambled over the river in a small boat with a handful of his officers, with Cromwell already at the bridges. He now decided to leave a rearguard to hold the Ribble and Darwen bridges as long as they could while he retreated south with the main body of his foot to rendezvous with the horse, who had been ordered back from Wigan post-haste. They abandoned all their powder, except what the troops had in their flasks, and before nightfall Cromwell had smashed his way across the bridges, killing at least a thousand Scots and taking four thousand prisoner, and captured the rest of the enemy baggage train.

Chaos ensued in a night of pouring rain. There were two roads between Preston and Wigan, and while the Scots infantry marched down the westerly road, via Standish, Middleton's cavalry were riding hard up the other road, via Chorley. They missed each other, of course, and though Middleton guessed the truth when he clashed with Cromwell's advance guard just outside Preston, and at once turned back down the Standish road, it was a tired, dirty and demoralised army which reassembled at Wigan early that morning, the 18th. Cromwell's army was still inferior in numbers, most of the Scottish losses being offset by his need to leave a garrison at Preston and send detachments north to look for Monro. But there was no thought of making a stand; instead the Scots retreated further south, towards Warrington. (It was now very much a retreat, not an advance.) By the following day, the 19th, Cromwell was in hot pursuit, and though he was held up for a few hours by a last-ditch stand at Winwick, just north of Warrington, where the Scots lost another thousand killed and more than two thousand captured, this was really the end. What powder the infantry still had in their flasks was now damp, and there was no more to be had. Hamilton ordered Baillie to make the best terms he could for the infantry while he himself rode on south in search of Byron's

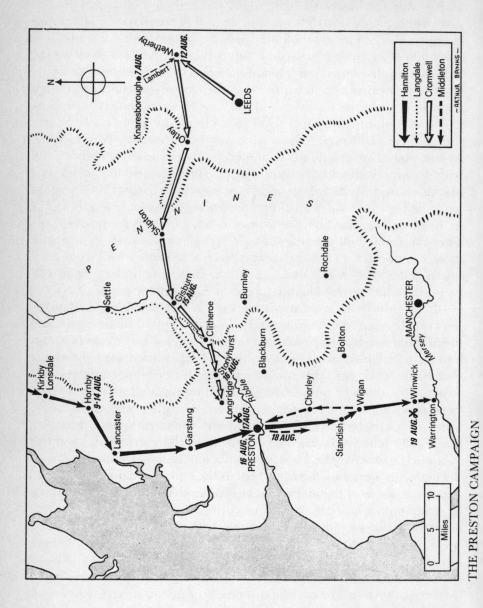

THE PRESTON CAMPAIGN

elusive rebellion in Cheshire. It was Lostwithiel all over again, and Baillie melodramatically implored his officers to shoot him rather than let him submit to such a disgrace. However, reason prevailed, and at a personal interview under a flag of truce Cromwell gave a guarantee of personal safety for all those who laid down their arms. Estimates of the number who then surrendered vary between 2,600 and 4,000, and that number of prisoners would normally have been an acute embarrassment; but so hated were the Scots by the local people that, as Cromwell wryly said, 'Ten men will keep a thousand from running away.'

Cromwell, still worried about Monro, now turned north again, while Lambert went after Hamilton with 2,000 horse and 1,400 foot. Still bereft of any English support, the flight of the Scots horse now became a *sauve qui peut*. Middleton was run down and captured at Stone, in Staffordshire, Hamilton at Uttoxeter on 25 August; Langdale, trying to escape via the east Midlands, was taken at Nottingham. All three were sent to London. Only Callander got clear away to the Continent.

By the end of the month Lambert had rejoined Cromwell and together they pressed slowly north, Monro retreating before them. The news of Preston had provoked an extraordinary mass rising in Ayrshire, Clydesdale and Galloway known as the 'Whiggamore Raid'. Led by the Earl of Eglington, the old Earl of Leven and David Leslie, thousands of armed men marched on Edinburgh to overthrow the Engager regime, which was still holding on to Berwick and Carlisle and was even trying to raise the Highland clans for another invasion of England. In the first week of September there was sporadic fighting in the Stirling area between Engager and 'Whiggamore' forces, and on the 12th Argyll, coming up with his own private army, was routed with heavy losses at Linlithgow. The Engagers now occupied Stirling, and the Committee of Estates, which had fled into the Borders, returned to Edinburgh.

Both sides were now trying to patch up a peace which would keep Cromwell out, and they both sent emissaries to his camp with soothing assurances that no help was required. But by 18 September he had reached the Border near Berwick, which still refused to surrender, and he told the Westerners that he still thought it necessary to advance further, 'in the end that we might be in a posture more ready to give you assistance'. He crossed the Border on the 21st, and next day had a long conference with Argyll and the Earl of Loudon. His arrival was sufficient. Leaving Lambert encamped with the army at Seaton, he entered Edinburgh on 4 October and was greeted by Argyll and a chastened Committee of Estates as 'the deliverer of their country'. The terms of a simple treaty were quickly hammered out: Berwick and Carlisle were surrendered, Monro was ordered back to Ulster, and all other military forces, including those of the Westerners, were to be disbanded. A final settlement of Scots politics was left to a new Estates (parliament) to be summoned in January 1649. Lambert stayed behind for another month with three regiments of horse to supervise the disbandment, but on 7 October Cromwell himself with the bulk of his army took the road to England.

In England, too, the war was drawing to a close. News of Preston reached the defenders of Colchester on 24 August, and three days later they surrendered. The Scots' defeat also frustrated Prince Charles's plan to take his nine remaining ships up to Berwick, and, surrendering to his sailors' clamorous demand for prize money, he returned to the Thames mouth. There he was confronted by eleven 'loyal' ships under the Earl of Warwick, but neither commander was anxious for an engagement. A change in the wind made the decision for them, and on 1 September the Prince retired to Helvoetsluys to take on fresh supplies. Warwick appeared off the port on the 19th, but he did not press an attack; the Dutch fleet under Van Tromp stationed itself between the two unenthusiastic adversaries and stalemate ensued, leading to Warwick's dismissal once more, for inaction. Charles retired ill to The Hague and was replaced by his cousin Rupert. In the end four of the rebel ships returned to their allegiance; the rest were organised by Rupert as a privateering squadron which had no more than a nuisance value. The great naval mutiny was over.

Meanwhile there was a sinister epilogue to the siege of Colchester. Lord Capel and Lord Norwich were sent prisoners to London, but Fairfax ordered Sir Charles Lucas and Sir George Lisle to be shot on the spot as 'mere soldiers of fortune'. Sir Bernard Gascoigne received the same sentence, but was reprieved when it emerged that he was an Italian citizen.* Fairfax reported that this was done 'for some satisfaction to military justice', and 'with the advice of the chief officers', and his conduct does not seem to have been questioned either by Parliament or by the Derby House Committee. Some royalists blamed it on the malign influence of his second-in-command, Henry Ireton,

---

* Bernardino Guasconi was born at Florence in 1614 and served as a mercenary captain in Italy and Germany in the 1630s. He took a commission in the King's army in 1642 and was knighted. He went abroad in 1646, but turned up in Kent in 1648; he was now deported. He returned to England in 1660, was naturalised, and became something of a favourite of Charles II.

but as we have seen ruthlessness was a feature of Fairfax's character too. In his handling of the Kent Rebellion he had already made a distinction between local men and footloose cavaliers who had come into the county to make trouble, and Lisle and Gascoigne were clearly in this category. Lucas had estates in Essex, but he was held to have broken the parole he had given when he surrendered at Stow-on-the-Wold in 1646. The siege of Colchester had been conducted with unusual severity, and in general the second Civil War had been fought with much greater bitterness and ruthlessness than the first – qualities which were now to be turned against the King himself.

As soon as the war began to turn against the royalists Parliament was under strong pressure to reach agreement with the King and present the Army with a *fait accompli* when it returned from the field. Early in August the eleven excluded Members were restored, and on the 24th the Vote of No Addresses was repealed. Their deliberations were only hastened by a 'Humble Petition' from the London Levellers on 11 September asserting that the House of Commons was the only supreme authority and demanding the immediate abolition of the monarchy and the House of Lords. They agreed that their commissioners should meet the King at an inn in Newport, Isle of Wight – he having given his parole – but that the negotiations, which began on 18 September, should last no longer than forty days. The peers, led by Lord Saye and Sele, were desperate for a settlement, foreseeing what was to come, but even in this ultimate crisis neither side was prepared to abandon its entrenched position. The best Parliament would offer was a slightly softened version of the Newcastle Propositions of 1646; Charles stuck to the 3:10 formula – three years' Presbyterianism on a trial basis, Parliament to control the armed forces for ten. No meeting of minds took place, and Charles's insistence that he would only accept a complete package prevented any partial compromise. On 27 October Parliament had no choice but to declare the negotiations at an end. Both sides had boxed themselves into a corner, and the King's hopes of help from France were disappointed. The Thirty Years' War had ended at last, that summer, but the war between France and Spain dragged on, and the outbreak of the Fronde that autumn seriously imperilled Cardinal Mazarin's regime.

As early as 21 September the garrisons of Newcastle and Berwick appealed to Fairfax to stop these negotiations at Newport. He had retired with his army to St Albans, where it was growing increasingly restless for lack of pay, any attempt to levy the assessment having been abandoned during the war. But he gave no sign, nor did he respond to Ireton's advice that he reoccupy London and purge the House of Commons. Ireton then retired to Windsor to draw up a document which later emerged as the *Remonstrance of the Army*; in his father-in-law's absence he was now the acknowledged spokesman of the hard-line elements in the officer corps.

Cromwell was in no hurry to return from Scotland; on 14 October he was still at Berwick, and few doubted that his procrastination was deliberate. After a visit to Carlisle he turned south, only to settle down before Pontefract, the last major royalist stronghold, spurred on by a raid mounted by the garrison on 29 October in which Thomas Rainsborough was deliberately murdered – an atrocity in which Cromwell was rumoured to have colluded in order to remove the chief Leveller spokesman in the officer corps. On 15 November he reported to the Derby House Committee that the castle was well victualled and could sustain a long siege:

> The men within are resolved to endure to the utmost extremity; expecting no mercy, as indeed they deserve none. The place is very well known to be one of the strongest inland garrisons in the kingdom; well watered; situated upon a rock in every part of it, and therefore difficult to mine. The walls very thick and high, with strong towers, and if battered very difficult of access, by reason of the depth and steepness of the graft.

He asked for pay and provisions for three regiments of foot and two of horse, five hundred barrels of powder, 'six good battering guns, none less than demi-cannons', with three hundred shot for each gun, to be shipped up to Hull, and if possible 'two or three of the biggest mortar pieces with shells'.*

Meanwhile Fairfax was forced to summon a Council of Officers at St Albans on 7 November, and they spent four days discussing Ireton's *Remonstrance*. (No more was heard of the pre-war General Council, with enlisted men as well as officers.) The *Remonstrance* set out Charles's conduct in the two Civil Wars at some length, and also examined in general terms the record of kingship in the modern world. It accordingly demanded that Charles himself be brought to justice, and the monarchy abolished. This was much too strong for Fairfax and a majority of officers, but the only result was to radicalise the *Remonstrance* still

---

* It eventually surrendered on 21 March 1649, and six of the defenders were excepted from pardon. Two of them were later tried at York assizes for Rainsborough's murder, convicted and executed.

further by driving Ireton into the arms of the Leveller leaders, his chief opponents at Putney. They had a long conference at the Nag's Head tavern in the Strand on 15 November, as a result of which clauses were added requiring Parliament, once it had dealt with the King, to dissolve itself, having made prior arrangements for the election of its successors annually or biennially on a revised electoral system, though Ireton still insisted on an unreformed franchise. Such parliaments, it was declared, would wield supreme authority, and if they chose to elect a king, apparently as a matter of administrative convenience, he was to have no veto on legislation. The House of Lords was ignored, as was the problem of the Church.

Meanwhile Fairfax and the Council of Officers had sent their own terms direct to the King. Again, they made no mention of religion, but the armed forces were to be controlled by a Council of State chosen by Parliament for the first ten years, after which each new member was to be chosen by the King from three names submitted by Parliament. Parliaments were to be elected biennially on a reformed electoral system, but the House of Lords was to continue. When Charles rejected these terms on 18 November Fairfax had no choice but to fall back on Ireton and the Levellers; the *Remonstrance* was accordingly approved by the Council of Officers and sent to the House of Commons on the 20th. It was accompanied by a peremptory demand for cash to pay the Army, but it was now so difficult to bring in taxation that the Lords were considering pardoning the Duke of Hamilton if he paid a fine of £100,000.

The Commons adjourned any discussion of the *Remonstrance* for a week. In a way this is understandable; it now ran to over 25,000 words, covering seventy-seven closely printed pages in the *Old Parliamentary History*; but the delay was fatal. On the 27th the debate was again postponed, until 1 December, but that same day Fairfax ordered the King to be brought from the Isle of Wight to Hurst Castle in Hampshire under strict guard. He vetoed Ireton's demand for the forcible dissolution of Parliament, with unexpected support from the Levellers, but on the 30th he announced that he had no choice but to re-occupy London, which he did on 2 December, demanding £40,000 from the City in arrears of assessment to pay the troops. He also sent orders to Cromwell to return from Pontefract.

The leading Presbyterian MPs fled once more, but Fairfax's idea of establishing a caucus of Independent MPs as a provisional government was rejected by all parties. At 8.00 a.m. on 5 December, after an unprecedented all-night session, the Commons voted that the King's removal to Hurst Castle was illegal. That afternoon the Council of Officers conferred with the leading Independent MPs, but Ireton's arguments for a forcible dissolution were again rejected. However, later that day, apparently without Fairfax's knowledge, Ireton and some of the Independent MPs decided to purge the House of Commons more thoroughly. Next morning, 6 December, Colonel Thomas Pride went down to Westminster with a file of soldiers, accompanied by Lord Grey of Groby, who picked out for him the offending Members. About 186 MPs were turned away, and forty-one arrested; a further eighty-six subsequently stayed away in protest, leaving a 'Rump' of 154 Members. Fairfax was furious but declined to intervene, and Cromwell, arriving from the north at last that evening, announced his approval of these proceedings.

The rest followed inevitably. On 1 January 1649, the Rump House of Commons passed an ordinance setting up a High Court of Justice to try the King for having wilfully betrayed the trust vested in him by the people. It appointed 150 Commissioners, with a quorum of twenty, who were to act as judge and jury alike. In the event the existing high court judges declined to serve, and the presidency was assumed by an obscure lawyer, John Bradshaw. The Lords rejected the ordinance next day, but on the 4th the Commons voted that ultimate constitutional power resided in the people, that by electing them to Westminster the people had delegated this power to them, and therefore they enjoyed sole legislative authority. In token of this they at once re-enacted the ordinance setting up the High Court of Justice as an 'Act'. Charles was brought up from Windsor to St James's Palace, entering his capital for the first time since January 1642, and on 21 January he appeared before the High Court. Cromwell and Ireton were present of course, but when Fairfax's name was called his wife shouted from the public gallery, 'He has more wit than to be there!', and one of the guard levelled his musket at her. In fact, Fairfax boycotted the whole proceedings, and publicly strove to prevent the King being sentenced, then executed; so much so that for the first time he quarrelled openly with Cromwell. In later years he regretted that he had not done more, but there were limits to his power. His prestige and authority in the Army were as high as ever, certainly higher than Cromwell's, but if he had ordered the Army to defend a hopelessly discredited monarch he would certainly have split the officer corps down the middle, and probably the troops themselves; it could even have led to a third civil war, this time between rival army contingents.

Charles himself expected the worst, and was prepared. When the negotiations at Newport collapsed the previous November he wrote to his eldest son, 'The commissioners are gone; the corn is in the ground; we expect the harvest.' He had rejected every conceivable compromise put before him, and just as his opponents had decided that the only way to end the constitutional impasse was to remove him, so he had concluded that only his death, in the most tragic and meaningful circumstances, could preserve the monarchy in the long run. 'The deception will soon vanish,' he told his son, 'this mask of religion on the face of rebellion will not long serve to hide some men's deformities. . . . Time will dissipate all factions, when once the rough horns of private men's covetous and ambitious designs shall discover themselves.' 'When they have destroyed me,' he said later, 'I doubt not my blood will cry aloud for vengeance in heaven.' In a final interview with his thirteen-year-old daughter Elizabeth he told her 'that he should die a martyr, and that he doubted not but the Lord would settle his throne upon his son, and that we should all be happier than we could have expected to have been if he had lived'.

He appeared before the Court a gaunt and sombre figure, clad from head to foot in black, relieved only by the insignia of the George and Garter. He declined absolutely to recognise the Court's jurisdiction. This was tantamount to suicide. Had he entered a plea of 'not guilty' lawyers would have been assigned to him and they would have demanded weeks, perhaps months, to prepare his defence. In these circumstances his fellow rulers in Europe would surely have come to his aid with more than words, perhaps the Scots too, and public order in England could well have broken down. But that was not his aim; he was furious, and momentarily unmanned, when he was not allowed to read out a statement of his case, but otherwise he acquiesced in his accusers' haste. On the 26th he was sentenced to death; on the 29th he was warned to prepare himself for execution next day. On the morning of the 30th he walked with his guard across the Park to the Banqueting House in Whitehall with perfect composure, a composure unruffled by an agonising wait from ten o'clock until two while the Rump rushed through an Act barring his sons from the succession. Then he walked through the great Hall, under the wonderful painted ceiling he had commissioned from Rubens in the 1630s, depicting the Apotheosis of King James and the triumph of Kingship over Injustice and Rebellion, through the window and onto a scaffold erected at first-floor level.

What followed has been recounted a score of times in different

versions, but never better than in the lean, unsparing verse of Andrew
Marvell, who in a few lines created two legends: that of Charles the
Martyr and Cromwell the Manipulator of Thrones and Powers:

> What field of all the Civil Wars,
> Where his [Cromwell's] were not the deepest scars?
> > And Hampton shows what part
> > He had of wiser art.
> Where, twining subtle fears with hope,
> He wove a net of such scope,
> > That Charles himself might chase
> > To Carisbrooke's narrow case.
> That thence the royal actor born
> The tragic scaffold might adorn;
> > While round the arméd bands
> > Did clap their bloody hands.
> He nothing common did or mean
> Upon that memorable scene,
> But with his keener eye
> The axe's edge did try;
> Nor called the Gods with vulgar spite
> To vindicate his helpless right
> > But bowed his comely head,
> > Down as upon a bed.
> This was the memorable hour,
> Which first assured the forcéd power.

Indeed, the 'royal actor born' was more than equal to the occasion.
With Christ-like charity he forgave his judges and his executioners.
With a glance at the files of cavalry round the scaffold, facing outwards
on the milling crowd which filled Whitehall, he said, 'If I would have
given way to an arbitrary way, for to have all the laws changed
according to the power of the sword, I needed not to have come here;
and therefore I tell you, and I pray God, it be not laid to your charge,
that I am the martyr of the people.' His last words were: 'I have
delivered my conscience; I pray God you do take those courses that are
best for the good of the kingdom and your own salvation.' He lay down,
and after a few moments gave the signal. His head came off cleanly,
with one blow. The cavalry at once thundered away from the scaffold
in both directions, clearing the street.

Before the day was out printed copies of his last speech were sell-
ing like hot cakes; within a week appeared the *Eikon Basiliké: the*

*Portraiture of his Sacred Majesty in his Solitudes and Sufferings,* a mixture of pietistic moralising and shrewd historical revisionism which was to prove one of the best-sellers of the century. In the furrow of his own death Charles had sown the seeds of his son's restoration in 1660.

# 10

# THE BITTER END

The Army's wrath was not appeased by the death of the chief war criminal. Blood still cried out for blood. On 6 March 1649, the Duke of Hamilton, the Earls of Norwich and Holland and Lord Capel were tried for treason by the High Court of Justice and convicted. Capel, Holland and Hamilton were duly executed, and Norwich was reprieved only by the casting vote of the President. In April five officers associated with the rising in South Wales the year before were tried by court martial; three were found guilty, though only their leader, Colonel Poyer, was shot. Fortunately for him, Sir Marmaduke Langdale escaped from Nottingham Castle and fled with many lesser refugees to the Continent, though it is difficult to imagine this lanky, cadaverous man disguised as 'a milkmaid in print gown and bonnet', as we are assured he was.*

The Levellers objected fiercely to the use of the High Court or courts martial, even against war criminals; they objected even more to the bastard oligarchic republic now instituted, consisting of the Rump and an executive Council of State elected in rotation from amongst its own Members. Radical officers like Ireton were also dismayed and enraged

---

* He took service with the Venetians, and was prominent in the defence of Candia (Crete) in 1652. Somewhere along the way he turned Roman Catholic.

by the Rump's failure to make provision for a permanent settlement then dissolve itself, as demanded in the *Remonstrance of the Army* and promised by the Rump itself in the Act abolishing the monarchy in March. The Levellers, who were now busy with the rank and file of the Army again, demanded in February that the old General Council of the Army be reconstituted, with elected agitators from each regiment, but the Council of Officers refused. They riposted with a long pamphlet bearing the self-explanatory title, *England's New Chains Discover'd*, followed up in March by other pamphlets which were a direct incitement to mutiny.

Mutiny duly came. On 17 April three hundred men of Hewson's regiment threw down their arms rather than muster for Ireland. They were promptly demobilised without arrears of pay, and their places were taken by men drafted in from other regiments. A week later Whalley's regiment mutinied in London, and Fairfax and Cromwell had to restore order in person; they tried fifteen men by drumhead court martial and sentenced five of them to death. Though only one of these, the young Leveller Robert Lockyer, was executed, the Levellers turned his funeral into a mass demonstration, the more impressive for being entirely orderly. However, the most serious mutiny broke out in May, when Scrope's regiment mutinied at Salisbury on its way to Ireland, and was joined by a majority of Ireton's regiment nearby. The discipline of other regiments in the area was in the balance, and at Banbury, to the north of Oxford, William 'King' Thompson, a seasoned agitator already dismissed from the Army, provoked a quite separate rising, though he was driven north by one of the 'loyal' regiments under Colonel Reynolds. Fairfax and Cromwell chose two reliable regiments of horse and three of foot from the London garrison to quell the Salisbury mutiny, but it was thought wise to parade them in Hyde Park before they set out on 9 May, where Cromwell harangued them. They reached Andover on the 13th by forced marches, only to find that the mutineers had fled north to Marlborough, then over the Thames to Burford, hoping to join up with Thompson. Fairfax swung north in pursuit, and after driving his cavalry forty-five miles in a day, reached the outskirts of Burford after dark; he at once sent Cromwell in. After a brief exchange of shot, about four hundred mutineers were captured; the remaining seven or eight hundred, quartered in the surrounding villages, hastily decamped and no doubt slunk back individually into civilian life. Next morning a court martial was convened and sentenced two cornets (second lieutenants) and two corporals to death, and three of them were shot on the spot. Colonel Eyres, previously associated with the mutiny at Corkbush Field in 1647, was lucky to be released, apparently because he was now a civilian. 'King' Thompson's supporters now melted away, and he was trapped and shot down in a wood near Northampton on 17 May, refusing quarter.

If there were no further mutinies it is not only because Fairfax and his colonels now took pains to weed out any further Levellers or suspected Levellers, but because the Rump succeeded in solving the financial problems which had dogged Parliament ever since 1646, though how it did it is not entirely clear. In March 1648, at the beginning of the second Civil War, Parliament had imposed an assessment of £60,000 a month for six months to pay the Army, extended in October for another six months, but as we have seen (p. 195 above) Fairfax complained throughout this campaign, and on into December, that his men's pay was not coming through. Nevertheless, on 6 March 1649 the Rump resolved to maintain a home army of 32,000 men, plus a strike force of 12,000 for Ireland, the whole costing £120,000 a month. The shortfall in taxation was to be made up by the sale of the remaining Church lands, and the estates of leading royalists already attainted for their part in the second Civil War, but this took time. The City of London refused a bridging loan of £120,000, and the mutinies in May further delayed the expedition to Ireland. However, on 7 April Parliament passed an ordinance imposing a further assessment of £90,000 a month for six months, together with another which (according to its sunny preamble) would entirely solve the problem of free quarter. In the event of the soldiers' pay not coming through, local magistrates were empowered to levy a rate to pay for their food and lodging which could be offset against payments due on the assessment; they were also empowered 'to assign so many soldiers as they think fit, to be billeted upon the refusers'.

This was all too reminiscent of the 'dragonnardes' employed by the despotic kings of France, but it worked, and the strike force for Ireland was certainly supplied. When Cromwell arrived at Bristol on 14 July to review the troops he promised them he would not sail until their arrears of pay had been settled and adequate provision made for the future. On the 31st £100,000 was sent down from London, and presumably more followed, for he embarked almost at once, and as soon as he arrived in Ireland he issued a proclamation guaranteeing cash payment for any goods or services supplied or requisitioned, a promise he apparently kept.

*      *      *

We left Ireland in August 1647, with Michael Jones's decisive victory over the Confederates at Dungan's Hill (p. 164 above). This put fresh heart into Murrough O'Brien, Lord Inchiquin, the royal governor of Munster who had defected to Parliament in 1644, and he at once began to clear the Confederates out of the south-west. On 12 September he stormed the Rock of Cashel with hideous slaughter, which earned him the name in legend of 'Murchdah na Atoithean', or Murrough of the Burnings. His fanatical Protestant troops gave the inhabitants no quarter, dragging priests from the very altar to slit their throats. His conduct caused lasting animosities in Munster, but in the short term his methods were certainly effective, and on 13 November he destroyed the only viable Catholic army in the south-west at Knocknannus, near Mallow.

Meanwhile in September, despite the worsening crisis in England, Parliament scraped together another 5,000 foot and 850 horse and sent them to Ulster under Monck, designating him Commander-in-Chief of all the English and Scots forces in that province. These comprised an army of Protestant settlers under Sir Charles Coote the Younger, known as the 'Laggan Army', and Robert Monro's 'New Scots', still numbering 3,000–4,000 foot and 200–300 horse. Neither was willing to acknowledge Monck's authority, and stalemate ensued. Coote had been fighting his own war for the past two or three years against Owen Roe O'Neill, and Monro was not likely to put himself under a London government increasingly at odds with his masters at Edinburgh. On the other hand, Monro's credibility was certainly undermined by his crashing defeat at Benburb the year before and his almost total inactivity since.

In fact, all of them, including Michael Jones at Dublin, could do little but hold on until a major field army arrived, and with the outbreak of the second Civil War in 1648 the arrival of such an army seemed more remote than ever. United, the Confederates could have driven their opponents into the sea, but they were more disunited now than they had ever been. Dungan's Hill, followed by Knocknannus, had thrown the Supreme Council into confusion. The Nuncio Rinuccini persuaded them to send envoys to the Pope asking him to accept a protectorate over Ireland, but even if he accepted (and he did not) it was difficult to see what practical effect it could have, and the Old English on the Council decided to send their own delegation to Paris to seek help from the Queen. Here they met up with Ormonde, whose last letters from Charles I had empowered him to resume the Lord

Lieutenancy if he saw fit. By now it was April 1648, the outbreak of another civil war in England opened up new horizons, and they decided to throw in their lot with Ormonde again. On hearing the news Inchiquin also declared for the King. The delegates to Rome returned in March not entirely empty-handed; the Pope had sent Owen Roe O'Neill the legendary great sword of his uncle Hugh O'Neill, but this only gave rise to damaging rumours that he endorsed the O'Neills' tenuous claim to the title of High Kings of Ireland. This strained relations between the Old English and the Old Irish to breaking point, and in April the Nuncio vetoed a proposed truce with Inchiquin and fled to O'Neill's camp at Maryborough in Leinster. There he formally excommunicated the members of the Supreme Council who had defected to Ormonde. He denounced the Old English as 'Catholics only in name; the ideas they hold are almost the same as those of Henry VIII and Elizabeth'. However, he soon had to seek a refuge further west, in Galway.

A kind of wary stalemate ensued over the summer, while civil war raged in England; only Monck made a move, and then not until the autumn. In July Monro was obliged to send 1,500 foot and 400 horse to Scotland under his nephew Sir George Monro to join Hamilton's expedition to England, and Monck took advantage of the situation on 16 September to seize Carrickfergus, and later in the same month Belfast and Coleraine. Monro was arrested and sent to London. But the practical effect of these manoeuvres was negligible; Monck was no better able than Monro to advance out of Ulster into central Ireland.

Ormonde finally landed at Cork in September 1648, made sure of Inchiquin's allegiance, then proceeded to Kilkenny to negotiate with the Supreme Council. As always, the main stumbling block was the proposed status of the Catholic Church and clergy in the new Ireland. All Ormonde could offer was a truce on this question until the King was in a position to take the advice of a free parliament, but the news of Charles's impending trial provoked a wave of loyalist emotion which left Rinuccini helpless. An interim agreement between the Council and the Lord Lieutenant was signed on 17 January 1649 and a month later the Nuncio left Ireland in disgust. Charles II subsequently confirmed Ormonde's appointment.

By the spring it was obvious that Fairfax or Cromwell would arrive with a field army in the near future, and there was every need for haste. Monck was still penned up in Ulster by O'Neill, and otherwise the

London government held only the Dublin Pale; Inchiquin, now royalist, had consolidated his grip on Munster and was encroaching on
Leinster. However, of the Catholic generals Thomas Preston was decidedly uneasy at being forced to act with Inchiquin, a ferocious anti-
Catholic, and O'Neill was actively negotiating with Sir Charles Coote
at Londonderry and Monck at Dundalk, while at the same time he
was being courted by Ormonde. (Part of O'Neill's price for joining
Parliament was a high command in the New Model Army!) They were
all acutely short of supplies; indeed Ormonde remarked, 'If Cromwell
come over, we shall more dread his money than his face'. But in July
Inchiquin suddenly struck north, captured Drogheda, Dundalk, Newry
and Trim, and forced Monck to surrender. (When Monck was released
and returned to England he faced some embarrassing questions about
his parleys with the arch-papist O'Neill, but a new realism prevailed
in London, and he was exonerated.) Inchiquin now turned back to join
Ormonde and Preston, who were moving up to invest Dublin. However,
Michael Jones, providentially reinforced at the last moment by 2,600
fresh troops from England, sallied forth on 2 August and comprehensively routed them at Rathmines, just south of Dublin. On the
15th Cromwell at last arrived, with a commission as Lord Lieutenant
as well as Commander-in-Chief.

Rathmines had already broken the back of Irish resistance, and
though it provoked O'Neill to declare for the King Ormonde could
never put together another field army. Cromwell brought with him
8,000 foot and 4,000 horse, all highly trained and experienced veterans,
and he took over the 8,000 already there under Michael Jones, flushed
with recent victory. (Jones was appointed second-in-command to
Cromwell, with Ireton Commissary-General.) He had plenty of money,
he had command of the sea, and he had brought with him an artillery
train capable of knocking out any castle or fort he was likely to
meet. He had eleven siege guns, two 8-inch cannon and two 7-inch,
two 24-pounders and three culverins, as well as twelve smaller field
pieces.

His first objective was Drogheda, which straddled the main line of
communication between Dublin and the north, and was an obvious
rallying-point for Inchiquin and O'Neill. The royal governor was Sir
Arthur Aston, the one-legged Catholic veteran who had commanded
the dragoon regiments in Charles I's army in 1642 and was later
governor of Oxford; he had presumably returned with Ormonde from
France, with a few other English officers. Cromwell arrived before the

town on 3 September, then waited a week for his artillery to arrive by sea, but with O'Neill seriously ill (in fact, dying) and Inchiquin holed up again in Munster, Ormonde could not pull together a relief army. As soon as his siege guns arrived on the 10th Cromwell brought them into play, and by that evening they had torn two breaches in the town walls. Next day he concentrated his fire on the larger of these breaches, and at five o'clock he ordered in three of his foot regiments. They met with strong resistance, but, rallied by Cromwell in person, they finally broke into the southern sector of the town. Most of the defenders then fled for the bridge over the River Boyne, which divides Drogheda into North Town and South Town, but Aston and his senior officers, with about three hundred men, took refuge on top of Mill Mount, an artificial mound which dominated the South Town. What happened next is best told in Cromwell's matter-of-fact report to Parliament:

> The Governor, Sir Arthur Aston, and divers considerable officers being there [on Mill Mount], our men getting up with them were ordered by me to put them all to the sword. And indeed, being in the heat of action, I forbad them to spare any that were in arms in the [rest of the] town; and I think that night they put to the sword about two thousand men, divers of the officers and soldiers being fled over the bridge into the other part of the town, where about a hundred of them possessed St Peter's Church steeple, some the West Gate, and others a strong round tower next the gate called St Sunday's. These being summoned to yield to mercy, refused. Whereupon I ordered the steeple of St Peter's Church to be fired, when one of them was heard to say in the midst of the flames: 'God damn me, God confound me; I burn, I burn'.

St Sunday's and the West Gate surrendered next day, and the officers, in Cromwell's laconic words, were 'knocked on the head' and their men shipped to Barbados. On a rough estimate at least 3,000 troops and civilians were slaughtered. It was said that Aston was beaten to death with his own wooden leg, and with him fell Sir Edmund Verney, the son of King Charles's standard-bearer of the same name who had been killed at Edgehill in 1642.

This fearful atrocity was technically justified by the laws of war as they were then understood. Certainly the English government took it in its stride, and so did Cromwell's officers; to them the Irish were a despised and evil race, and Englishmen who joined them were if anything worse. As Cromwell said: 'I am persuaded that this is a righteous judgment of God upon those barbarous wretches who have imbrued their hands in so much innocent blood, and that it will tend to prevent the effusion of blood for the future'; and to some extent he was right. The towns of Trim, Dundalk, Carlingford and Newry now surrendered without a blow, leaving him free to turn to the south.

On 2 October he appeared before Wexford, a noted privateering base on the south-east coast, and he at once sent Michael Jones to take Fort Rosslare, at the end of a long spit of land commanding the harbour entrance. This enabled him to land his siege guns from the waiting ships. Colonel David Synott, the garrison commander, was reinforced on the 6th by 1,500 troops sent from Ulster by the Earl of Castlehaven on Ormonde's behalf, but the soldiers and townspeople were divided in their allegiance between the Old English and the Irish, between Ormonde and what was still known as the Nuncio's party. Synott therefore opened negotiations with the besiegers. However, to speed up these negotiations Cromwell ordered his batteries into action against the castle, and on the 11th one of Synott's officers treacherously surrendered it. The defenders on the town walls promptly panicked and rushed for the shore, where many were drowned. The English troops poured over the walls and down the streets of the little town, and when they met with resistance from a small body of enemy troops and townsmen another indiscriminate massacre ensued. This was much more reprehensible than the sack of Drogheda, because Cromwell launched his attack when negotiations for a surrender were in full swing, but in his report to Parliament he showed more concern for the damage to the town, which he had planned to use as a base, than for the loss of 2,000 lives, as against twenty of his own men killed, and he complacently put the blame (if blame there was) on Almighty God:

> It hath, not without cause, been deeply set upon our hearts that, we
> intending better to this place than so great a ruin, hoping the town might
> be of more use to you and your Army, yet God would not have it so, but
> by an unexpected providence, in his righteous justice, brought a just
> judgment upon them.

From Wexford Cromwell now headed west towards Munster, and he took the surrender of New Ross on terms on 19 October. But he was plagued by incessant rain, and with the onset of winter he was beginning to lose momentum. When he arrived before Waterford on 24 November he could make no impression on the fortifications, perhaps because his siege guns were bogged down far behind him on the atrocious Irish roads. Dysentery was raging in camp – it took off Michael Jones that

December – and it is estimated that by now, allowing for garrisons left behind and detachments sent to the north, he had only about 3,000 effectives. When he settled down in winter quarters he admitted that he had secured 'a great tract in longitude along the shore, yet it hath but little depth in the country'.

Nevertheless Ormonde, plagued by inter-Catholic feuds and chronic lack of money and supplies, still could not raise another field army, and he and Inchiquin now lost control of Munster without a fight. Over the winter Cromwell's emissary Lord Broghill, son of Richard Boyle, Earl of Cork, secretly toured the Munster garrisons and persuaded most of them, including Cork itself, to declare for Parliament. From the north, too, the news was dire. Owen Roe O'Neill finally died on 6 November, and was irreplaceable. In December the fall of Carrickfergus completed the reconquest of Ulster as far west as Derry, and a pronouncement from the Irish bishops at Clonmacnoise on 13 December, enjoining all Irish Catholics to support Ormonde, came far too late. Cromwell's proclamation in reply, 'For the Undeceiving of Deluded and Seduced People', was for the most part an unedifying piece of anti-Catholic and racialist rant, but he justified his mission to Ireland in ringing tones:

> If ever men were engaged in a righteous cause in the world, this will scarce be a second to it. We are come to ask an account of the innocent blood that hath been shed, and to endeavour to bring to an account – by the blessing and presence of the Almighty, in whom alone is our hope and strength – all who, by appearing in arms, seek to justify the same. We come to break the power of a company of lawless rebels, who having cast off the authority of England live as enemies to human society, whose principles, the world hath experience, are to destroy and subjugate all men not complying with them. We come, by the assistance of God, to hold forth and maintain the lustre and glory of English liberty* in a nation where we have an undoubted right to do it, [and] wherein the people of Ireland may equally participate.

Mild winter weather set him on the road again at the end of January 1650, from Youghal into Tipperary, to link up with the defecting Munster garrisons. He then swung north-east towards Kilkenny, the headquarters of the Confederation since 1642, and on 19 March he was joined by a fresh contingent from Dublin under Colonel John Hewson.

---

* Carlyle shrewdly remarks that by 'liberty' Cromwell meant 'rigorous settled obedience to laws that are just'.

Kilkenny surrendered on 28 March without bloodshed, though the Catholic churches in the town were heavily pillaged, and on 10 April at Macroom Lord Broghill defeated the last Confederate force in Munster under Lord Roche and the Bishop of Ross; the Bishop was captured and hanged. Being an Irish bishop in these times was a dangerous job. The Bishop of Clogher, who had taken command of O'Neill's army, was defeated that June by Sir Charles Coote at Scarriffhollis, near Letterkenny in Donegal; he was captured and shot. Meanwhile Cromwell and Hewson had taken the surrender of Clonmel on 27 April. Essentially the whole of Ireland except for Connaught was now under English control, and the rest was largely a matter of guerrilla warfare and the reduction of the Atlantic towns. On 26 May Cromwell turned over his command to Ireton with the title of Lord Deputy and sailed for England, in order to meet a new threat from Scotland.

The execution of Charles I had provoked a storm in Scotland. The Scots had their own quarrel with Charles, but it is doubtful if they would have proceeded to the same lengths as the English government, and that government's total failure to consult them in the disposal of what after all was Scotland's anointed king as well as theirs was deeply humiliating. The Scots reacted predictably. On 5 April 1649 the Committee of Estates, headed by Argyll, recognised Charles II as king, though they stipulated that he could not execute that office until he had taken the Covenant. Emissaries were at once despatched to The Hague, where Charles was living on the charity of his brother-in-law, William II of Orange.

They found the new king very different from the old. 'The Black Boy' was not quite nineteen, but already disconcertingly adult; swarthy of face, with black curly hair, elegant in purple from head to foot, the colour of royal mourning. At five foot ten inches he was tall for that period, and certainly head and shoulders taller than his father; he was fluent and ostensibly outgoing, whereas his father had been tongue-tied, introspective and reserved. He already had at least one mistress, and his eldest son, the future Duke of Monmouth, was born only a fortnight after the Scots Commissioners arrived on 26 March.* Still, they made the best of it, and one of them reported back to Argyll: 'He is one of the most gentle, innocent, well-inclined princes, so far as yet

---

* His mother was Lucy Walter. A daughter, Charlotte Jemima, was born to Elizabeth, Lady Boyle, later Viscountess Shannon, in 1650, after his departure to Scotland.

appears, that lives in the world; a trim person, and of a manly carriage; understands pretty well, speaks not much.'

However, they were disconcerted to find their enemies well established at Court; not only the Engager leaders, the 2nd Duke of Hamilton and the Earl of Lauderdale, but the ineffable Marquess of Montrose, outlawed in Scotland. Not surprisingly, Charles agreed to impose the Covenant in Scotland, but not in England without the consent of a free parliament.

Charles, in fact, was now considering pleas from Ormonde that he come to Ireland in the hope of reuniting the Confederates: a more attractive prospect to him and the Queen Mother than presbyterian Scotland. He left Holland in June to join his mother in Paris, in search of money, but he consigned his heavy baggage by ship to Ireland (and consequently lost it all). At the same time he bowed to Montrose's wishes, and appointed him his Lieutenant-General for Scotland; the Marquess promptly departed to Denmark, Sweden and Poland in search of mercenary recruits, and, so far as the exiled Court was concerned, disappeared. In fact, his advance guard of five hundred men landed on Orkney in September, though Montrose himself, with a further 1,500 men, did not arrive until the following March, 1650. The unlucky Lord Eythin, whom he had winkled out of retirement at Stockholm, was to follow with more recruits, but he was certainly late (as at Marston Moor), and it is not clear that he arrived at all. Early in April Montrose crossed to the mainland at Thurso and cut across to the east coast, heading south; but he could not take Dunrobin Castle on the way, and from there he struck west into Sutherland, hoping to recruit men from the clans. However, the clans were rent by their usual feuds and thoroughly disillusioned with the royal cause, and the Scots army was no longer distracted, as in 1644–5, by distant campaigns in England. Colonel Archibald Strachan marched from Inverness with a strong force of cavalry and cut Montrose's makeshift army to ribbons at Corbisdale in Sutherland on 27 April. Of his 1,200-odd men Montrose lost at least six hundred killed and four hundred captured. He himself escaped for the moment, but he was taken a week later, brought to Edinburgh and hanged on 21 May.

Charles II's conduct, in first encouraging Montrose then abandoning him, was to leave an indelible stain on his reputation, which the execution of Argyll in 1661 could not erase. But his cause was now at its nadir. News reached him at Paris of Ormonde's defeat at Rathmines in August, and Cromwell's arrival in Dublin. After a quarrel with his

mother, who wanted him to appoint his father's evil genius Lord Digby
as Secretary of State again, he repaired to Jersey on 12 September,
where news of further disasters in Ireland began to come through.
There was no news of Montrose. He delayed as long as he could by
making an appointment to meet the Scots Commissioners again at The
Hague the following spring, but on 27 April 1650, still with no news of
Montrose, he finally agreed to take the Covenant himself and impose
it on England and Ireland,* and to repudiate Montrose as well as the
Engagers. By a secret clause he also agreed to disown Ormonde. After
a hazardous journey he eventually landed at Garmouth-on-Spey, north
of Aberdeen, on 24 June with a handful of English followers, including
the young Duke of Buckingham and Henry Wilmot, though to his fury
Argyll insisted that he leave Hamilton and Lauderdale behind. He
received a warm welcome from the people of Aberdeen and Dundee
on his way south, but he was at once removed to the privacy of the
royal palace of Falkland, then to Dunfermline, where he remained a
virtual prisoner, his conduct and his correspondence closely monitored,
subjected to a lowering regimen of four-hour sermons from Argyll's
Calvinist ayatollahs, and forbidden so much as to play cards. His
coronation was put off from month to month, and there was sinister
talk of a marriage between him and Argyll's daughter, Lady Anne
Campbell.

By now Cromwell was back in London, and he and a majority of the
Council of State were all for a pre-emptive strike against the Scots, who
seemed certain to invade England the following spring, if not before.
Fairfax, however, stood out against it. He had never made any secret
of his aversion to the new regime in England, and it is evidence of his
immense prestige that the government still clung to him; they even
allowed him to take an amended version of the 'Engagement', or oath
to the republic, imposed on all office-holders. But both sides had now
reached the end of the road. Cromwell and other senior officers pleaded
with him to take command of the Scottish expedition now being
prepared, and there is no reason to doubt their sincerity, but he
continued to denounce the whole idea as unethical, and the Council of
State rejected a compromise which would have allowed him to take
titular command of the expedition while remaining at home. He
resigned on 26 June, offering as his reasons 'debilities both in mind and

---

* Actually, he promised to give his assent to legislation tendered to him for that end. Assuming
that the ordinances of the Long Parliament had lapsed, it is unlikely that any further legislation
would have been passed except under extreme pressure.

body, occasioned by former actions and businesses', but apart from his recurrent gout this was very far from the truth. He retired to his estates at Nunappleton in East Yorkshire with a pension of £5,000 a year, and Cromwell took his place as Commander-in-Chief.

His task was eased by the more assured financial position of the government; it had even raised the pay of infantrymen from 8d to 10d a day. In August 1649 it extended the excise to 'every the commodities, merchandises and manufactures, as well imported or exported, as [well] made or growing, put to sale or consumed', and made free use of troops to suppress the subsequent unrest. In December 1649 the assessment was imposed for a further six months at £90,000, then reduced to £60,000 for another three. And, whether because of improved administration or the threat of force – though we have no record of force being used – the yield improved dramatically; between March 1649 and December 1650 £1,133,071 was collected out of £1,260,000; from December 1650 to January 1652, £1,514,445 out of £1,560,000.

This was as well, for new regiments had to be raised to guard against a possible Scots counter-invasion, and by an ordinance of 11 July the militia was resurrected for home defence, well-stocked with Civil War veterans; even then, when Cromwell left for the North in the first week of July he left behind four regular regiments of horse and four of foot. He took with him about 5,000 horse and 10,000 foot, and his infantry commander, George Monck, raised another regiment on the Border as they went, later to form the 2nd Regiment of Foot, the Coldstream Guards. Charles Fleetwood was nominally second-in-command, but Cromwell relied more on the advice and initiative of his Commissary-General, John Lambert. He reached Newcastle on the 15th, whence he issued an extraordinary *Declaration*, 'To all that are Saints, and Partakers of the Faith of God's Elect, in Scotland', which bears the mark of his hand. For the execution of Charles I and the proclamation of a republic, they were told, the authority of the English Parliament was quite sufficient:

> That they are not accountable to any other nation, is sufficient to say to you, except it be to excite you to rejoice in this wonderful work of God, and to be thankful to him for so much deliverance as you have thereby, and leave the rest to the State of England, to whom it doth only and properly belong.

As for Charles II, he pointed out, quite pertinently, that the young King's first hopes had been pinned on 'Montrose and his accomplices' and 'his popish Army in Ireland', and he 'would never be induced to comply or close with the Covenant and Presbytery, till utterly disappointed of all those his malignant and popish hopes and confidences'. Nevertheless, he undertook this unwelcome task with compassion:

> We undertake this business in the fear of God, with bowels full of love, yea, full of pity to the inhabitants of the country; and if it shall please God to make Scotland sensible of the wrongs done to us, and to give to the Commonwealth of England a satisfying security against future injuries, we shall rejoice.*

The Scots had no intention of giving way, and by this time David Leslie had recruited a much larger army than Cromwell's, estimated at 26,000. Unfortunately the Act of Classes passed the previous year denied him the use of the Engagers, and with them most of the trained veterans left over from 1648. Still, he deployed his forces with considerable skill; he retreated on Edinburgh and ordered the farmers of the Border counties to remove their cattle and stores of corn, so that Cromwell had no choice but to stick to the Great North Road (the modern A1) along the coast, and make as fast as he could to Dunbar, the nearest port through which he could be supplied by sea.

He reached Dunbar on the 26th, and duly got his supplies, but now things began to go badly wrong. He advanced on Edinburgh on the 29th, but finding its defences too strong for him he fell back on Musselburgh, to make contact with his fleet. On the way his rearguard was badly mauled – Lambert was injured and temporarily captured – and when he reached Musselburgh late at night he found the weather too stormy to land supplies on the open beach. Another attack by Leslie forced the Army back on Dunbar, where they arrived tired, disheartened and thoroughly soaked. As in the two previous summers, the rain was relentless, and despite the use of tents† sickness was now rife; it is estimated that in the first six weeks of this campaign Cromwell lost four or five thousand effectives, most of them to various fevers. Nevertheless, he was back at Musselburgh on 12 August, and he now

---

* This was endorsed by the Rump on 19 July, but from Berwick on the 23rd he issued a much more moderate declaration, no doubt framed by more sober minds. However, the sense was the same.

† Tents were rarely used in the English Civil Wars, except by officers of field rank; a large and elaborate tent was supplied for Fairfax when he took command of the New Model. But Cromwell took them with him on his Irish campaign, and he ordered them for Scotland as well, one tent for every six men. However, it seems they were not landed until mid-August.

tried to cut Leslie off from his ultimate base at Stirling by a flanking movement round Edinburgh to the south, linking up with the fleet at Queensferry. But in a long series of marches and counter-marches across the countryside west of Edinburgh, round the present suburb of Corstorphine and the future site of Edinburgh Airport at Ingliston – then a wilderness of bogs and lakes – Leslie completely outwitted and out-manoeuvred him. Unable to force a pitched battle, outgeneralled and thoroughly discomfited, Cromwell pulled back first to Musselburgh and then on 1 September to Dunbar once more, with Leslie in close pursuit.

This time Leslie pressed home his advantage. He cut Cromwell's only escape route by land, at Cockburnspath, and posted his army on the heights overlooking the port. True, under pressure from the Committee of Estates, who wanted Cromwell driven into the sea, he advanced next day further down the hill, but his position was still overwhelmingly strong, and he had about 6,000 horse and 16,000 foot; Cromwell about 3,500 and 7,000 respectively. Cromwell complained that 'Our lying here daily consumeth our men, who fall sick beyond imagination.' He now had the choice of evacuating his army by sea, and giving up the whole venture for that year, or sending it uphill against a much superior force in driving wind and rain.

It was a tactic born of desperation, but on the night of 2–3 September this is just what he and Lambert decided to do. Actually it was four or five in the morning before the troops were marshalled and deployed, and Lambert and Fleetwood, with six regiments of horse, backed up by Monck with three regiments of foot, could launch their attack. The Scots were taken completely by surprise; no one had expected an attack on a night like this, or any attack at all; few of the infantry even had their matches lit. Lambert hammered the Scots cavalry on the left, many of them still in their tents, while Monck came in from the right against the main body of the infantry. A furious struggle ensued in the light of an overcast dawn, but as the sun broke through Cromwell himself led two regiments of horse and the reserve of foot under Thomas Pride in a charge against the Scots centre. Leslie's horse now broke, and streamed off down the road towards Cockburnspath, and the infantry, most of them unable even to fire their muskets in the rain, laid down their arms and fled. The whole action lasted no more than an hour. Cromwell estimated that about 3,000 Scots were killed and 10,000 soldiers and three hundred officers captured. Leslie's army had virtually ceased to exist.

In a triumphant despatch to Parliament Cromwell called this 'one of the most signal mercies God hath done for England and this people', but he was under no illusion that it marked the end of the campaign. Ordering Sir Arthur Haselrigg to join him with the reserve regiments he had left behind at Newcastle, he remarked: 'It's probable the Kirk has done their do, [but] I believe their king will set up upon his own score now, wherein he will find many friends.' Indeed, Dunbar did increase Charles's freedom of action, and Scots and English royalists began to rally round him, but he was still firmly under Argyll's tutelage, and the Kirk continued to forbid the enlistment of Engagers.

On 4 September, with his army scarcely rested, Cromwell sent Lambert to occupy Edinburgh, where only the Castle now held out. Leslie collected four or five thousand men, mostly refugees from Dunbar, and locked himself up in Stirling Castle. Cromwell arrived before Stirling on 17 September, but he decided not to attempt the castle perched high on its precipitous rock, and withdrew again. He paid a brief visit to Glasgow in October, and left a garrison at Hamilton. Strathclyde was more or less subdued, and he spent the rest of the year consolidating his position in Lothian and the Borders.

On 14 December the Kirk at last faced up to reality, and relaxed its restrictions on enlistment; Engagers and other royalists now poured in to form something like a national army again. Even so, there were still many extreme Covenanters, some of Leslie's officers amongst them, who rejected King Charles II and regarded Cromwell as the lesser of two evils. One of them tamely surrendered Edinburgh Castle on 24 December.

On 1 January 1651 Charles II, having expressed suitable remorse for his father's sins and his mother's 'idolatry', and having publicly disowned Ormonde as well as Montrose, was finally crowned at Scone. Argyll himself placed the crown on his head, and at once proclaimed a day of fasting for the sins of the royal family. In February Cromwell unwisely made another attempt on Stirling, but he was forced back by foul weather, fell ill on the way, and was *hors de combat* until June. By then he had been substantially reinforced from England, bringing him up to ten regiments of horse, fifteen of foot and two of dragoons.

On the other hand the King's coronation, however humiliating the circumstances, had strengthened his position immeasurably. He had escaped Argyll's tutelage and could move in public with complete freedom, as befitted an anointed king. He now undertook a personal recruiting campaign up and down the Lowlands, with excellent results.

'He is very intelligent, industrious and active', said one observer, 'his judgment and activity, both in civil and martial affairs, are to a degree you would not imagine.' He presided over a new session of the Estates in March, and his birthday on 29 May was celebrated with much public rejoicing. In June he persuaded the Estates to repeal the Act of Classes, enabling him to call once more on the services of Engager peers like Hamilton. By this time he and David Leslie had recruited an army of about 15,000 foot and 6,000 horse. John Middleton was in command of the horse again, and there was a sizeable English contingent, led by those Presbyterian veterans of the first Civil War, Richard Browne and Edward Massey. However, the army was decidedly top-heavy. In May the King was appointed Commander-in-Chief, with the old Earl of Leven nominally general in charge. David Leslie was in effective command, but Charles insisted that the Duke of Buckingham be given independent command of the English regiments, with Massey as his Major-General. In fact there were at least three lieutenant-generals and five major-generals* to control an army much smaller than Hamilton's in 1648, which had made do with one of each.

As in 1648, decision-making was slow and contentious, and Leslie complained that while the generals and politicians bickered, his men, unpaid and half-starved, were melting away. Moreover, Cromwell had now risen from his sickbed refreshed. In July he made a feint towards Glasgow, inducing Leslie to send ten regiments of horse from Fife in pursuit; he next pulled all his garrisons out of Strathclyde and doubled back with them on Edinburgh; then he threw four or five thousand men under Lambert across the Firth of Forth to Inverkeithing. An impetuous attack by Leslie on his bridgehead was bloodily repulsed, as many as 2,000 Scots being killed, and Cromwell continued to pour men over the river to the number of 14,000 or more, leaving only eight regiments in Lothian. At the end of the month he set off for Perth, and took the surrender of that city on 2 August.

Cromwell had now cut Leslie's communications with the North and at the same time left the road to England via Glasgow and Carlisle invitingly open. He saw no point in attacking Stirling from the south only to drive the Scots back on the Highlands; much better chase them into England, where they would meet the same fate as Hamilton's army in 1648.

Leslie saw the trap, and argued for an immediate attack on Perth,

---

* Including the Dutchman Jonas van Druske (see p. 152n above).

but the King wanted to march on England and his will prevailed. At this stage Argyll cautiously pulled out. On 31 July the army left Stirling, and reached Cumbernauld near Glasgow that night; it crossed the Border, bypassing Carlisle, on 6 August, and two days later it reached Penrith, meeting with no opposition. It numbered about 13,000 men, Scots and English, and in contrast to Hamilton's army it was well-equipped and well-disciplined, but many Scotsmen, who had not bargained for a campaign in England when they enlisted, were beginning to peel off and trickle back to Scotland. David Leslie was plunged in deep melancholia, riding by himself and speaking to no one, and when the King tried to rally him, 'and asked him with great alacrity how he could be so sad when he was at the head of so brave an army', he replied in an undertone 'that he was melancholic indeed, for he well knew that army, how well soever it looked, would not fight'. Nor was he the only one of like mind; the 2nd Duke of Hamilton, no doubt with his brother's fate in mind, wrote gloomily: 'We have quit Scotland, being scarce able to maintain it; and yet we grasp at all, and nothing but all will satisfy us, or to lose all. But we have one stout argument, despair – for we must now either stoutly fight, or die.'

The trap was already closing. Having detached Monck with about 4,000 men to take care of Stirling, Cromwell sent Lambert on ahead with 4,000 horse to join the reserve regiments in the North of England commanded by Harrison and Rich. He came on himself as fast as he could with the foot and artillery. He also sent Fleetwood on ahead to raise new regiments in the Midlands, while the government called out the militia nationwide. On 15 August Lambert joined Harrison and Rich at Newcastle, and on the same day the King marched into Wigan; Lambert thrust across the Pennines and pursued him as far as Warrington. At Warrington he was joined by the Earl of Derby with a few hundred Manxmen, but otherwise scarcely any English volunteers came in. The whole area had had its bellyful of the Scots in 1648, and Charles was handicapped by his public adhesion to the Covenant, a fact underlined by the gaggle of vociferous Scots ministers attached to the army. On the other hand it was noticed that he lodged almost exclusively with Catholic gentry families on the road south. At Warrington he decided not to turn south-east towards London and risk being intercepted by Cromwell, but when he pressed on due south instead, along the Welsh border, it was an admission of defeat. Shrewsbury closed its gates to him, and Gloucester resisted the blandishments of its old governor, Massey. On 22 August he found refuge at last at

Worcester, true to its loyalist past, but the 2,000 men he recruited there scarcely made good his losses by desertion; he was now reduced to about 12,000 men.

Cromwell caught up with Lambert and Rich on the 24th at Warwick, sixty miles from Shrewsbury, and Fleetwood was coming up fast from the Midlands. By the 29th he had assembled more than 30,000 men to the south of Worcester, as against Charles's 12,000. The parliamentary army included 3,000 militiamen from Essex and Suffolk; indeed, the general response of the militia was remarkable, and said a lot for the stability of the regime as well as the unpopularity of the Scots. The militia also garrisoned Gloucester, Ludlow, Hereford and Bristol, releasing hundreds of regular troops, and a mobile force of 2,000 patrolled Yorkshire; two regiments from Norfolk and two more from Suffolk were marching west towards Worcester.

With this superiority in numbers victory was inevitable, and Cromwell's main concern was to minimise casualties and capture the 'King of Scots'. As for Charles, he could only hope for some lucky accident: 'For me', he said, 'it is a crown or a coffin.' Cromwell's problem was to get his men across the Severn, which ran north–south through the city, and the Teme, which joined the Severn from the west about two miles to the south. The Scots had supposedly destroyed all the bridges, but when Lambert reconnoitred the bridge at Upton-on-Severn, about six miles to the south, on the 28th, he found he could throw planks across a narrow gap in the centre span and push his vanguard over. There was a bit of brisk fighting at the bridgehead, in which Massey was wounded, but by the next day Lambert had put 11,000 men over and was marching north.

The next step was to build a bridge of boats across the Teme near its junction with the Severn, and another across the Severn itself about half a mile north. This took until the afternoon of 3 September, the anniversary of Dunbar. As Cromwell and Fleetwood pushed their men across the river to join Lambert they met with stiff resistance, but they steadily drove the Scots back towards the town. Charles then ordered a diversionary attack from the western salient, where the enemy forces were now at their weakest; but Cromwell himself hastened back over the bridge with reinforcements, and after a tense struggle lasting three hours he stormed Fort Royal, at the south-east corner of the city, and turned its guns on the Scots, jammed in the streets below. Lambert and Fleetwood's men flooded in from the south and it was all over. Cromwell's verdict was that it was 'as stiff a contest, for four or five hours, as I have ever seen', yet he did not think he had lost more than two hundred men. Thousands of infantry surrendered after sporadic street-fighting while the horse streamed off towards the North, though very few, if any, reached Scotland again. The Duke of Hamilton died of his wounds on the way; David Leslie and John Middleton were captured at Rochdale and sent to the Tower; Middleton later escaped, but Leslie stayed there until 1660. They were luckier than the Earl of Derby, who was convicted of treason and executed at Bolton the following month. Charles II also rode north a while with Henry Wilmot, then turned off to Whiteladies in Shropshire, where he spent a day in the branches of the celebrated royal oak at Boscobel. He then doubled back towards the South West, and after six harrowing weeks on the run with a price on his head he and Wilmot at last took a small boat from Brightelmstone (Brighton) in Sussex on 14 October and reached France in safety.*

'The dimensions of this mercy are above my thoughts,' said Cromwell, 'it is, for aught I know, a crowning mercy.' Everywhere men were conscious of the fact that the long struggle which had begun in 1642 was over at last. Dismissing a regiment of militia drawn up at Powick Bridge a few miles up the Teme, where Rupert had led the first cavalry charge of the Civil Wars in September 1642, Hugh Peters told them: 'When your wives and children shall ask you where you have been, and what news, say you have been at Worcester, where England's sorrows began, and where they are happily ended.'

Back in Scotland Monck took the surrender of Stirling Castle on 14 August, and a fortnight later he captured the Committee of Estates *en bloc* at Alyth and shipped them off to England. On 1 September he stormed Dundee and put it to the sack, killing five or six hundred townspeople, and Montrose and Aberdeen hastened to surrender on terms. In the next campaigning season the remaining major fortresses at Dumbarton and Dunottar surrendered. In January 1652 English Commissioners arrived at Dalkeith to take over the government, and in April the union of the two nations was officially proclaimed at Edinburgh, while the Army pressed remorselessly on towards the Highland Line.

The remaining strongholds of royalism further out, some of them

---

\* Charles's hectic adventures on the run form no part of a narrative of the Civil Wars. The best account is by Richard Ollard, *The Escape of Charles II* (London 1966).

half-forgotten, now surrendered or were easily subdued: the Isle of Man on 31 October 1651, Jersey on 12 December, Castle Cornet in Guernsey on the 17th. Meanwhile a naval detachment under Admiral Ayscue, having taken the Scillies, went on to the West Indies, arriving off Barbados in October; in January the royalist garrison there capitulated, followed in March by Bermuda, then Virginia and Maryland.

That left only Ireland. In the autumn of 1650, after Cromwell's departure, Ireton had gone on steadily reducing the remaining fortresses in the south and south-west. Carlow fell on 24 July, Waterford on 6 August, Duncannon on the 13th, followed next day by Charlemont, which surrendered to Coote in the north. Limerick, Athlone and Galway were now the only substantial towns in Irish hands. Ireton, always a much better politician than he was a general, muffed a joint attack on Galway and Athlone in October, but he had all the time in the world. Ormonde's authority as Lord Lieutenant, never very strong, was steadily weakening; that summer Galway and Limerick pointedly declined to admit his troops, and news was coming through from Scotland that the new King had disowned him. In August the Irish bishops, meeting at Jamestown, County Antrim, performed another *volte face*, and solemnly forbade the Catholics to obey him. In December he agreed to hand over what slight authority he had left to the Catholic Earl of Clanricarde and sailed for the last time for France, together with Inchiquin and other Protestant notables.

The Confederates' last hope was the Duke of Lorraine, who had been dispossessed of his duchy by the French in 1633 and had turned soldier of fortune. He had been denied any redress at the Peace Congress of Westphalia in 1648, but he had taken refuge in the Spanish Netherlands, and he apparently still had plenty of men and money. But when his envoy arrived in Ireland in February 1651 he could find no one to negotiate with; the Supreme Council was on the run, and Clanricarde refused to see him. In any case, though he was a Catholic, Clanricarde was no more trusted by the Confederates than Ormonde had been. In May Ireton emerged from winter quarters, crossed the Shannon, and on 14 June opened the siege of Limerick, while Coote invaded Connaught from the north. Limerick finally surrendered on 27 October after a hard siege, and Ireton proceeded to reduce County Clare. The citizens of Limerick and Waterford were now given notice to quit, to make way for English colonists. Ireton died of pneumonia on 26 November, and his body was shipped back to England by his grieving father-in-law for a state funeral in Westminster Abbey – 'What is of this world', said Cromwell, 'will be found transitory'. His second-in-command, Edmund Ludlow, took over for the final mopping-up operations.

Clanricarde made a last desperate offer to treat in February 1652, but Ludlow told him that the issue was not one for negotiation but capitulation: 'The settlement of this nation doth of right belong to the Parliament of the Commonwealth of England, to whom we leave the same, being assured they will not therein capitulate with those who ought to be in subjection, yet stand in opposition to their authority.' On 12 April Galway surrendered, and a month later the so-called 'Leinster Army', the last official army of the Confederacy. Clanricarde finally gave up on 28 June; he surrendered his powers as Lord Deputy, *vice* Ormonde, to Parliament, and though he was formally excepted from pardon he retired to his English estates at Somerhill, Kent, where he died unmolested five years later. The remaining forts and roving guerrilla bands surrendered over the autumn and winter; the castle of Cloghoughter on remote Lough Oughter held out until 27 April 1653, but that was the last.

Thus began the long night of Ireland's troubles. Scotland deeply resented the Union of 1652 as the rape of her independence, but though the authority of the Kirk was drastically reduced she suffered no religious persecution, and order and justice were imposed, even on the Highlands. But in Ireland it was another matter. The Catholic Church was proscribed and over a thousand priests driven into exile, together with an estimated 34,000 rebels taken in arms, the 'Wild Geese' who were to be a longstanding element in many Continental armies; after them went the Old Irish and most of the Old English nobility, stripped of their estates and outlawed. Virtually the whole of Munster, Leinster and Ulster was handed over to the Adventurers, to redeem the investment they had made in 1642, or to demobilised English officers and soldiers. The native landowners who were not exiled, to the number of 44,000, were transferred to Connaught, though they were forbidden to settle within four miles of the River Shannon or the sea. With the Irish landowning class penned in this huge 'reservation' the rest of the island was handed over to the Protestant ascendancy. When Ormonde returned as Lord Lieutenant in 1661 he and the other royalist leaders of the 1640s regained their own estates, but they could not alter the main structure of the Cromwellian settlement.

# 11
# EPILOGUE

The continuing odyssey of Oliver Cromwell, which took him to heights of power attained by no other English commoner, is no direct concern of ours; but that of his Army is.

The aim of all governments after 1651 was to retain an army of the minimum size to police the country and repel royalist attacks from abroad; to reduce its cost as much as possible and minimise its impact on the civil population. Legend to the contrary notwithstanding, this was accomplished to a substantial degree. In the winter of 1651–2 Cromwell disbanded five regiments of foot and two of horse, as well as thirty 'loose' companies; he also reduced the size of the remaining foot regiments to 700 men (from 1,200) and of troops of horse to sixty (from seventy or eighty). By January 1653 he had demobilised another 5,000 men, bringing the Anglo-Scots establishment down to about 35,900 men, costing £76,000 a month. The assessment continued at £120,000 a month partly because of the expense of the Irish establishment, but mainly because of the outbreak of war with the Netherlands, which occasioned a huge increase in Navy expenditure. In fact, the Navy was a growing burden; by 1657, by which time England was at war again, with Spain, the Navy was costing over £600,000 a year, the Army only £400,000.

The assessment, we may assume, was paid with reluctance, but so far as we can tell there was no sign of a further taxpayers' strike until 1659, after Cromwell's death. In July 1653 another Army Committee was appointed to supervise its collection, and behind it was always the ultimate threat of military force, but as before there is no known instance of its being specifically invoked. However, it was the aim of all successive governments to reduce it – hopefully to the magic figure of £30,000 a month.

Cromwell forcibly dissolved the Rump in April 1653, and the following December he took office as Lord Protector under the Instrument of Government, drawn up by John Lambert and the Council of Officers. The Instrument of Government provided for a 'home' army of 30,000 (20,000 foot and 10,000 horse), and in December 1654 the first Protectorate Parliament demanded that it be reduced to that figure, and the assessment accordingly. In August 1654, just before Parliament assembled, he had cut the assessment from £120,000 a month to £70,000; in February 1655 he cut it again, to £60,000, and in July he promulgated a new Army establishment. By October the total establishment in the three kingdoms had been reduced to about 40,000 men, and their pay had also been reduced: from 10d a day to 9d for a foot soldier (8d in garrisons), and from 2s 6d a day to 2s 3d for a cavalry trooper.

Nevertheless, the government continued to run at a deficit, accumulating an ever increasing debt. Foreign expeditions were financed from separate heads of taxation, but Ireland was not. As early as December 1654 the Anglo-Scots establishment had fallen to 29,950, but an Irish establishment of 23,515 pushed the total to over 53,000. In 1657, under a revised protectoral constitution known as the Humble Petition and Advice, Parliament gave the government an established income of £1,300,000 a year, £1,000,000 of it for the armed forces, but none of it was to be raised by a land tax. In fact, the assessment (which was now essentially a land tax) remained indispensable, but an attempt was made to spread the financial burden over the other two kingdoms; by now the Irish establishment stood at 14,520 men, the Scots establishment at 10,260, and the English at 11,733. So in June 1657 an assessment of £60,000 a month was imposed on England, £20,000 on Ireland and £5,000 on Scotland, totalling £85,000; but a few weeks later Parliament adjusted these sums to £35,000, £9,000 and £6,000 respectively, a total of £50,000, though this was imposed for the unprecedented term of three years – six months was the usual maximum. Serious efforts were now made to reduce the Army establishment all round, partly by sending regiments overseas, and by 1659 the figures for England, Scotland and Ireland respectively had fallen to 12,549, 7,700 and 10,560 – a total of 30,809, the lowest yet. Even so, Army pay was now so far in arrears that it was reckoned that the government was at least £2 million in debt, and to some extent further demobilisation only exacerbated the problem, in that the arrears of men demobilised could only be met by 'borrowing' from current income which should have been used to pay those remaining in service. In addition there was the awkward fact that though the assessment was levied by the calendar month the men were paid by the lunar month, thirteen to the year, not twelve. But this was a problem which had plagued the Long Parliament from the beginning.

Even so, and despite these horrid actuarial problems at government level, the common soldier was apparently unaffected. There was no free quarter and not a flicker of mutiny, and we must assume that the troops were paid *something* week by week, however far it might be in arrears. Under these conditions the army merged quite well into society. Discipline was strict, and friction between soldiers and civilians was kept to the minimum – at least until the general breakdown in 1659, when we hear of some units going on the rampage. Care was taken to ensure that the regiments were scattered in small garrisons, mainly round the coasts, and well away from London. Much of the friction between the public and the Army in 1647, and the Army's propensity to intervene in national politics, had arisen from its concentration in the south-east quadrant of the country – a mistake which was not made again. On the other hand the military life had considerable appeal to the working classes, and recruitment was never a problem. Garrison officers took their natural share in local government; many of them served as JPs, and a few as sheriffs. Thus the appointment of nine major-generals in 1655 to supervise local government in the wake of Penruddock's Rising, a rather pathetic rural *émeute* in Wiltshire, was merely an extension of an existing trend, and occasioned little comment except from committed royalists. The Parliament of 1657 forced their withdrawal not because they objected to the major-generals as such, but because of the decimation tax on former royalists levied to support them, which was regarded as an infringement of the principles of natural justice. The idea that the 1650s was a period of bitterly unpopular and oppressive military tyranny is a fabrication of the post-Restoration era, blown up to even greater proportions during the 'Standing Army' controversy in the 1690s.

Cromwell himself did his best to 'civilianise' his government. After 1654 he abandoned military uniform, and saw that his senior officers who came to 'Court' did so too. The dispersal of the Army gave no occasion for military reviews or parades in London. Many of the more radical general officers, notably Thomas Harrison and Edmund Ludlow, could not stomach the semi-monarchical Instrument of Government and resigned or were cashiered in 1654. John Lambert, Cromwell's most trusted lieutenant, some said his *alter ego*, resigned in 1657 when Parliament gave him the right to choose his own successor. His place in Cromwell's entourage was taken by Charles Fleetwood, a career soldier of no great ability who had married Ireton's widow. It is noticeable by this time how few of the Protector's advisers, including Fleetwood, had risen to the top in the 1640s, or had had any share in the King's execution. In fact, the tide was running strongly against the 'swordsmen', and it was clear that Cromwell would nominate as his successor his elder son Richard, a civilian of retiring disposition, not his younger brother Henry, a career army officer and now Lord Deputy in Ireland.

Opposition to the regime, from Presbyterians, Levellers and Royalists, was persistent but shallow, striking no deep roots. The only serious threat came in 1655, when the Levellers and the Royalists concluded an unholy alliance; but an ambitious nationwide conspiracy petered out in Penruddock's Rising. Two or three hundred Yorkshire royalists gathered on Marston Moor – surely a field of ill omen – before helplessly dispersing again, an incident repeated in various locales up and down the country. Indeed, when Cromwell died on 3 September 1658, the anniversary of Dunbar and Worcester, there seemed little to threaten the protectoral constitution.

But Richard Cromwell ('Tumbledown Dick') tried to press on too vigorously with his father's policy of demilitarisation, and came up against Fleetwood, now Commander-in-Chief, and the other general officers: 'The Wallingford House Party', as they were known from their meeting-place in London. They eased him from power in April 1659, then found that an apparently depoliticised army was still embarrassingly committed to 'The Good Old Cause' of republicanism. Like the 'grandees' of 1647, their preoccupation with politics and 'Court' life in London had caused them to lose touch with the officers and men in the provinces on whom their power depended. In May they were forced to recall the Rump of the Long Parliament and re-establish the Commonwealth.

However, it soon emerged that the Rump was intent on emasculating the power of the Army, which had unseated it in 1653. They bypassed Fleetwood by appointing a seven-man committee to review and confirm Army commissions, which gave them the opportunity, freely used, to cashier officers of suspect loyalty. They also recalled Lambert, to offset Fleetwood and his chief lieutenant, John Desborough (or Disbrowe). But Lambert was speedily alienated by the Rump's failure to pass a satisfactory Act of Oblivion to indemnify officers like him for their complicity in Oliver's 'tyranny' and its refusal to impose further taxation. Their only answer to the pressing problem of soldiers' pay was a swingeing cut in the salaries of senior officers.

The spell was broken by the Royalists, now allied with the Presbyterians.* As in 1655 a projected national uprising only resulted in a localised revolt. The Cheshire landowner Sir George Booth, a staunch parliamentarian even in 1651, raised the county on 1 August, calling for the election of a new parliament. He made no mention of the King, though some of his supporters did. The revolt spread to Wrexham and Denbigh in the West, Liverpool to the North, but it was thinly supported, and when Lambert arrived with two regiments of horse and three of foot the end was inevitable. He caught up with Booth at Hartford Green near Northwich on 19 August and routed him completely. Lambert lost one man killed, Booth about thirty killed and over three hundred captured. This minor skirmish may be termed the last military action of the Civil Wars. The rest of Booth's followers quietly dispersed, while he was sent to the Tower; Wrexham, Denbigh and Liverpool hastened to surrender.

Lambert's victory, puny as it was, polarised the issues at large. It enhanced his personal ascendancy and it underlined the Rump's dependence on the Army to protect it from a multitude of enemies. In mid-September his officers at Derby, no doubt with his connivance, sent up a petition to the Rump calling for the appointment of a 'select senate', the speedy dissolution of Parliament and the confirmation of Fleetwood as Commander-in-Chief, with Lambert second in command.

---

\* 'Presbyterian' is almost as difficult a word to construe as 'Puritan'. Believers in a Presbyterian form of church government had opposed Charles I's execution and accused Cromwell of betraying the Covenant; their leaders were proscribed, and many of them, as we have seen, joined Charles II and the Scots in 1650–1. But by 1659 the name embraced many moderate Puritans who had come to believe that only the King's restoration on terms could bring an end to the prevailing anarchy in politics as well as religion. Most of them (including Booth himself and George Monck) passed over into moderate royalist Anglicanism after 1660.

To use the words of one historian, this was 'the spark which started the conflagration that destroyed the Commonwealth'. The Rump ordered Lambert to discipline the officers concerned, but it was soon apparent that they enjoyed the firm support of their counterparts in the London garrison, who presented an even stiffer petition on 5 October. The Rump's answer was to cashier Lambert and eight other senior officers, but he simply threw an armed guard round the Palace of Westminster and once more prevented the Rump from sitting.

But Lambert was not Cromwell, and this was not 1653. Officers loyal to the Commonwealth promptly seized Dublin Castle, and George Monck, still Commander-in-Chief Scotland, stepped in. Monck had always been one of Cromwell's most trusted lieutenants, despite his royalist past, and from Edinburgh he had watched the drift of events in England with growing dismay, meanwhile tightening the discipline of his army and imposing a censorship which isolated it from the political epidemic now raging south of the Border. He now demanded the recall of the Rump as the only legally constituted authority, but he entered into prolix negotiations with Lambert while he made his preparations to advance into England. Members of the defunct Council of State sent him a commission as Commander-in-Chief in England as well as Scotland, and the morale of the English Army began to crumble, especially now that all legal sources of pay and supply had dried up. Faced with the day-by-day disintegration of their authority, Lambert and Fleetwood recalled the Rump on 26 December; the Rump immediately hastened that disintegration by cashiering five hundred veteran officers and NCOs for supporting the Wallingford House Party in their recent coup.

Monck duly crossed the Border on 1 January 1660. Facing him in Yorkshire were 12,000 men under Lambert's command, but he was in touch with Fairfax at Nunappleton, and the sudden emergence from retirement of their old commander, calling for a free parliament, dissolved the loyalties of the Northern army in a matter of hours. Fairfax entered York in triumph on 3 January, and he was there to greet Monck when he marched in on the 11th. Lambert fled south with a few companions and was promptly thrown into the Tower. Uncertain of the loyalty of his remaining troops, Fleetwood made no move, and the Army of Scotland entered London unopposed on 3 February. Monck's first act was to disperse the London garrison to the provinces.

Monck told the Rump that the nation would be satisfied with nothing less than a new parliament, freely elected, but they still refused to fix a date for their dissolution, and it would have been contrary to his previous declarations of loyalty for him to coerce them. But after two weeks his patience snapped. On 20 February he interviewed the Members excluded by Thomas Pride in 1648, and exacted certain pledges from them. He then withdrew his guards from Westminster and the newly returned Members were as good as their word. They annulled the Engagement to the republic, voted to dissolve themselves at last on 16 March, and ordered the Speaker to issue writs for a new parliament, to assemble on 25 April. The loyalties of the Army were still ambiguous, but none of the senior officers questioned Monck's authority; on 7 March he held a meeting at which he told them roundly that 'he brought them not out of Scotland for [to be] his nor the Parliament's counsel; that for his part he would obey the Parliament and expected they should do the same'. Later he sent out a letter to the provincial garrisons pointing out that only a properly constituted parliament could raise the taxation needed to satisfy their demands for pay and arrears.

A day or two after the dissolution of the Long Parliament Monck had a secret interview with Charles II's emissary, Sir John Grenville, and told him that the King must promise all men as full and liberal a pardon as possible, confirm land sales concluded during the Interregnum, undertake to pay all arrears owed to members of the armed forces and offer 'a liberty for tender consciences' in matters of religion. These points were embodied in a declaration issued by Charles II from Breda on 4 April, which he sent with a covering letter to the Speaker of the new Parliament. Lambert escaped from the Tower on 10 April and called for a rendezvous at Edgehill. (The attachment of veterans on both sides to old battlegrounds is remarkable.) A few troops of horse under John Okey joined him at Daventry, but his support melted away as soon as Colonel Richard Ingoldsby arrived with a couple of loyal regiments. Lambert implored Ingoldsby to let him escape, but he was returned to the Tower. It was Easter Sunday, 21 April. Monck then insisted that all regiments subscribe to a declaration that they would not only obey him without question but would abide by any decisions of the new Parliament.

Parliament, of course, decided to recall the King, and the Army never stirred. In fact, when Charles II rode into London on 29 May – his thirtieth birthday – his route was lined by the redcoats of the New Model, which had destroyed his father's cause and his own. The diarist John Evelyn 'stood in the Strand and beheld it, and blessed God'. 'And all this', he added, 'was done without one drop of blood shed, and by that very army which rebelled against him.'

However, the first task of the restored monarchy was to disband the Army, and in this it had the full co-operation of Parliament. One of the last convulsive acts of the Rump, on 29 January 1660, had been to impose an assessment of £120,000 a month for six months. How much of this was collected, if any, is not clear, but on 1 June the Convention* imposed another assessment of £70,000 a month for three months, followed in August by an emergency poll tax, and in September by a further three months' assessment. By January 1661 this burst of taxation had produced £560,000, against total arrears of £835,819 8s 10d. In July 1661 the Cavalier Parliament voted the King a 'free and voluntary present', followed in December by an eighteen months' assessment at £70,000. Not all of this was earmarked for the Army, and the figures are obscure, but it apparently disposed of the problem.

The sudden re-entry to civilian life of thousands of highly trained, independently minded men – 'every soldier', it was said, 'able to do the functions of an officer' – kept Charles II's ministers in a constant state of alert for the next ten years or more, but when we consider the enormous numbers of men blooded in war who had already been demobilised since 1645 it is remarkable that they had so little discernible effect on the texture or nature of English society; and so it was now. Pepys remarked in 1663:

> Of all the old Army now you cannot see a man begging about the street –
> but what? You shall see this captain turned a shoemaker, the lieutenant a
> baker; this, a brewer; that, a haberdasher; this common soldier, a porter;
> and every man in his apron and frock, &c., as if they had never done
> anything else – whereas the other [the Cavaliers] go with their belts and
> swords, swearing and cursing and stealing.

He could also have mentioned those many veterans who used their accumulated arrears, often a considerable sum, to set up inns or ale-houses; thus the many 'Royal Oaks' which adorn our towns and villages, and probably many of the 'Crowns' as well.

Nevertheless, not all the Ironsides were demobilised. The atmosphere in 1660 and 1661 was electric; every minor ruckus was anxiously scrutinised, and rumours of plots abounded. In November 1660 Charles

---

* The name accorded to a parliament summoned without the king's writ. The Convention speedily declared itself to be a parliament, but the name stuck.

commissioned the royalist veteran John Russell to form the 1st Regiment of Foot Guards, 1,200 strong, but they were hard put to it to suppress a Fifth Monarchy uprising which suddenly erupted in London the following January, and for a few hours seemed likely to engulf the whole city. So, when Monck's regiment of foot came up for demobilisation in February, most of them were remustered as the 2nd Regiment of Foot, the Coldstreams. Similarly, Cromwell's former regiment of horse was divided between the Duke of York's lifeguard, which he brought over from Flanders, and a new regiment captained by Aubrey de Vere, Earl of Oxford; the Royal Horse Guards, later the 'Blues'. This was the beginning of the British regular army.

Otherwise the permanent effects of the Civil Wars are difficult to assess. It was once thought that the confiscation of some royalists' estates, and the sale of others to pay 'delinquency' fines, ruined many landowners, who were replaced by unscrupulous *arrivistes* and war profiteers, thus consummating a 'Land Revolution'. However, this thesis has crumbled under the pressure of more detailed research. In the same way destruction of crops and wholesale confiscation of supplies by the armies in the 1640s undoubtedly brought many areas to the edge of destitution, and this was exacerbated by the poor harvests of 1647–9; but farmland soon recovers from this kind of treatment, and there is no suggestion that the agricultural crisis – if there ever was one – persisted into the 1650s. Internal trade soon recovered, and external trade may well have been stimulated by the wars; industry certainly was. From 1642 well into the 1650s the army was the largest customer for manufactured articles: uniforms, shoes, small arms of all kinds, swords, bandoliers, saddles, even drums; and it may well be that the pronounced economic slump of 1659 was partly caused by the falling-off of such orders as the Army establishment shrank and money began to run out. However, the unprecedented levels of taxation imposed in the 1640s and 1650s betrayed the fact that pre-war parliaments had been less than ingenuous when they represented England as a poor nation, and post-war governments took notice. In 1661 Charles II was given a funded income of £1,200,000 a year, but this was merely a foretaste of what was to come after the Revolution of 1688.

On individuals the effects of the wars were curiously random. The Act of Indemnity and Oblivion which Charles and his chief minister Clarendon (formerly Sir Edward Hyde) pushed through the Convention before the hard-line Royalists came back to Westminster in the Parliament of 1661 was a remarkable piece of statesmanship. It exonerated all those who had fought against the King and his father and did its best to wipe from the record the events of the previous eighteen years. It even imposed fines on those who publicly criticised their neighbours' conduct during the 'Late Troubles'. The regicides – those who had sat on the High Court which tried Charles I, or had signed his death warrant, or had participated in any way in his execution – were not unnaturally excepted, and measures were even taken against the dead. Thus the bodies of Cromwell, Ireton and Bradshaw were disinterred from Westminster Abbey and gibbeted. (The opportunity was also taken to remove a few other embarrassing corpses less ostentatiously, and throw them in the 'common pit'; amongst them John Pym's, though not, of course, the Earl of Essex's.) Ten surviving regicides, six of them Army officers, were tried and executed in 1661, though their bearing was such that the government soon abandoned the practice as counter-productive. The last words of the veteran Thomas Harrison, who had fought at Edgehill, Marston Moor, Naseby, Basing, Langport, Preston and Worcester, were especially poignant: 'By God,' he said, 'I have leaped over a wall; by God, I have run through a troop; and by God, I will go through this death, and He will make it easy for me.' In 1662 two more Cromwellian field officers, John Barkstead and John Okey, were captured in Holland and brought back to be tried as regicides, then butchered by the archaic process of hanging, drawing and quartering: hung by the neck for a few minutes, then cut down and their bowels and sex organs cut out and burned before their eyes, then their head and limbs cut off. There was much public sympathy for Okey, who had commanded the dragoon regiments of the New Model ever since 1645. 'Some of the sheriff's officers, when Okey came to the cart, said of him that he was a lusty, stout, brave man as ever fought in England', and instead of drawing and quartering him the government took the unusual step of offering his body intact to his wife for burial. However, such crowds gathered at Christchurch, Stepney, in anticipation of the funeral that the government took fright and hastily interred him somewhere in the Tower of London. However, cruel as Okey's fate was, it was arguably better than that of John Lambert, his close friend and associate, who was sentenced to life imprisonment, first in Guernsey, then on tiny St Nicholas Island in Plymouth Sound. He was only forty-one at the Restoration, and at the height of his powers, but he was reduced to drivelling idiocy long before his death in 1683. Sir Arthur Haselrigg might well have gone the same way, but he died in the Tower in January 1661. Sir Henry Vane, the leading republican in the Commonwealth of 1649–53, was also excepted from the Act of Indemnity, though not a regicide. Charles II thought him too dangerous to live, and he was arraigned on a trumped-up charge of treason in 1662 and beheaded.

Slightly less spectacular offenders were simply ignored. Charles Fleetwood, for instance, was barred from public life, but he lived out his days in some affluence at Stoke Newington with his wife Bridget, Cromwell's daughter and Ireton's widow. Desborough, though he had married Cromwell's sister as far back as 1636, and had been closely associated with Lambert in 1659, also went free, though he soon left for Holland. He was suspected of plotting there, and in July 1666 the government summoned him home and put him in the Tower. In February 1667 he was examined by a high-powered committee consisting of Clarendon, Monck (now Duke of Albemarle) and Secretary of State Arlington, but they let him go, and nothing more is heard of him until his death at Hackney in 1680, aged seventy-two, when he was possessed of estates in Cambridgeshire, Lincolnshire and Essex.

Even Oliver's sons went unmolested. Richard Cromwell felt it wiser to go abroad, where he remained twenty years, but he returned in 1680, taking an assumed name but making no other attempt at concealment, and lived out the rest of his long life as a modest country squire at Cheshunt, Bucks, dying in 1712. His younger brother Henry made his peace with the new government in 1660, and even hung on to some of his ill-gotten Irish lands; he also used his handsome arrears of pay to buy an estate in Cambridgeshire worth £700 a year, where he died in comfortable circumstances in 1674.

In fact, there was some truth in the cynics' comment that Charles's Act of Indemnity and Oblivion offered 'indemnity to his enemies, oblivion to his friends', but this merely reflects the ineluctable fact that Parliament had won the Civil Wars handsomely and the restoration of the monarchy was an act of grace. The distribution of rewards and favours after 1660 has never been fully assessed, but it seems that though the King was generous in his award of honours he was unable to offer the old royalists much compensation for their financial losses; they had invested in the monarchy, and its restoration was a sufficient dividend. Nor did royal favour necessarily survive the recipient. Henry Wilmot, for instance, had been one of Charles's closest companions in exile and undertook many perilous missions to England; in 1652 he was created Earl of Rochester. Unfortunately he died in 1658, and though his son, the rakehell poet, was also one of Charles's boon companions, it seems he derived little financial benefit from the connexion. The best Clarendon could suggest was marriage to a wealthy heiress. As for Charles I's favourite, Lord Digby, his career in exile was typically rackety. He joined the French army in 1647 and served with distinction, rising to lieutenant-general in 1651, but Charles II refused to reinstate him. In 1653 he succeeded his father as Earl of Bristol, but he was almost at once disgraced for complicity in a plot to unseat Louis XIV's chief minister, Mazarin. In 1657 Charles gave way to his mother's urging and appointed him his Secretary of State, but he dismissed him a few months later when he found he had turned Roman Catholic. In 1660 he was made a Knight of the Garter but nothing else. Sir Marmaduke Langdale was another who probably suffered because of his conversion; he was raised to the peerage but he died in some penury in 1661.

For the rest, the Marquess of Newcastle received a dukedom, but he was never repaid the huge sums he had spent raising the Army of the North in 1642. Nor did Edward Somerset, 2nd Marquess of Worcester, ever recover the huge loans (said to amount to £300,000) his father had made to Charles I in 1642 and 1643. Charles would not even confirm the Dukedom of Somerset promised his father in 1643; it went instead to a less active royalist, Essex's brother-in-law William Seymour, Marquess of Hertford, who had compounded in 1646 and lived a tranquil life thereafter on his estates. In 1660 he was automatically made Duke of Somerset by the removal of the attainder passed on his great-grandfather, the Protector Somerset, in 1552; he was also appointed a Gentleman of the Bedchamber and a member of the Privy Council. The Marquess of Winchester, however, received no further honours, perhaps again because he was a Roman Catholic; nor did he recoup the losses he had sustained in his heroic defence of Basing House throughout the first Civil War. These were assessed by the Convention at £19,000, then reduced in 1661 to £10,000; but even this was never paid. Most noblemen regained their estates, though often in a ruinous condition, by a special resolution of the House of Lords or a private Act of parliament, but the 8th Earl of Derby, who had been left destitute after his father's execution in 1651 and had sold some of his estates to local speculators, was frustrated by the Act in Confirmation of Judicial Proceedings (1660), which confirmed all such sales 'freely' undertaken, whatever the circumstances. Already angered by the refusal of the government to except his father's 'murderers' from pardon, he launched a series of ruinous law suits which preoccupied him until

1670, and before his death he erected a monument on his estates testifying to Charles II's ingratitude.

Lesser men may well have fared better in their modest way. In 1662 the King set aside the inadequate sum of £60,000 to assist 'loyal and indigent' ex-officers, and more than 5,000 applied, but it is estimated that over and above this Charles spent about £31,600 a year between 1660 and 1667 in 'royal bounty', much of it directed towards deserving cases like the destitute sister of Sir George Lisle, executed at Colchester in 1648, who received £2,000. (The young Lord Capel was also created Earl of Essex in memory of his father's 'martyrdom'.) On a lower level, when the Lord Steward of the Household, in response to persistent rumours, ordered an investigation in December 1661, it was found that out of 298 servants appointed or reappointed since the King's return only two were ex-Cromwellians.

But the treatment received by several notorious parliamentarians of the 1640s understandably attracted greater public attention. Viscount Saye and Sele, for instance, one of Charles I's most implacable opponents, was made Lord Privy Seal. The Earl of Manchester was appointed Lord Chamberlain, admitted to the Privy Council and made a Knight of the Garter. Major-General Richard Browne, who had returned to his old trade of wood-monger, was Lord Mayor of London in 1660 and one of the City's MPs; he was made a baronet and received over £2,000 in back pay for his service in the 1640s. By a singular irony he was also appointed one of the commissioners appointed to hear appeals from royalist ex-officers. Edward Massey was knighted and received all his back pay plus an additional £3,000 from the excise; he was also given command of an Irish regiment and appointed to the Irish Privy Council. He returned to his old stamping ground at Gloucester, and sat as MP for that city from 1660 till his death in 1674. This contrasts with the treatment meted out to another convinced Presbyterian and opponent of Cromwell, Sir William Waller; he received nothing at the Restoration and died in reduced circumstances in 1668. The point is that Browne and Massey had fought with Charles on the Worcester campaign, whereas Waller had always held off from the royalists. But even late converts like Sir George Booth were not forgotten; he was raised to the peerage as Lord Delamere.

But the strangest case of all is that of Thomas Fairfax, enigmatic to the end. His opposition to Charles I's execution and the establishment of the republic was well-known, and his intervention at York in December 1659 had been a decisive contribution to the Restoration. His only child Mary was married to one of the King's closest friends, the 2nd Duke of Buckingham, who had returned secretly to England in 1657 and successfully wooed her and, more surprisingly, her father. He was elected to the Convention for Yorkshire, and usually sat next to Monck, MP for Devon, though he took little part in debates, and he headed the Commons delegation sent to The Hague in April 1660 to invite Charles to return. He had several private interviews with Charles in Holland; what they discussed we do not know, but he was given a full pardon under the Great Seal there and then. If he was offered any further favours he declined them, and he did not stand for election to the next parliament in 1661; instead he retired to Nunappleton to indulge his hobbies of gardening and horse-breeding, and there he died in 1671, almost forgotten. But in a last extraordinary gesture he offered the King one of his best horses to ride to his coronation in April 1661; its dam was the chestnut mare he had ridden to victory at Naseby. It is typical of Charles II that his offer was graciously accepted.

# 12

# A NATION DISARMED

The Civil Wars cast a long shadow over the thinking of the next few generations, although it was a shadow men did their best to ignore, publicly at least. But as late as 1689 we find Lord Wharton, a veteran of the Committee for Both Kingdoms, demanding that the 2nd Earl of Clarendon, son of the great royalist statesman, be summoned to the bar of the House of Lords 'for calling the Civil War a Rebellion'. Meanwhile framers of public documents took refuge in phrases like 'the Late Troubles', or 'the late Unhappy Troubles'.

After the Revolution of 1688, and especially after the abandonment of press censorship in 1695, a full-dress debate broke out on the rights and wrongs of the Civil Wars, and particularly on the merits and demerits of Charles I, but it was difficult to reach any objective conclusion (as it still is), and even Clarendon's enormously influential *History of the Rebellion and Civil Wars*, published in 1702–4, handed down what was in effect a hung verdict. The eighteenth century saw in the whole episode an unacceptable degree of royal tyranny and irresponsibility and at the same time an even less acceptable eruption of political radicalism and vulgar religious enthusiasm; it preferred to rest its case on the 'Glorious Revolution' of 1688, a conserving or preserving revolution – in fact, in the words of Edmund Burke, 'a revolution not made but prevented'. The Hampden societies founded in the 1770s and

1780s had a strong whiff of radicalism which would have dismayed the great John Hampden himself, especially since many of them came out in support of the American and French Revolutions. The French Revolution itself put radicalism under a cloud, and led most Englishmen to believe that they had had a lucky escape in 1649. Lord Macaulay, who set the seal of mid-Victorian orthodoxy on the late seventeenth century, dismissed the men of the Long Parliament as at best irresponsible.

Cromwell's reputation plummeted at the Restoration, too, as was only to be expected, and James Heath's violently hostile biography *Flagellum* (1663) set the prevailing tone. The Protector was denounced as a monster of evil, power-obsessed, devil-driven and crafty; personally and deliberately responsible for the death of Charles I and for every ill which followed therefrom. Samuel Pepys and his ex-Puritan friends might reminisce in private about 'Old Noll's' statesmanlike care for trade and the improvement of the Navy, and the publication of Slingsby Bethel's *The World's Mistake in Oliver Cromwell* (1668) shows that they were not the only ones. But by the 1680s these whispered, nostalgic voices were dying away, and Cromwell's reputation subsided into a slough from which it emerged only in the mid nineteenth century. The conservatives, Whig or Tory, blamed him not only for the death of Charles I but for the perpetuation of rebellion into a second decade; the radicals, when they re-emerged in the late eighteenth century, bitterly denounced him as the man who had stopped a revolution single-handed.

On the other hand, in the short term at least the posthumous reputation of 'King Charles the Martyr' rapidly assumed mythic proportions. A statute of 1661 imposed a day of fasting and humiliation in perpetuity on the anniversary of his execution, 30 January (in fact it was not repealed until 1858), and provided for a special church service which often tottered on the edge of blasphemy in comparing his sufferings and sacrifice to those of Christ at Calvary:

> Blessed lord, in whose sight the death of thy saints is precious; we magnify thy name for thine abundant grace bestowed upon our martyred sovereign; by which he was enabled so cheerfully to follow the steps of his blessed Master and Saviour, in a constant meek suffering of all barbarous indignities, and at last resisting unto blood, and even then according to the same pattern praying for his murderers. Let his memory, O Lord, be ever blessed among us; that we may follow the example of his courage and constancy, his meekness and patience, and great charity... [etc., etc.].

On that sacred day churchmen zestfully obeyed the injunction to preach on the perils of disobedience to the powers that be and the sinfulness of rebellion, and indeed they did so at every conceivable opportunity otherwise. They perpetuated the myth that Charles's death was due to his obstinacy with respect to religion and the church, not politics or law, and it was not until after 1688 that sacrilegious hands began to rock the pedestal upon which the martyr king was now firmly enthroned.

For the Church believed, with some superficial justification, that it owed its restoration in 1660–2 to the restoration of the monarchy, just as its fall had been directly linked with the fall of the monarchy in 1640–2, and it now set out to reaffirm and strengthen that special relationship between Crown and Mitre which had been the hallmark of the English Reformation since its beginnings under Henry VIII. In truth, it owed its unexpected restoration not to the Laodicean Charles II but to the general desire of the upper classes to close the door once for all on religious radicalism and experimentation and return to an older, steadier, more colourful, more dignified and less demanding form of worship. They had also been brought to realise that the clergy, from the parish priest upwards, were a crucial factor in maintaining the hierarchical structure of civil society. King James had once said, 'No bishop, no king'; he could just as easily have said, 'No bishops, no earls', or 'No deans, no viscounts', and so on. In retrospect one of the most disquieting aspects of the Interregnum had been its (much exaggerated) tendency towards the 'levelling' of class distinctions and even their inversion. England, thundered one clergyman, had been 'a kingdom quite inverted, a body without a head, with its heels upwards, and the dregs of the people lording it over their betters and superiors'. 'The estates of the realm were made slaves,' moaned another, 'and (which is the vilest of all servitude) slaves to their own servants.' They found an appreciative audience.

So, although the King and Clarendon approached the religious problem with extreme caution, and showed a marked willingness to compromise, an irresistible momentum, particularly after the dissolution of the Convention in December 1660, swept them on to the full-blown restoration of the pre-war Church. As for Puritanism, that mighty force which, it was supposed, had powered the Great Rebellion, engineered the King's defeat and death, and sustained the manic rule of Cromwell, it simply faded away like a ghost at cock-crow. True, more than 2,000 ministers resigned their livings rather than comply with the new Uniformity Act of 1662, which meant, incidentally, that the Church had to relinquish its monopoly of English Protestantism; but the former Puritans, now 'Dissenters', grouped in scattered congregations proscribed by the Conventicle Acts of 1664 and 1670, presented no real threat to the establishment, ecclesiastical or political; indeed, they showed an increasing disposition towards political quietism. The great 'Presbyterians' who had taken a decisive part in the King's restoration – Monck, Anthony Ashley Cooper, Edward Montagu, and their like – took their seats in the House of Lords and in public embraced a moderate Anglicanism. What they did in private was different no doubt, but even the Conventicle Acts allowed for heterodox worship within a man's household or family.

Animosity against the bishops still lingered, and again this is evident in Pepys's diary, but it never surfaced with any marked political force. However, with the great Uniformity Act of 1662, which governed the conduct of the Church of England well into the twentieth century, Parliament reasserted its right to legislate for and on behalf of the Church, an issue which had bedevilled relations between the last three monarchs and the House of Commons. Charles II cared little for his rights as Supreme Governor of the Church, and under his easy-going superintendence it embarked on one of the most glorious periods in its history, throwing up some of its greatest leaders and its most charismatic preachers and controversialists: Gilbert Sheldon, Gilbert Burnet, Edmund Stillingfleet, William Sherlock, William Sancroft, and many more, before it was thrown into further confusion by the Revolution of 1688.

Otherwise the constitution, and the structure of society and government, continued on its way apparently untouched by the traumatic events of the 1640s and 1650s. It was tacitly agreed that all the legislation of 1641 and 1642 to which Charles I had given his assent stood. This meant that the king could never again exact any money payment from the citizen without his consent expressed through Parliament; a tenet which was to have momentous consequences when it was invoked in the next century by the American colonists. Nor could he ever again operate outside the courts of common law through Star Chamber and High Commission. (Star Chamber had been extraordinarily useful, to the private citizen as well as the government, but it had acquired such a baleful reputation in the 1630s that tentative proposals to revive it in 1661 came up against a brick wall.) Other restrictions were never explicitly imposed, but imposed they were all the same. For instance, the days were now gone when the king could imprison contumacious MPs at the end of a session, order them into protective custody or rifle their papers for incriminating documents, as James I and Charles I had regularly done right up to 1640.

On the other hand the actual and effective power of the monarchy was enhanced in several important respects. The immediate cause of the first Civil War had been the dispute between Charles I and the Long Parliament over the command of the army, and Parliament now felt it imperative to settle this once for all. Therefore the Militia Act of 1661 stated that:

> The sole supreme government, command and disposition of the militia and of all forces by sea and land and of all forts and places of strength is and by the laws of England ever was the undoubted right of his Majesty and his royal predecessors, kings and queens of England, and that both or either of the houses of Parliament cannot nor ought to pretend to the same.

Another act of the same year put Parliament even more firmly in its place, with this blanket proviso:

> That by the undoubted and fundamental laws of this kingdom, neither the peers of this realm nor the Commons, nor both together, in Parliament or out of Parliament, nor the People, collectively or representatively, nor any persons whatsoever, ever had, hath, have or ought to have any coercive power over the persons of the kings of this realm.

This made Charles II's legal position unassailable, at the same time as his theoretical, even his spiritual position as ruler by Divine Right was being exalted to the skies by a grateful and subservient Church. For the Restoration divines went far beyond anything contemplated by their Laudian predecessors or even James I; they rejected the saving proviso that the subject could passively disobey the unlawful commands of the ruler, enduring such punishment as came his way with the assurance of eventual recompense and restitution (if only in the next world). He must now positively obey *any* command sent down to him from on high, even if it seemed to him unlawful or immoral. (Fortunately Charles II did not issue such commands; but James II did.)

But in practical terms, too, Charles II's position was much stronger than his father's had ever been. For instance, he not only had the *right* to keep an army, he actually *had* an army. The four regiments retained after Venner's Rising in 1661 (p. 230 above) were almost insensibly reinforced as the reign progressed: by the Cromwellian regiments recalled from Dunkirk in 1662, and others from Portugal in 1668, and by a few contingents recalled from the Army of France in 1674, these last distinctly Irish and papistical in tone. Moreover, one of the strange by-products of Charles's marriage in 1662 to the Portuguese princess Catherine of Braganza was the acquisition of a North African base at Tangier, which led to the recruitment of further regiments to resist the almost incessant pressure of the Moors. When Tangier was evacuated in 1684 these cynical and battle-hardened men also returned to England; amongst them the Queen's Own Regiment of Foot under its rakehell colonel Percy Kirke – 'Kirke's Lambs', they were called, because their standard featured the Paschal Lamb of the House of Braganza – though they were to prove the opposite of lamb-like in their suppression of Monmouth's Rebellion in 1685 in the West Country. (They were, in fact, the direct equivalent of the French 'Paras' recalled from North Africa by de Gaulle.) By the end of Charles's reign in 1685 the army stood at 9,000–10,000 men; smaller, obviously, than most Civil War field armies, and quite inconsiderable compared with the armies of France or the Netherlands at this time. But apart from the Scots and Irish armies, also firmly under the King's control, it was the only team on the ball park, and it was certainly able to deal with any rebellion not supported by a foreign power. Moreover, one of the unnoticed features of the Restoration and the years immediately following was the government's determined campaign to confiscate all weapons, and certainly muskets and hand-guns, held by the people at large. Thus the right, indeed the duty, of all Englishmen to bear arms, laid down in the Statute of Winchester in 1285, was quietly negatived. As for the Militia, that supposed citizen army, it continued to suffer from the studied neglect of the government and local authorities alike. With one exception. Charles II was determined never to be overborne by mob violence in his own capital as his father had been in 1641. He exercised strict control over the Lieutenancy of the City of London, and through them the London trained bands, and even in the frenzy of the Popish Plot, in 1678–81, that control never wavered. It is equally significant that when he transferred the Parliament of 1681 to Oxford he went down to meet it flanked by two of his elite regiments of guards. In short, after 1660 England was a nation disarmed, with all the guns in the King's hands.

Moreover, to maintain what we may call his physical authority Charles II had inherited from the Interregnum regimes a flexible and efficient taxation system, of a kind his predecessors could only dream of. It was ironic that in pioneering the Assessment and the Excise the Long Parliament had gone far towards solving the fiscal problems of the Stuart monarchy. True, the assessment was laid aside in 1661 by a Parliament which remembered with aversion two decades of grinding taxation, and the handsome £1.2 million it voted the King for life from the customs and excise fell short of its anticipated target in the 1660s and early 1670s, but thereafter the mushroom growth in England's overseas trade soon drove the Crown's income nearly up to the £1.5 million mark, and James II, voted nearly £2 million a year by his first Parliament in 1685, was easily the best-endowed of all the Stuarts. Meanwhile the assessment was always there, ready for use; it was reimposed as a war-time tax in 1665–7, in 1672–4 and again in 1678, and from 1692, as the 'Land Tax', it became the permanent basis of the tax system for the next hundred years.

Charles II also enjoyed a psychological advantage which is less easy to define. We might say that the national sense of guilt for the wasted years left the initiative with the King. Viewing the activities of the Cavalier Parliament, which Charles retained from 1661 to 1679, it is difficult to believe that this was the same institution that had once mobilised the nation for war, raised army after army to defeat the King, then defeated him again, tried and executed him, then conquered Scotland and Ireland. Of course, the very fact that it had done these now outrageous things paralysed its thinking as it confronted a new era. It uneasily settled down into a pattern of conduct reminiscent of the period 1604–29: carping at royal mismanagement and financial waste, attacking with limited success incompetent or delinquent ministers, bickering about religion, clamouring for a greater share in foreign policy. It was all very reminiscent of James I's reign. There was always some sort of opposition, but it was difficult to find a name for it; in the 1660s it was usually the 'Old Parliamentary Party', in the 1670s the 'Country Party'. Later it assumed, or was given, the name of 'Whig', but its programme was still essentially negative and destructive.

Indeed, for all the constitutional safeguards enacted in 1641 and confirmed twenty years later, it seemed that the England of the Restoration, with Scotland and Ireland battered into passivity, was destined for a lightly modified version of that military despotism which was the prevailing contemporary form of government on the Continent; in Spain, France, much of Germany, and even (from time to time) in the Dutch Republic under the House of Orange. Scotland and Ireland, it is true, nursed smouldering resentments, but Charles II chose his gauleiters well. The great James Butler, Marquess of Ormonde (Duke 1661), Charles I's Lieutenant-General in Ireland in the 1640s, and the leader of the Protestant Ascendancy, was removed from the Lord Lieutenancy in 1669 by Court intrigue, but had to be restored in 1677, and rode out the reign almost to the end. In Scotland John Maitland, Earl of Lauderdale, an early convert from the Covenant, who had signed the Engagement with Charles I in 1648, and had been captured at Worcester in 1651 and spent the next nine years in prison, emerged as the King's High Commissioner. He presided over the restoration of the episcopal Church in Scotland and ruthlessly reimposed monarchical authority in every sphere of government, so much so that by the late 1670s he was virtual dictator of Scotland. He was unseated by a serious rising of Covenanters in 1679, which had to be suppressed by troops sent from England, but this only led to what is known in Scots history as the 'Killing Time', that vicious and remorseless persecution of the Covenanters led by John Graham of Claverhouse ('Bonny Dundee') and Judge Advocate General Sir George Mackenzie ('Bluidy Mackenzie').

That the three kingdoms did not lapse into complete subservience to the monarchy was not due to the opposition of the ruling classes, but rather to certain abiding tendencies in the Stuart dynasty. Charles II was no more able than his father to operate a successful foreign policy, which could have consolidated his finances, given him a much larger army, and made his position as leader of the nation unassailable. Secondly, like his father he chose to marry a Catholic princess, and in the same way he was always suspected of a penchant for that religion, this time with much more justice. Though he postponed his final conversion until he lay on his deathbed, there is no doubt that from some time in the 1660s he was a 'closet Catholic'.

Thus his two wars against the Dutch, England's great trading rivals, were lamentable fiascoes, which weakened his position rather than strengthened it, and the second, in 1672–4, was undertaken in close alliance with Louis XIV of France, who was fast replacing the dreaded King of Spain as the principal bogeyman of the over-heated Protestant imagination. His attempt in 1678 to re-enter what had now become a major European war only resulted in further humiliation. Worse still, in 1673 his blatant partiality for Catholicism, and still more so that of his brother James, Duke of York, led Parliament to drive through a new Test Act, which at once revealed that James, heir-presumptive to the throne, was in fact a full-blown Roman Catholic. The ferocious reaction which followed was intensified in 1678 by the criminal mendacity of Titus Oates and other informers, who invented a 'Popish Plot' to assassinate Charles and put James on the throne. There followed an impassioned crisis stretching over two and a half years during which successive parliaments fought to exclude James from the line of succession. The monarchy seemed to sway on its foundations.

Nevertheless, Charles and James fought their way through. In the 'counter-backlash' after 1681 they even improved their position. Despite its visceral fear of Catholicism, the Church stood foursquare behind the Crown: better a Catholic king than another civil war and no king – which seemed not impossible in the overcharged atmosphere of 1679 and 1680. And the Church's stance was eventually adopted by the laity; royalist MPs warned the House that this was '1641 come again', and the Whig opposition's links with republicanism, evinced by the re-emergence of the great Interregnum republican Algernon Sidney, exiled for twenty years, told heavily against it, as did the pressure mounted by some of its fringe supporters for electoral reform. There was great talk of a rising in London when the Parliament of 1680 met, and the Whig leader, the Earl of Shaftesbury (formerly Anthony Ashley Cooper) was supposed to be bringing up his 'brave boys' from Wapping (unemployed watermen) any hour to over-awe the two Houses; but the King, with the London militia obedient to his orders, had the capital firmly under his control, and the moment passed. Another, more decisive moment passed on 28 March 1681, when Charles peremptorily dissolved the next parliament, summoned to Oxford, after a sitting of only seven days. The decision burst on the Commons like a thunderclap, their resentment and frustration were intense, but they did nothing. As the historian David Ogg points out:

> Round them were tennis courts and college gardens on which [they] might have reunited themselves by an oath more solemn than any which they had yet sworn; but they dispersed; some to London, others to the country, and many to the horse races at Burford.

In fact the English ruling classes had no stomach for a fight, and much of their pusillanimity must be blamed on the trauma of the Civil Wars, which many had experienced directly, virtually all of them indirectly through their fathers or their uncles. Despite its fear of Catholicism the nation could not be mobilised for rebellion, even when James II came to the throne in 1685 and soon after embarked on a policy of blatant romanisation which threatened the Protestant Ascendancy in all three kingdoms. So in 1688, as in 1638, England had to seek outside assistance to bring its ruler under control: in 1638 from Scotland; in 1688 from Holland. (Indeed as late as 1709, in the Barrier Treaty, the English were looking to the Dutch to underwrite the Protestant Succession.) Even so, in the Revolution of 1688 the ruling classes appropriated all the gains made by the monarchy in 1660 and thereafter. They used a taxation system invented by the Long Parliament, a naval tradition going back to Charles I's ship money fleet and a military tradition originating with the Ironsides to wrest from France the position of dominant political and military power in Europe and from the Dutch the position of dominant economic power. All these trends, of course, can be traced back to the Civil Wars.

The only serious casualty of the Civil Wars, ironically enough, was reform as we understand it. The great efflorescence of radicalism culminating in the Putney Debates came to nothing, though it has captured the imagination of the twentieth century. Persecuted by republican, protectoral and royal governments alike, the Levellers sank from sight, and the brief re-emergence of radical ideas in the Rye House Plot of 1683 and Monmouth's Rebellion in 1685 was greeted with horror. 'Blessed God!' said Judge Jeffreys, 'What is the way that this devil of sedition comes to bewitch people to such a height, when Almighty God has so lately delivered us from the misery and confusion of a civil war?' The Levellers struggled briefly into view again in the 1770s and 1780s, only to be swamped by a conservative reaction to the French Revolution of 1789, and their final re-emergence did not begin until 1845, with the publication of Thomas Carlyle's maverick edition of Cromwell's *Letters and Speeches*. Needless to say, Carlyle also began the rehabilitation of Cromwell himself, assisted by the interest roused during the bicentenary decade of the Civil Wars (though the centenary in the 1740s had gone virtually unnoticed). By 1859 one Augustus Leopold Egg could exhibit at the Royal Academy a portrait of 'Cromwell before Naseby' in which the future Protector kneels at the door of his tent in the moonlight, his eyes uplifted, the Bible before him, in mimicry of a medieval knight performing his vigil before the altar.

But this was far, far in the future. One of the unforeseen and now largely unnoticed effects of the Great Rebellion was to put a stopper on basic constitutional and legal reform. Because Cromwell had tried in 1655 to reform the cumbersome, creaking, overloaded Court of Chancery it must now lumber on into the nineteenth century unchanged, there to shock the readers of Dickens's *Bleak House*. Because

Ireton in the *Heads of the Proposals* had suggested a much-needed redistribution of parliamentary seats, and Lambert had carried this through in the *Instrument of Government*, any such reform was now unthinkable. As for the Leveller idea that the franchise should be extended so that Parliament was truly representative of the people, any change in that direction, however slight, was now anathema. Clarendon told Parliament in 1661, to general applause:

> It is the privilege, if you please the prerogative (and it is a great one), of the common people of England to be represented by the greatest, and learnedest, and wealthiest and wisest persons that can be chosen out of the nation; and the confounding the Commons of England, which is a noble Representative, with the common people of England, was the first ingredient in that accursed dose which intoxicated the brains of men with the imagination of a commonwealth.

This was a prescription for oligarchy, and though Charles II and James II, the one by serpentine manoeuvre, the other by bull-headed aggression, put off the evil day for a generation, by an oligarchy was Britain ruled from 1689 well into the nineteenth century, it could be said right up to 1914. It is strange that an episode which historians from Gardiner in the 1860s to Lawrence Stone in the 1970s have cried up as the 'English Revolution' should have had such an anti-revolutionary effect.

# BIBLIOGRAPHICAL ESSAY

There are many general accounts of the early seventeenth century, but in the present flux of historical scholarship the last is usually the best, and this is the case with *Authority and Conflict: England 1603–58* by Derek Hirst (1986).* For introductory treatments of Scotland and Ireland, see Rosalind Mitchison, *Lordship to Patronage: Scotland 1603–1745* (1983), and Margaret MacCurtain, *Tudor and Stuart Ireland* (Dublin 1972), respectively. The European background is covered by Geoffrey Parker, *The Thirty Years' War* (1985) and J. R. Hale, *War and Society in Renaissance Europe 1450–1620* (1985).

The basic authority on the Civil Wars proper is still S. R. Gardiner, *History of the Great Civil War 1642–9* (4 volumes 1893) and *History of the Commonwealth and Protectorate 1649–56* (4 volumes 1903), completed by C. H. Firth in *The Last Years of the Protectorate 1656–8* (2 volumes 1909), and Godfrey Davies in *The Restoration of Charles* II *1658–60* (San Marino, California 1955). Unfortunately C. V. Wedgwood's uncompleted history of the Great Rebellion only covers the first Civil War: *The King's War 1641–7* (1958). Incomparably the best of many one-volume histories is *The English Civil War 1642–51* by Peter Young and Richard Holmes (1974). *Sieges of the Great Civil War* by Young and Wilfred Pemberton (1978) is also valuable, as is P. R. Newman's *Atlas of the English Civil War* (1985), though unfortunately it does not show natural features.

There are biographies galore of the leading protagonists, none of them entirely conclusive. Pauline Gregg's biography of *Charles* I (1981) can be

---

* Unless otherwise stated all books mentioned here are or were published in London.

recommended with some reservations, and the same may be said of Antonia Fraser's *Cromwell: Our Chief of Men* (1973). The most complete study of Fairfax is *The Great Lord Fairfax* by Clements Markham (1870); and M. A. Gibb in *The Lord General* (1938) and John Wilson in *Fairfax* (1985) do not have a great deal to add. Vernon F. Snow's *Essex the Rebel* (Lincoln, Nebraska 1970) is comprehensive, but ponderous and not very perceptive. John Adair's much shorter study of Waller, *Roundhead General* (1969), gets much nearer its subject. Information on lesser figures can sometimes be found in *The Dictionary of National Biography* or *The Complete Peerage*, or in P. R. Newman's *Royalist Officers in England and Wales 1642–60: A Biographical Dictionary* (New York 1981).

Most of the major battles, certainly those of the first Civil War, have been covered in individual monographs of varying quality; the best are *Cheriton* by John Adair (1973) and *Marston Moor* by P. R. Newman (1981). Austin Woolrych's *Battles of the English Civil War* (1961) is full of sound common sense. Similarly there are many studies of the Civil Wars in individual counties; in fact it is difficult to think of a county which has been left out. To my mind the most valuable are Mary Coate, *Cornwall in the Great Civil War* (Oxford 1933), Alan Everitt, *The Community of Kent and the Great Rebellion* (Leicester 1966), and John Morrill, *Cheshire 1603–60* (Oxford 1974). Morrill's *Revolt of the Provinces* (1976) is a seminal book which amongst much else examines the effect of the wars on the provinces in general.

On Ireland the prime authority is now the *New History of Ireland*, vol. III: *Early Modern Ireland 1534–1691*, ed. T. W. Moody, F. X. Martin and F. J. Byrne (Oxford 1976). Scotland is covered by Maurice Lee in *The Road to Revolution: Scotland under Charles I 1625–37* (Chicago 1985), and by David Stevenson in *The Scottish Revolution 1637–44* (Newton Abbot 1973), *Revolution and Counter-Revolution in Scotland 1644–51* (1977) and *Scottish Covenanters and Irish Confederates* (Belfast 1981).

Strangely enough, the tactics used in the Civil Wars have never been properly assessed, and this applies across the board to what may be called the 'concrete' aspects of the war. For instance, the best account of Civil War fortifications and siegeworks is a paper presented to the Royal Corps of Engineers by Lieutenant-Colonel W. G. Ross in 1887, 'Military Engineering during the Great Civil War 1642–9' (*Professional Papers of the RCE*, vol. XIII, 1888; reprinted in book form, Ken Trotman 1984), though some further enlightenment is to be had from B. H. St J. O'Neill, *Castles and Cannon* (Oxford 1960), D. E. Lewis, 'The Use of Ordnance in the English Civil War 1642–9' (Manchester MA thesis, 1971), and Christopher Duffy, *Siege Warfare: The Fortress in Early Modern Europe 1494–1660* (1979).

C. H. Firth first considered the organisation of the war effort in his pioneering book *Cromwell's Army* (1901), but it is only recently that his work has been taken up again by a new generation of historians: notably Clive Holmes, *The*

*Eastern Association and the English Civil War* (Cambridge 1974), Ronald Hutton, *The Royalist War Effort 1642–6* (1982) and Joyce Lee Malcolm, *Caesar's Due: Loyalty and King Charles 1642–6* (1983). Ian Roy has also edited *The Royalist Ordnance Papers 1642–6* (2 vols, Oxfordshire Record Series, 1964, 1975), and D. E. Lewis investigates the other side of the question in 'The Parliamentary Board of Ordnance 1642–9' (Loughborough Ph.D. thesis, 1976). But apart from Dr Lewis's thesis there is precious little available on the logistics of the Civil Wars, only a couple of articles in the *Journal of the Arms and Armour Society*: Walter M. Stern, 'Gunmaking in Seventeenth-Century London', vol. I (1954), and Gerald Mungeam, 'Contracts for the Supply of Equipment to the New Model Army in 1645', vol. VI (1968). Other valuable research on the pay and organisation of the royalist armies is still buried in unpublished dissertations such as Ian Roy's 'The King's Army in the First Civil War' (Oxford D.Phil., 1963), P. R. Newman's 'The Royalist Armies North of the Trent 1642–6' (York Ph.D., 1978), and M. D. G. Wanklyn's 'The King's Army in the West 1642–6' (Manchester MA, 1966). However, there are three important articles in print: Ronald Hutton on 'The Structure of the Royalist Party', *Historical Journal*, 1981; P. R. Newman, 'The Royalist Officer Corps', *ibid.*, 1983; and Ian Roy on 'The Royalist Council of War 1642–6', *Bulletin of the Institute of Historical Research*, 1963.

Unfortunately there is little on the parliamentary armies apart from Holmes's *Eastern Association* and Firth's *Cromwell's Army*, already mentioned. Firth devoted much of the rest of his life to *The Regimental History of Cromwell's Army*, and it was completed and published after his death by Godfrey Davies (2 volumes, Oxford 1940); but he was hampered by his failure to find the original list of the line regiments and their officers, which has been published only recently by R. K. G. Temple, 'The Original Officer List of the New Model Army', *Bulletin of the Institute of Historical Research*, 1986. Mark Kishlansky's *The Rise of the New Model Army* (Cambridge 1979) is extremely valuable, but is focused mainly on the Army's politics 1646–8; it is now supplemented and corrected by Austin Woolrych, in *Soldiers and Statesmen: the General Council of the Army and its Debates 1647–8* (1987). There is very little on the Army in the 1650s, and here H. M. Reece's unpublished dissertation 'The Military Presence in England 1649–60' (Oxford D.Phil., 1982) is especially valuable. Otherwise there is only a short essay by Derek Massarella, 'The Politics of the Army and the Quest for a Settlement', in Ivan Roots (ed.), *Into Another Mould: Aspects of the Interregnum* (Exeter 1981).

The finances of the Protectorate are dealt with by Maurice Ashley in *Finance and Commercial Policy under the Cromwellian Protectorate* (Oxford 1934), but he would be the first to admit that this needs updating and expanding. As for the finances of the Long Parliament, virtually all we have is a short paper by D. H. Pennington, 'The Accounts of the Kingdom 1642–9', in *Essays in the Economic and Social History of Tudor and Stuart England*, ed. F. J. Fisher (Cambridge 1961). Documentary evidence for royalist finances is sketchy, but they are roughly assessed by Jens Engberg, 'Royalist Finances during the English Civil War 1642–6', *Scandinavian Economic History Review*, 1966. However, one topic which has been thoroughly explored is the financial implications of the crisis of 1647: by John Morrill in 'Mutiny and Discontent in the English Provincial Armies 1645–7', *Past and Present*, 1982, and 'The Army Revolt of 1647', in A. C. Duke and C. C. Tamse (eds), *Britain and the Netherlands VI*, (The Hague 1977); and by Ian Gentles, in 'The Arrears of Pay of the Parliamentary Army', *Bulletin of the Institute of Historical Research*, 1975, and 'Arrears of Pay and Ideology in the Army Revolt of 1647', in Brian Bond and Ian Roy (eds), *War and Society* (1975).

The more general economic effects of the wars have been little discussed, which is surprising in view of the intensive debate in recent years on the effects of the Thirty Years' War on Germany, but historians have now begun to examine this question; notably Ian Roy in 'England turned Germany?' *Transactions of the Royal Historical Society*, 1978, and Donald Pennington, 'The War and the People', in John Morrill (ed.), *Reactions to the English Civil War* (1982).

The best assessment of the Restoration in so far as it affected the royalists is Paul Hardacre, *The Royalists during the Puritan Revolution* (The Hague 1956), ch. 8. The taxation needed to disband the Army is described by C. D. Chandaman, *The English Public Revenue 1660–88* (Oxford 1975), and the establishment of the regular army by John Childs, *The Army of Charles II* (1976).

Finally, first-hand accounts. The most celebrated is Clarendon's *History of the Rebellion and Civil Wars* (best edition by W. D. Macray, 6 volumes, Oxford 1888). On the other side we have the *Historical Collections* of Fairfax's secretary, John Rushworth (7 volumes, 1659–1701), and *Anglia Rediviva* by his chaplain, Joshua Sprigge (1647) (reprinted in facsimile, Ken Trotman 1984). Carlyle's edition of *Oliver Cromwell's Letters and Speeches* (re-edited by S. C. Lomas, 3 volumes, 1904) is unfailingly interesting, and is to be preferred to most biographies. (The definitive collection is *Writings and Speeches of Oliver Cromwell*, ed. W. C. Abbott (4 volumes, Cambridge, Mass. 1937–47), but for ordinary use Carlyle is sufficient.) Many despatches from other commanders, and the papers of the Committee for Both Kingdoms, are printed in the *Calendars of State Papers Domestic* for the relevant years, which also contain such gems as the letters home of one of Essex's soldiers, Nehemiah Wharton, on the Edgehill campaign, and the statements and counter-statements drawn up by the quarrelling generals in the winter of 1644–5. Other military despatches were published in the *Commons Journals*.

In addition there is an abundance of personal reminiscences, letters, diaries and accounts of individual actions, such as Sir Hugh Cholmley's vivid narrative of the siege of Scarborough 1644–5 in *English Historical Review*, 1917, or the anonymous contemporary *Journal of the Siege of Lathom House* (published 1823), and this list could be extended almost indefinitely. For a view of the fortunes of one royalist family in the wars, the soldiers and those they left behind, *The Memoirs of the Verney Family*, ed. Frances Verney, vols 1–2 (1892), are invaluable. Lucy Hutchinson's famous *Memoirs of the Life of Colonel Hutchinson* (best edition by James Sutherland, Oxford 1973) is written from the other side of the fence.

# DRAMATIS PERSONAE

People whose careers are adequately covered in the text are excluded, as are those of minor importance, mentioned only once or twice.

ASTLEY, Jacob, Baron (1579–1652). After a distinguished military career in Flanders and Germany returned as governor of Plymouth, 1638. Major-General of Foot in the Bishops' Wars 1639–40, continuing into the Civil Wars. Fought at Edgehill and First and Second Newbury, after which last he was raised to the peerage. Commanded the royalist foot at Naseby, and surrendered the last organised royalist forces at Stow-on-the-Wold, March 1646. Thereafter lived in retirement.

ASTON, Sir Arthur (1590–1649). Born of a Catholic family in Cheshire; fought with distinction in the Russian army 1613–18, the Polish army 1618–31 and the Swedish 1631–40. Fought in the Scots campaign 1640; gazetted major-general and knighted 1641. Colonel-General of Dragoons in the royal army 1642–3, but because of his religion transferred to the governorship of Reading, then Oxford. Lost a leg in a riding accident 1644 and invalided out, but joined Ormonde in Ireland 1646 and was killed at the siege of Drogheda, 1649.

BRERETON, Sir William (1604–61). Of Handforth, Cheshire. Baronet 1627. One of the leaders of Cheshire society, who emerged 1642–3 as one of Parliament's best provincial commanders. With Fairfax he defeated Byron (q.v.) at Nantwich, January 1644, and frustrated Rupert's attempt to relieve Chester that August. Continued to police the Midlands, and took Astley's surrender at Stow-on-the-Wold March 1646. But apparently took no part in public life thereafter.

BROOKE, Robert Greville, 2nd Baron (1608–43). An extreme Puritan and one of the most committed parliamentarian peers. Refused to join the Scots campaign 1639, temporarily imprisoned 1640. As Lord Lieutenant of Warwick and Stafford fought one of the first engagements of the Civil Wars, against Lord Northampton at Kineton, August 1642. Appointed Commander of the Midlands Association, but killed at the siege of Lichfield, March 1643.

BUCKINGHAM, George Villiers, 1st Duke of (1592–1628). Prime favourite of James I and Charles I, Lord High Admiral 1619–28. His maladroit foreign policy, his unsuccessful prosecution of the war against Spain and France and his monopoly of royal favour and patronage were predominant factors in the breach between Charles I and Parliament 1625–8, and led to his assassination.

BUCKINGHAM, George Villiers, 2nd Duke of (1628–87). Raised with the future Charles II, who remained a close personal friend, with occasional interruptions, until 1674. Fought under Rupert at Lichfield 1643, then sent abroad on the Grand Tour. Returned 1648 with the Earl of Holland (q.v.), and after the failure of their rising escaped abroad. With Charles II in Scotland 1650, and at Worcester 1651, and again escaped. Quarrelled with the King and returned secretly to England 1657 determined to regain his estates, which had been granted to Fairfax. Wooed and won Mary Fairfax, and more surprisingly her father; when Cromwell threw him in the Tower it provoked a violent quarrel between him and Fairfax. Released into Fairfax's custody 1659, regained his estates 1660 and appointed Master of the Horse, etc. Thereafter led a life of increasing dissipation and irresponsibility and died a ruined man. Satirised as 'Zimri' in Dryden's *Absalom and Achitophel*.

BYRON, Sir John (1599–1652). Born of a wealthy family with estates in Lancashire and Nottinghamshire. Eldest of seven brothers, all of whom fought for the King. Knighted 1625, MP for Nottingham 1624, 1628. Served in Low Countries 1630s, and in the Scots campaign 1640. Briefly governor of the Tower 1641–2. Fought at Edgehill and First Newbury, then raised to peerage (1st Baron Byron) and appointed Commander-in-Chief Lancashire and Cheshire. Mismanaged and lost his army at Nantwich (January 1644) and was appointed governor of Chester. Served at Marston Moor, where his indiscipline was a prime factor in Rupert's defeat. Surrendered Chester (February 1646) and Caernarvon (May), after long sieges. Returned from exile 1648 to raise North Wales, without success. The title passed on his death to his brother Richard, governor of Newark 1643–5. (Ancestor of the famous poet, the 6th Lord Byron.)

CASTLEHAVEN, James Touchet, 3rd Earl of (1617–84). Born of an Old English Catholic family in Ireland. Father, 2nd Earl, executed 1631 for sodomy. Suspected, almost certainly wrongly, of complicity in Irish Rebellion of 1641 and indicted for treason. Willy-nilly became a leading Confederate commander until 1646, when he declared in favour of the 'Ormonde Peace' and compromise with Parliament. Retired to France, but returned in 1648 with Ormonde, who handed over to him the Lieutenant-Generalship in December 1650. Unable to rally Irish resistance, he finally retired to France in 1652, where he took part in the War of the Fronde, then commanded the Irish regiments in the Spanish Army of Flanders 1653–8. Was unable to regain all his Irish estates in 1660, but received various grants and pensions from the Crown. Fought briefly in the Anglo-Dutch War 1665–7, and re-entered the Spanish service in Flanders 1674–8.

CLANRICARDE, Ulick Bourke, 5th Earl of (1604–57). Succeeded to title 1635. Wealthy 'Old English' Catholic landowner; married the 3rd Earl of Essex's widowed mother. Served in Scots campaigns 1639–40, but stayed neutral in the Irish Rebellion, 1641. Ormonde appointed him Commander-in-Chief Connaught in 1644; created Marquess 1645. Held Galway and Connaught for the King into 1650. Ormonde appointed him Lord Deputy when he retired in December 1650, but he was forced to surrender two years later.

CRAWFORD, Lawrence (1611–45). Born at Jordanhill, Glasgow. Served from an early age in the armies of Christian IV of Denmark, Gustavus Adolphus of Sweden and Charles Lewis, Elector Palatine. From 1641 served as infantry colonel in Ireland, but refused to serve the King in England on the Cessation of 1643, and escaped to Scotland, then England, where he charmed Parliament by a recital of his sufferings. Appointed major-general of foot and second-in-command of the Eastern Association; quarrelled bitterly with Cromwell after Marston Moor and again after Second Newbury. Mustered out in 1645, he joined the Army of the Western Association, and was killed at the siege of Hereford later that year.

DERBY, James Stanley, 7th Earl of (1607–51) (Baron Strange until his father's death September 1642). Enormously wealthy Lancashire landowner and hereditary lord of the Isle of Man. Fought in the Scots campaigns 1639–40; tried unsuccessfully to take Manchester in 1642, but was ultimately driven out of his own county. Spent much time holed up on Man, the siege of his seat at Lathom being mainly sustained by his French wife, whom he had married 1626. Fought at Marston Moor, then retired with his wife to Man until 1651, when he tried to raise Lancashire and Cheshire for Charles II, without success. Fought at Worcester, after which he was captured, tried by court martial, and executed at Bolton, 15 October 1651.

DIGBY, George, Baron (1612–77). Eldest son of John, 1st Earl of Bristol. Active royalist in Long Parliament and summoned to House of Lords May 1641. Impeached in January 1642 for an attempt on the arsenal at Kingston-on-Thames with Lunsford (q.v.), fled to Holland, but returned to join the King at York. Took a cavalry regiment and fought at Edgehill and Lichfield, but quarrelled with Rupert and returned to Court. Appointed Secretary of State on Falkland's (q.v.) death at First Newbury and was regarded as Charles I's evil genius. Commanded the Northern horse 1645, and after fleeing to Dublin retired to France. Gazetted Lieutenant-General French Army 1651 and Commander-in-Chief Normandy. Succeeded as 2nd Earl of Bristol 1653, but cashiered for complicity in a plot against Cardinal Mazarin and joined the Spanish Army of Flanders. Charles II appointed him Secretary of State in 1657, but dismissed him when he found he had turned Catholic. After the Restoration he resumed his old rivalry with Sir Edward Hyde (q.v.), now Earl of Clarendon, but took little part in politics after 1663.

FALKLAND, Lucius Cary, 2nd Viscount (1610–43). One of the most highly regarded young men of his generation, who presided over a renowned intellectual and literary coterie at his mansion at Great Tew, Oxford, in the late 1630s. Like his friend Hyde (q.v.) he was a late convert to royalism in the autumn of 1641, but was appointed Secretary of State in January 1642. Fought at Edgehill, but fell a prey to serious depression, and his death at First Newbury in 1643 smacks of suicide.

FIENNES, Nathaniel (1608–69). Younger son of Saye and Sele (q.v.). MP for Banbury and prominent opposition leader in Long Parliament. Fought at Edgehill, but was disgraced for his surrender of Bristol in 1643, and never entirely rehabilitated. Excluded in Pride's Purge, 1648, but favoured by Cromwell, under whose Protectorate he was appointed to the Council of State and made a Commissioner of the Great Seal. Took no part in politics after 1658.

GELL, Sir John, of Hopton, Derbyshire (1593–1671). Baronet January 1642, but organised the Derbyshire County Committee and in January 1643 was made governor of Derby. Held Derbyshire throughout the war and sustained Leicestershire and Nottinghamshire with local forces notorious for plundering. He himself was suspected of blatant self-serving, and even of planning to join the King just before Naseby, and fell out of favour. In 1650 found guilty of plotting against the Commonwealth, but released in 1652. Took no further part in public life.

GOMME, Sir Bernard de (1620–85). Dutch military engineer, born in Lille. Trained in the Dutch army but came to England with Rupert in 1642 and was knighted. As royalist Engineer-in-Chief he designed most of the new fortifications erected at Oxford, Liverpool, Newark, etc. Returned in 1660 as Surveyor-General of Fortifications; 1661, Engineer-in-Chief to the Crown; 1682, Surveyor-General of Ordnance. Built new fortifications throughout the three kingdoms. Buried in the chapel of the Tower.

GORING, George, Baron (1608–57). Eldest son of 1st Earl of Norwich. Married in 1629 Lettice, daughter of millionaire Irish land speculator Richard Boyle, Earl of Cork, who in 1632 purchased for him command of the Earl of Oxford's foot regiment in the Dutch army. Severely wounded at Breda in 1637, and left semi-disabled. Governor of Portsmouth 1638–9; commanded a regiment in the first Scots War, 1639, and a brigade in the second, 1640. MP for Portsmouth 1640–2. Betrayed First Army Plot to Parliament 1641, and by them reappointed governor of Portsmouth. Declared for the King in August 1642, surrendered Portsmouth to Waller in September, and went to Holland. Returned in December to command the horse in the Army of the North; captured at Wakefield May 1643; exchanged for Earl of Lothian March 1644. Returned to Northern army, fought at Marston Moor, then came south and was appointed Lieutenant-General of Horse in the King's army, August 1644, displacing Wilmot (q.v.). Insisted on being appointed Commander-in-Chief West, May 1645, but defeated at Langport in July, and in November retired to France, pleading illness. Appointed Colonel-General of the English contingent in the Spanish Army of Flanders, 1646; took up a similar command in Spain, 1650, and distinguished himself at the siege of Barcelona, 1652. Died at Madrid ill, destitute and almost certainly a Catholic convert.

HAMILTON, James, 1st Duke of (1606–49). Succeeded as 3rd Marquess 1625. Master of the Horse 1628, and close confidant of the King, but in 1638–43 found himself 'squeezed' between Charles and the Covenanters. Fell out with the King, but refused the Covenant 1643 and returned to Oxford. Imprisoned by the royalists until 1646, when Fairfax released him from St Michael's Mount. Nevertheless, led the invasion of England in 1648 on Charles's behalf, was defeated at Preston and executed in 1649.

HAMILTON, William, 2nd Duke, 4th Marquess of (1616–51). Brother to 1st Duke, and until 1649 styled Earl of Lanark. Arrested with 1st Duke 1643, escaped 1644, reconciled with Charles I 1646. Negotiated the Engagement of 1647 with Charles at Carisbrooke. Did not join the invasion of 1648, and fled to Holland 1649. Returned with Charles II 1650, but mistrusted by the Scots government. Joined the Worcester campaign in 1651 as a Colonel of Horse and died of wounds.

HAMPDEN, John (1594–1643). Wealthy Buckinghamshire landowner, MP for county in Long Parliament. Famed for his refusal to pay ship money in 1635, leading to the famous case Rex v. Hampden 1637–8. One of the most respected, even revered, of the parliamentary leaders. Raised a troop of horse and fought at Edgehill; his death at Chalgrove Field in 1643 was a severe blow to the cause of moderation.

HASELRIGG (or Hesilrige), Sir Arthur, baronet (d. 1661). Brother-in-law to Lord Brooke (q.v.) and like him an extreme Puritan and parliamentarian. MP for Leicestershire. Raised regiment of cuirassiers at own expense, fought at Edgehill, and from 1643 to 1645 was Waller's second-in-command. After 1645 transferred his loyalties to Cromwell, whom he followed on his two Scots campaigns, 1648 and 1650. But broke with Cromwell when he dispersed the Long Parliament 1653, remaining a dedicated and active republican. Imprisoned 1660, died the following year in the Tower.

HERTFORD, William Seymour, 2nd Earl of (1588–1660). Distinguished for his love affair with Arabella Stuart and their clandestine marriage in 1610, which was at once severed by James I, both having a (remote) claim to the throne. Fled to the Continent, but made his peace and returned 1616 to marry Frances, sister to 3rd Earl of Essex. Staunch royalist, created Marquess 1640, Privy Councillor 1641, and governor to Prince of Wales. Met with disaster as Commander-in-Chief West Country 1642, but accompanied Hopton and his Western army on the campaign of 1643, though apparently not in command. Recalled to Court 1644 as Groom of the Stole. Attended Charles I in his imprisonment and was one of the royalist Commissioners at Newport, 1648. Retired on King's death, but was made KG and had the dukedom of Somerset revived in his favour, 1660.

HOLLAND, Henry Rich, 1st Earl of (1590–1649). Younger brother of Earl of Warwick (q.v.). Favourite of James I, Buckingham and Charles I, and an adroit courtier; created Baron Kensington 1623, Earl of Holland 1624, for no obvious reason. In the 1630s he secured great influence over the Queen, and was appointed Groom of the Stole 1636 and Lieutenant-General of Horse in 1649, superseding Essex. Nevertheless, declined to join the King at York in 1642, and was appointed to the Committee of Safety; but went over to the 'Peace Party' in Parliament and joined the King at Oxford in 1643, in time to distinguish himself at the siege of Gloucester and First Newbury. However, the Queen's hostility frustrated his ambitions on high office at Court, and he returned to London in 1644 under the aegis of the Earl of Essex; but he was barred from the House of Lords, and treated with arctic coldness. Went into exile, and returned to lead a royalist insurrection in the Home Counties in 1648; captured at St Neots, he was condemned and executed, despite the intervention of his brother Warwick and Fairfax.

HOTHAM, Sir John, baronet, of Scorborough, East Riding (d. 1645). Served in Germany *c.* 1618–24 under the Elector Palatine, then Count Mansfeld. Ally of Strafford as Lord President of the North, but dismissed governorship of Hull 1639, and went into opposition. MP for Beverley continuously 1625–43. Restored to Hull by Parliament 1642 and held it against two personal approaches by the King. But entered into negotiations with the royalist commander Newcastle in June 1643, was arrested and brought to London. Tried by court martial (presided over by Waller) December 1644, executed January 1645. His eldest son, also John Hotham, was executed with him.

HYDE, Sir Edward, 1st Earl of Clarendon (1599–1674). Professional lawyer, member of the Great Tew circle (see 'Falkland'). Member for Saltash in Long Parliament and prominent opposition spokesman until autumn 1641, when he went over to the King, becoming his chief speechwriter and constitutional adviser. Privy Councillor 1642, Chancellor of the Exchequer 1643. Accompanied the Prince of Wales to the West in 1645, and in 1646 to Jersey. Opposed Charles's removal to France and subsequently his expedition to Scotland 1650, but after 1651 became one of his leading advisers and the architect of the Restoration. Lord Chancellor 1658, Earl of Clarendon 1661. Impeached in 1667, he went into exile where he completed his classic *History of the Rebellion*, not published until 1702. He died in France.

INCHIQUIN, Murrough O'Brien, 6th Baron, 1st Earl of (1614–74). Apart from Ormonde (q.v.) the leading Protestant peer amongst the Old English in Ireland. Served in the Spanish Army of Italy 1636–9; Vice-President of Munster 1640, President 1641. Held Cork and the south-west against the rebel Confederates with a mixture of ruthlessness and duplicity until the Cessation of 1643, when his army was shipped to England. Charles I refused to confirm him as President of Munster 1644 (against Ormonde's advice) and he went over to Parliament. Consolidated his hold on the south-west in a series of anti-Catholic atrocities, and decisively defeated the Confederates at Knocknannus in November 1647. Declared for the King again in 1648 and embraced the 'Ormonde Peace', and in 1649 conquered much of Ulster, but through the machinations of Cromwell his own province, Munster, rose against him, and he went into exile with Ormonde in 1650. Found favour with Charles II, who gave him an earldom 1654, and fought in the French army in Italy and Catalonia 1654–5, when he was converted to Rome. On his way to Lisbon 1660 captured by Algerine corsairs, ransomed 1661. Recovered his estates, but not his influence in Munster; High Steward to dowager Queen Henrietta Maria, and commander of the English expeditionary force to Portugal 1663.

LAMBERT, John (1619–83). Born of obscure Yorkshire gentry family. Served under the Fairfaxes in Yorkshire from 1642; colonel 1643, and distinguished himself at Nantwich, January 1643; second-in-command of the Yorkshire horse at Marston Moor. Left in command of the Northern Association army when both Fairfaxes left in 1645, but was defeated by Langdale at Wentbridge and superseded by Sydenham Poyntz (q.v.). Joined New Model Army, fought in Western campaign 1645–6, and won the confidence of Cromwell, which was enhanced by his conduct in the Preston campaign of 1648 and the Scots campaign of 1650, when he shared the credit for the victory at Dunbar. Became Cromwell's *alter ego* and the most powerful man in the Army and the State; framed the Instrument of Government 1653. Fell out with Cromwell 1657, when it became apparent that he would not name him as his successor, and resigned. Reappeared as one of the chief Army spokesmen in the confusion of 1659–60, but ended up in the Tower. Exempted from pardon in 1660 and imprisoned until his death in 1683.

LESLIE, David (d. 1682). Scotsman of obscure origin. Served under Gustavus Adolphus in the 1630s; wounded in 1640 and returned home. Second in command to Alexander Leslie, Earl of Leven (no relation), 1644–5. Recalled from England in 1645 to face Montrose and defeated him at Philiphaugh. Commanded the post-war Scots army, but was exonerated from blame for Dunbar; effectively commanded the royal army on the Worcester campaign 1651, when he was captured, and imprisoned in the Tower until 1660. Raised to the peerage as Baron Newark 1661 and pensioned. Took no further part in public life.

LUCAS, Sir Charles (1613–48). Younger son of Sir Thomas Lucas of Colchester. His sister Margaret married the Earl of Newcastle (q.v.). Served as cavalry officer in Flanders in 1630s, and in the Scots campaigns 1639–40; knighted 1639. Served under Rupert 1642–3 and recommended by him to brother-in-law Newcastle. Fought with distinction at Marston Moor 1644, but was wounded and captured. Exchanged in 1645 and appointed governor of Berkeley Castle, then Lieutenant-General of Horse. Captured with Astley (q.v.) at Stow-on-the-Wold 1646; released on parole. Led the Essex rebellion 1648, and was shot by Fairfax after the siege of Colchester for breaking his parole. His two brothers, Sir Thomas and John (created Baron Lucas 1645) were also prominent royalist officers.

LUNSFORD, Sir Thomas (1611–43). Born of a Sussex gentry family. Indicted for attempted murder of Sir Thomas Pelham 1633; escaped from Newgate 1634 and joined the French army; outlawed 1637, but pardoned 1639, when he fought in the Scots campaign, and again in 1640. Briefly governor of the Tower (22–6 December 1641); knighted 28 December. Fought under Hertford (q.v.) 1642, captured at Edgehill and imprisoned at Warwick until May 1644. Fought in the Marches area thereafter and was captured again at Hereford,

December 1645. Released 1648 and emigrated to Virginia 1649, where he died 1653. His two brothers, Herbert and Henry, were also royalist officers, the latter being killed at the siege of Bristol in 1643.

MANCHESTER, Edward Montagu, 2nd Earl of (1602–71). Born of a wealthy Huntingdonshire family. Intimate of Prince Charles, whom he accompanied to Madrid 1623. Created Baron Montagu of Kimbolton 1626, but took courtesy title Viscount Mandeville when his father was made an Earl the same year. Through his father-in-law Warwick (q.v.) he was drawn into opposition, and he was impeached with the Five Members 1642. Raised a regiment in August 1642 and served under Essex; appointed Commander of the Eastern Association army 1643. After the Self-Denying Ordinance continued an active political role up to 1649, but refused to take the Engagement to the Republic and was deprived of all his offices in 1650. In 1660 reappointed Chancellor of Cambridge University and Lord Lieutenant of Huntingdonshire and Northamptonshire; appointed a Commissioner of the Great Seal and Lord Chamberlain. Carried the sword of state at Charles II's coronation and dubbed KG.

MELDRUM, Sir John (d. 1645). Of obscure Scots origin; served in the Irish army c. 1610–13, and the Low Countries 1613–22. Knighted in 1622 by James I, who liked him. Received a lucrative patent for lighthouses which was sharply questioned in Parliament. In 1642 wrote an open letter explaining why he was abandoning Charles I despite thirty-six years' service to him and his father, and thereafter was used by Parliament as a military trouble-shooter. Killed before Scarborough, May 1645.

MONRO, Robert (d. c. 1680). Of the Monros of Foulis, County Ross. Fought in the Swedish army in the 1630s with his uncle Robert, the 'Black Baron', and his nephew, Sir George. Returned 1639 to join the Army of the Covenant, and was appointed Commander in Ulster 1642, where he met with mixed success. Arrested by Monck 1648 and imprisoned in the Tower until 1654, when he was released and allowed to live quietly on the estates of his wife, Lady Jane Alexander.

NEWCASTLE, William Cavendish, 1st Earl, Marquess, Duke of (1592–1676). Son of millionaire Sir Charles Cavendish of Welbeck. Created Viscount Mansfield 1620, Earl of Newcastle 1628. Served in the Scots campaigns 1639–40; raised his own army in the North 1642–3. Went into exile after Marston Moor, first to Hamburg 1644–5, then Paris 1645–8, Antwerp 1648–60. Returned 1660; never regained all his estates, or much of the estimated £1 million he had spent in the royal cause, but created Duke 1665. Lived in retirement until his death.

O'NEILL, Owen Roe (1590–1649). Nephew of Hugh O'Neill, Earl of Tyrone (1540–1616), whose flight abroad in 1607 precipitated the plantation of Ulster. Owen succeeded to his uncle's claim to be High Chief of Ulster, even King of Ireland, but spent most of his life in the Spanish army, achieving particular distinction at the siege of Arras in 1630. Returned in 1642 to serve as principal general of the Irish Confederates.

ORMONDE, James Butler, 12th Earl, 1st Duke of (1610–88). Born to one of the greatest of the Old English families in Ireland; made a ward of the Crown 1619 and raised a Protestant. Returned to Ireland 1633, colonel in the Irish army 1639–41. Served as the King's Lieutenant-General in Ireland 1642–7, then Parliament's 1647–8. Created Marquess 1642. Left Ireland 1650, and joined Charles II, becoming one of his principal advisers and a close ally of Edward Hyde (q.v.). Restored to his estates 1661 and created Duke; Lord Steward 1660–88, Lord Lieutenant in Ireland 1661–9, 1677–84.

POYNTZ, Sydenham (b. c. 1608). Born of obscure minor gentry at Reigate, Surrey. Apprenticed to a London tradesman, but ran away to join the Dutch army, then the Imperial army, where he rose to the rank of Major-General and was knighted. Returned 1645, appointed Commander of the Northern Association (May), governor of York (August); took part in the battle of Rowton Heath (September), and joined Scots in siege of Newark 1646. But could not control his mutinous troops 1647, who arrested him and sent him down to Fairfax in July. Retired to Holland and went with Lord Willoughby to the West Indies, where he was made governor of the Leeward Isles. When Ayscue arrived to reconquer the West Indian colonies 1651 he proceeded to Virginia, where he died, date unknown.

SAYE AND SELE, William Fiennes, 1st Viscount (1582–1662). Succeeded as 8th Baron 1613, created Viscount 1624, but from 1625 one of the strongest opponents of Charles I; nicknamed 'Old Subtlety'. One of the most determined and active leaders of the Lords, he remained a staunch Presbyterian, and desperately pushed the Newport Treaty 1648. Retired from public life 1649–60, spending much of that time on Lundy Island, which he owned. Privy Councillor 1660, and in moderately good standing.

VERNEY, Sir Edmund (1590–1642). Second son of Sir Edmund Verney of Claydon, Buckinghamshire. Knighted 1611; favourite of Henry Prince of Wales, the eldest son of James I, and like many in his circle never recovered from Henry's premature death in 1612. Accompanied Buckingham and Prince Charles to Madrid 1623; Knight-Marshal to Charles I 1626. Disapproved of Charles's policy thereafter, but of unwavering loyalty. Appointed royal standard-bearer at Nottingham, August 1642, but killed in October at

Edgehill. (His body was never found, only his severed hand, still grasping the broken shaft of the standard.)

WARWICK, Robert Rich, 2nd Earl of (1587–1658). Active colonial entrepreneur and sailor in the Drake–Raleigh tradition; also a noted Puritan and a strong opponent of Charles I in the 1630s. Appointed Admiral of the Fleet by Parliament 1642, Lord Admiral 1643. Resigned 1645 because of Self-Denying Ordinance, but chaired the Admiralty Commission of twelve which replaced him. On the fleet mutiny, May 1648, he was reappointed Admiral of the Fleet; dismissed later that year, and refused to recognise the Commonwealth. However, he was an ardent supporter of Cromwell, whose daughter Frances married his grandson and heir.

WILMOT, Henry (1612–58). Younger son of 1st Viscount Wilmot (d. 1644) of Irish family. Served in the Dutch army 1635–40, then Commissary-General of the royal army; captured at Newburn 1640. Expelled from the Commons December 1641 for complicity in the Second Army Plot; Commissary-General 1642–3; Lieutenant-General, April 1643; created Baron Wilmot, June 1643. Distinguished himself at Roundway Down and Cropredy Bridge, but was disgraced August 1644, and went abroad. Found favour with Charles II, went to Scotland 1650 and fought at Worcester 1651. After Worcester went on the run with Charles for six weeks before they regained the Continent; became one of his closest friends and his trusted secret agent in England. Created Earl of Rochester 1652; died at Sluys.

# INDEX

Persons whose names are printed in **bold** also feature in the Dramatis Personae, beginning on p. 252. *Italics* denote a battle or skirmish.

Aberdeen, 135, 149, 211, 219
*Adwalton Moor*, 78–9
'Agreement of the People', 172–3, 174
Aldbourne Chase, 95
*Alford*, 149
*Alton*, 87
*Ancaster Heath*, 75
Argyll, Archibald Campbell, 8th Earl, 1st Marquess of, 4, 19, 22, 135, 178, 191, 209–11, 215, 217
Arlington, Henry Bennett, 1st Earl of, 232
Armour, 53, 55
Artillery, 51, 56, 86
Arundel Castle, 62, 87
Assessment, 115, 161, 170, 202, 212, 223–4, 229, 242
**Astley,** Sir Jacob (later Lord), 16, 19, 34, 53, 57, 65, 155–6
**Aston,** Sir Arthur, 35, 205, 206

*Auldearn*, 40, 141
Ayscue, Admiral Sir George, 220

Baillie, Sir William, 109, 135, 149, 186, 189–91
Balfour, Sir William, 21, 26, 45, 49, 57, 113, 117, 118, 121
Barkstead, Colonel John, 231
Barnstaple, 69, 80
Basing House, 85–6, 117, 118, 121, 153, 185
Bath, 69–70
Battern, Sir William, 182, 183
Bedford, William Russell, 5th Earl of, 49, 52
Beeston, Lady, 101
Behre, Hans, 49, 113, 114, 143*n*
Belasyse, John, Lord, 37, 57, 79, 92, 95, 156, 179
*Benburb*, 163, 203

Berwick, Pacification of, 17
Bethel, Christopher, 148
Bethel, Slingsby, 237
Bideford, 69, 80
Birch, Sir Thomas, 47
Birmingham, 66
Bishops' Wars, 16–19
Blake, Robert, 94
Blakiston, Sir William, 108
Bolton, 101, 219
Booth, Sir George, 226, 234
Boscobel, 219
Bourke, John, 26
*Braddock Down*, 68
Bradshaw, John, 196, 231
Breda, siege of (1625), 11, 44; (1637), 35, 43
Breda, Declaration of, 223
*Breitenfeld*, 14
Brentford, 59
**Brereton,** Sir William, 46, 92, 155
Bridgnorth, 102
Bridgwater, 138, 148, 149
Bristol, 79–80, 97, 125, 137, 149, 150–1, 154, 202
Bristol, John Digby, 1st Earl of, 9, 11, 25
Broghill, Roger Boyle, Lord, 208, 209
**Brooke,** Robert Greville, 2nd Lord, 34, 41, 48, 59, 66, 67
Brown, Sir John, 49, 152
Browne, Richard, 96, 99, 100, 102, 113, 122, 234
**Buckingham,** George Villiers, 1st Duke of, 8, 9, 12, 32, 44, 185
**Buckingham,** George Villiers, 2nd Duke of, 162, 179, 184, 185, 211, 216, 234–5
Burford, 201
Burke, Edmund, 236
Burnet, Gilbert, 239
**Byron,** Sir John (later Lord), 26, 27, 28, 37, 49, 51, 57, 71–3, 82–3, 90, 92, 105, 151, 188, 189

Cadiz expedition (1625), 8, 9, 32, 43
Caernarvon, Robert Dormer, 1st Earl of, 83
Callander, James Livingstone, 1st Earl of, 186, 187, 188, 191
Capel, Arthur, 1st Lord, 184, 192, 200, 234
Carisbrooke Castle, 175, 198
Carlisle, 110, 141, 147, 154, 156, 178, 194
Carlisle Sands, 152–3
Carlyle, Thomas, 208*n*, 245
Carnwath, Robert Dalyell, 2nd Earl of, 145
**Castlehaven,** James Touchet, 3rd Earl of, 207
Castles, 3, 85–6, 101–2
Catherine of Braganza, 241
Cavalry tactics, 55–6
Cavendish, Charles, 75, 78, 80
*Chalgrove Field*, 67
Charles II as Prince of Wales, 125, 137, 154, 178, 180, 183, 192, 197; as King, 15, 112, 209–11, 212–13, 215–19, 228–9, 232 ff., 238, 240 ff.
Charles Lewis, Elector Palatine, 14, 35, 113
Chelmsford, 184, 185
*Cheriton*, 94, 95, 124
Chester, 151, 155
Chomley, Sir Hugh, 40
Cirencester, 65, 82, 84, 125
Clanricarde, Richard Bourke, 4th Earl of, 32
**Clanricarde,** Ulick Bourke, 5th Earl of, 24, 91, 220, 221
Clare, John Holles, 2nd Earl of, 38
Clarendon, Earl of *see* Hyde, Edward
Clavering, Sir William, 110

Clogher, Heber MacMahon, Bishop of, 209

Clubmen, the, 130, 147–8, 149

Cockburnspath, 214

Colchester, siege of, 184, 185–6, 192, 193

Committee for Both Kingdoms, 97–8, 182

Conway, Edward, 2nd Viscount, 19

Conyers, Sir John, 28

Cooper, Anthony Ashley Cooper, 1st Earl of Shaftesbury, 239, 244

Coote, Sir Charles, Sr., 25

Coote, Sir Charles, Jr., 203, 209, 220

Corbisdale, 40, 210

Corkbush Field, 174, 202

Corstorphine, 214

Covenant, the Scottish National, 15

Covenant, the Solemn League and, 91, 114, 131, 159, 177, 209

Crawford, Ludovic Lindsay, 16th Earl of, 87

**Crawford,** Lawrence, 46, 108, 113–14, 119, 139

Cromwell, Henry, 225, 232

Cromwell, Oliver, 1, 3, 14, 27, 36, 41, 42, 46, 48, 61, 75–7, 80, 84, 104, 105–8, 109, 113, 114, 116, 117, 118–19, 121, 123, 124, 128, 131, 133–5, 138, 140, 141, 142–6, 149, 153, 157, 162, 164, 166, 171, 172, 173, 175, 177, 179, 180, 181, 182, 187–92, 194, 195, 196, 198, 201, 202, 205–9, 211–19, 220–1, 222 ff., 225, 230, 231, 237, 245

Cromwell, Richard 225, 232

*Cropredy Bridge*, 99–100, 112

Dalbier, Jan, 153, 185

Denbigh, Basil Fielding, 2nd Earl of, 41, 67

**Derby,** James Stanley, 7th Earl of (formerly Lord Strange), 34, 52, 101, 217, 219

Derby, Charles Stanley, 8th Earl of, 233–4

Derby, Charlotte, Countess of, 101–2

Desborough, John, 148, 226, 232

Devizes, 3, 71–2, 129

**Digby,** George, Lord, 25, 28, 35, 51, 63, 98, 112, 117, 137, 150, 151, 153, 155, 211, 233

Dillon, Lord Robert, 36

*Drogheda*, 39, 205, 206

Donnington Castle, 118, 119, 153

Druske, Jones van, 99, 152, 216$n$

*Dunbar*, 213, 214

Dundee, 211, 217

Dunfermline, 211

*Dungan's Hill*, 164, 203

Eastern Association, the, 42, 46, 65, 75–6, 99, 113–14, 115–16, 132

*Edgehill*, 36, 39, 48, 53 ff., 62, 77, 78, 124, 228

Eglington, Alexander Montgomery, 6th Earl of, 108, 191

Elizabeth I, 7, 23

Elizabeth of Bohemia, 8, 9, 11, 14, 43

Elizabeth, Princess, 197

'Engagement', the, 176, 177

Essex, Robert Devereux, 3rd Earl of, 16, 26, 27, 30, 31–3, 39, 43, 48, 49–59, *passim*, 60, 62, 67–8, 73, 78, 81–5, 87, 93, 96–8, 102, 110, 111–13, 117, 118, 124, 128, 132, 157, 167, 231

Evelyn, John, 228–9

Excise, 115, 242

Exeter, 69, 154

Eythin, Lord, *see* King, James

Fairfax, Thomas, 1st Lord, of Cameron, 44

Fairfax, Ferdinando, 2nd Lord, 44, 52, 74, 79, 95–6, 103, 104, 108, 132

Fairfax, Thomas, 3rd Lord, 3, 31, 36, 44, 52, 74–5, 78–9, 84, 86, 92, 93, 95–6, 101, 103, 104, 108, 109, 125, 128, 131, 132, 133, 136, 138, 141, 142–6, 147–9, 150–1, 153–4, 156, 157, 159, 162, 164, 166, 168 ff., 177, 179–80, 182–4, 185, 192–3, 193–6, 201, 202, 211–12, 213n, 227, 234–5

Falkland, 211

Falkland, Henry Cary, 1st Viscount, 24

**Falkland,** Lucius Cary, 2nd Viscount, 34, 35, 36, 46, 61, 83

Farnham Castle, 62, 87, 112, 134, 138

Feilding, Basil, Lord (later Earl of Denbigh qv.), 57

*Ferrybridge*, 136–7, 152

Fielding, Colonel Richard, 67

**Fiennes,** Nathaniel, 79–80, 150, 151

Firth, Sir Charles, 2, 4

Fleetwood, Charles, 27, 212, 214, 217, 218, 225, 226, 227, 232

Forth, Patrick Ruthven, Earl of, 44, 53, 94, 95, 99, 117, 119, 123, 125

Frederick, Elector Palatine, 8, 9, 14

Frederick Henry, Prince of Orange, 11, 21, 35

Free quarter, 130

Gardiner, Samuel Rawson, 1, 246

Gascoigne, Sir Bernard, 184, 192, 193

Gainsborough, 80, 111

Gerard, Charles, 57, 117

**Gell,** Sir John, 46, 66

Glamorgan, Edward Somerset, Earl of, 30, 155

Glemham, Sir Thomas, 74, 110, 154, 156

Glasgow, 150, 151, 215, 216

Gloucester, 80–1, 217, 234

**Gomme,** Bernard de, 35, 105

**Goring,** George, Lord, 20, 34, 36, 43, 46, 60–1, 65, 74, 75, 96, 101, 108, 109, 110, 112, 134, 135, 140–1, 142, 147–8, 154, 182n

Gough, Richard, 41

Graham, James, of Claverhouse, 243

Grand Remonstrance, the, 25

Grantham, 75

Greenland House, 100

Grenville, Sir Bevil, 61, 68, 69, 71, 126, 153

Grenville, Sir John, 228

Grenville, Sir Richard, 27, 44, 46, 153–4

Grey, Thomas, Lord Grey of Groby, 97–196

Gunpowder, 128–9

Hambledon Hill, 149

Hamilton, 215

**Hamilton,** James, 1st Duke of, 14, 117, 186–91, 195, 200, 204, 216, 217

**Hamilton,** William, 2nd Duke of, 210, 211, 216, 217, 219

**Hampden,** John, 13, 27, 32, 34, 41, 48, 67, 237

Harcourt, Sir Simon, 26

Harrington, James, 5

Harrison, Thomas, 217, 225, 231

*Hartford Green*, 226

**Haselrigg,** Sir Arthur, 41, 48, 55, 62, 72, 99, 113, 119, 121, 215, 231

Hastings, Lord Henry (later Lord Loughborough qv.), 31

'Heads of the Proposals', the, 171, 246

Henrietta Maria, Queen, 10, 15, 16, 18, 20, 27, 28, 40, 66, 74, 78, 96, 127, 146, 154, 178, 203, 210

Henriette-Anne, Princess, 96, 111

Herbert, Edward Somerset, Lord (see also Glamorgan), 30, 65
Hereford, 149, 150
**Hertford,** William Seymour, 3rd Earl of, 33, 34, 51–2, 63, 68, 71, 233
Hewson, Colonel John, 208
Hexter, J. H., 1
Heydon, Sir John, 51
High Commission, 20, 239
Hodgson, Captain John, 39
**Holland,** Henry Rich, 1st Earl of, 16, 17, 30, 32, 40, 179, 182, 184–5, 200
Holles, Denzil, 32, 48, 59, 133, 168
Holmby House, 159, 166
Hopton, Sir Ralph (later Lord), 3, 51–2, 61, 68, 69–73, 79, 80, 85, 86, 90, 94, 95, 124, 126, 127, 129, 154
Horses, 56n
Horton, Colonel Thomas, 179, 180, 181
**Hotham,** Sir John, 30, 40, 52, 75, 79
Hotham, John, 40, 79
Hull, 21, 28, 30, 33, 34, 61, 78, 80, 84
Humble Petition and Advice, the, 223
Hurst Castle, 195, 196
Hutchinson, Mrs Lucy, 38
**Hyde,** Edward, 1st Earl of Clarendon, 25, 34, 35, 39, 46, 61, 66, 137, 142, 230, 232, 233, 236, 238
Hyde, Henry, 2nd Earl of Clarendon, 236

**Inchiquin,** Murrough O'Brien, 6th Lord, 1st Earl of, 91, 164, 203, 205–6, 208, 220
Indemnity, 165, 167, 169, 174
Ingliston, 214
Ingoldsby, Colonel Richard, 228
Instrument of Government, the, 223, 225, 246
Inverkeithing, 216
Inverlochy, 135

Ireton, Bridget, 232
Ireton, Henry, 27, 143, 145, 171, 172–3, 175, 192, 194–6, 205, 209, 220–1, 231, 246
Irish army (1640–1), 17, 21; (1641–3), 25, 26–7; (1643), 85, 89–90
Irish Cessation, the, 90–1, 113
Irish Rebellion, the, 23 ff., 28–9, 89, 155, 163–4, 203–9, 220–1
Islip, 67

James I, 7, 12, 32
James II, 15, 180, 230, 240, 243–4, 246
Jeffreys, George, 245
Jones, Michael, 164, 203, 205, 207
Joyce, Cornet George, 166
Juxon, William, 15

Kentford Heath, 167
Kilkenny, 208, 209
Kirke, Percy, 241
*Kilsyth*, 150
King, James, Lord Eythin, 35, 45, 74, 104, 105, 108, 110, 210
Kingston, Robert Pierrepoint, 1st Earl of, 38
*Knocknannus*, 203

**Lambert,** John, 36, 109, 132–3, 136, 182, 186, 187, 191, 212, 213, 214, 216, 217, 218, 223, 225, 226, 227, 228, 231, 232, 246
Lambton, Sir William, 74n., 109
Langdale, Sir Marmaduke, 74, 110, 117, 136–7, 141, 145, 151, 152, 153, 178, 186, 187, 188, 189, 190
*Langport*, 138, 148, 189
*Lansdown*, 70–7, 79, 94
La Rochelle, 10–11, 13
Lathom House, 52, 86, 101–2, 110
Laud, William, 11, 15
Lauderdale, John Maitland, 2nd Earl of, 177, 210, 243

Leeds, 74, 108
Legge, William, 154
Leicester, 128, 142, 147
Leicester, Robert Sidney, 2nd Earl of, 24, 46
Lenthall, William, 157
Leslie, Alexander, Earl of Leven, 11, 14, 16–17, 91–2, 96, 103, 104, 105, 108, 110, 141, 147–9, 150, 152, 191, 216
**Leslie,** David, 104, 108, 150, 151, 152, 166, 178, 186, 191, 213–15, 216, 219
Levellers, the, 160–1, 170–1, 172, 177, 193, 194–5, 200, 202, 225
Leven, Earl of *see* Leslie, Alexander
Lichfield, 35, 65–6
Lilburne, John, 160
Lincoln, 33
Linlithgow, 191
Lindsey, Montague Bertie, 2nd Earl of, 53, 57
Lines of Communication, the, 63–4, 167, 168, 169
Lisle, Sir George, 184, 192, 193, 234
Lisle, Philip. Lord, 164
Little Gidding, 156
Liverpool, 101, 111, 226
Livesey, Sir Michael, 184, 185
Lockyer, Robert, 201
Lorraine, Charles, Duke of, 154, 220
Lostwithiel, 61, 111–12, 116, 125, 146, 189
Lothian, William Kerr, 3rd Earl of, 96
Loudon, John Campbell, 1st Earl of, 191
Louis XIII, 18, 20 89
Loughborough, Henry Hastings, 1st Lord, 93, 133, 147
**Lucas,** Sir Charles, 57, 92, 108, 109, 156, 179, 184, 192, 193

Ludlow, Edmund, 27, 86, 221, 225
Luke, Sir Samuel, 129
**Lunsford,** Sir Thomas, 26, 27, 28
*Lutter*, 10
*Lützen*, 14
Lyme (Regis), 68, 94–5, 97, 98, 117, 149

Macaulay, Thomas, Lord, 237
MacColla, Alasdair, 135, 151
Mackenzie, Sir George, 243
Maidstone, 183
Manchester, 34, 42, 101, 188
**Manchester,** Edward Montagu, 2nd Earl of, 39, 46, 48, 75, 76, 77–8, 84, 94, 96, 97, 99, 104, 108, 110, 112, 113–14, 116–17, 118–22, 132, 234
Manwaring, Roger, 12
Maps, 3
*Marston Moor*, 36, 57, 102–9, 113, 136, 158, 210, 225
Marten, Henry, 40, 73
Marvell, Andrew, 198
Marwood, George, 36
Mary, Princess, 20
Massey, Edward, 66, 81, 98, 123, 124, 125, 128, 130, 131, 133, 139, 162, 163, 166, 167, 168, 216, 217, 234
Maurice, Prince, 36, 42, 43, 51, 66, 64, 71, 80, 88, 94, 98, 112, 118, 127, 145, 154
Maurice of Nassau, 6, 11, 43, 44
Maximilian of Bavaria, 8, 9
May, Thomas, 141
Mazarin, Cardinal, 154, 193, 233
**Meldrum,** Sir John, 34, 45, 52, 60, 74, 93, 95, 104, 110–11, 147, 153
Middleton, John, 99, 112, 113, 114, 186, 189, 191, 216, 219
Militia Act (1661), 240
Militia Ordinance (1642), 28, 34

Monmouth, James Scott, Duke of, 209

Monck, George, 26, 43–4, 90, 93*n*, 164, 203, 205, 212, 214, 217, 219, 227–9, 230, 232, 235, 239

Monro, Sir George, 186, 187, 188, 189, 204

**Monro,** Robert, 29, 91, 155, 163, 186, 203, 204

Montagu, Edward, 239

Montreuil, Jean de, 154–5, 156

Montrose, James Graham, 5th Earl, 1st Marquess of, 19, 40, 135, 141, 149, 150, 151–2, 159, 178, 210, 211, 212, 215

More, Robert, 26

Morgan, Sir Charles, 32

Morrill, John, 38

Mountjoy, Charles Blount, Lord, 23, 24, 25

Musgrave, Sir Philip, 178

Muskets, 53–4

Musselburgh, 213, 214

*Nantwich*, 90, 92, 101

*Naseby*, 36, 136, 140, 142, 143–7, 148, 152, 189, 235

*Newburn*, 19

*Newbury*, First, 46, 82–4, 119, 124, 129; Second, 118–19, 125, 131

Newcastle, 19, 52, 92, 110, 212, 215

Newcastle coalfield, 64

Newcastle, Propositions of, 159, 176, 178, 193

**Newcastle,** William Cavendish, Earl, Marquess, Duke of, 21, 28, 37, 45, 46, 52, 63, 73–5, 80, 84, 88, 92, 95, 104, 105, 109, 110, 233

New Model Army, 113, 127, 128, 132–3, 138–40, 141, 142, 161, 162–3, 164 ff., 179, 222 ff., 229

*Newnham*, 65

Newport, Treaty of, 193, 197

Newport Pagnell, 116, 129, 142

Newark, 33, 74, 75, 93–4, 96, 101, 104, 136, 145, 149, 151, 152, 154, 155, 156

Nineteen Propositions, the, 31; Answer to, 31, 37

Northampton, 49, 128, 136

Northampton, Spencer Campton, 2nd Earl of, 34, 66

Northampton, James Compton, 3rd Earl of, 140

Northern horse, the, 110, 117, 135–7, 142, 145, 151, 152–3

Northumberland, Algernon Percy, 10th Earl of, 21, 32, 130

Norwich, George Goring, 1st Earl of, 182, 183, 184, 192, 200

Nottingham, 34, 200

Oates, Titus, 244

Ogg, David, 244

Okey, John, 55, 145, 228, 231

Oldenbarneveldt, John, 6

O'Neill, Daniel, 21

O'Neill, Hugh, Earl of Tyrone, 23, 204

**O'Neill,** Owen Roe, 29, 163, 203, 204, 205, 208

**Ormonde,** James Butler, 12th Earl, Marquess, Duke of, 25, 89–90, 155, 163–4, 203–6, 208, 210, 215

Oxford, 60, 67, 95, 97, 141, 149, 154, 155, 156

Oxford, Aubrey de Vere, 20th Earl of, 230

Oxford Parliament, the, 95, 124–5, 137

Pay, 125–7, 169–70

Pembroke, 3, 181, 187

Pembroke, Philip Herbert, 4th Earl of, 28, 32

Penruddock's Rising, 224, 225

Pepys, Samuel, 229, 237, 239

Perth, 216

Peterborough, John Mordaunt, 1st Earl of, 48, 49

Peters, Hugh, 219

Petition of Right, the, 11, 12

Philip IV, 9

*Philiphaugh*, 151–2

Pike tactics, 54, 109

Plymouth, 68, 69, 80, 111, 113, 117

Pontefract, 74, 86, 136, 141, 147, 152, 194

Portsmouth, 20, 34, 60, 61

*Powick Bridge*, 49, 219

Poyer, Colonel John, 179, 200

**Poyntz,** Sydenham, 43n, 132, 150, 151, 162, 165, 167, 168

*Preston*, 188–9

Preston, Thomas, 29, 163, 205

Pride, Colonel Thomas, 196, 214, 228

Puritanism, 11–12

Putney Debates, 172–3, 195, 243

Pym, John, 21, 22, 25, 32, 61, 67, 91, 231

Queen, Queen Mother, *see* Henrietta Maria

Raglan Castle, 147, 149, 150, 151, 156

Rainsborough, Thomas, 150, 173, 177, 182, 194

Ramsay, Sir James, 49

*Rathmines*, 205, 210

'Remonstrance of the Army', the (1648), 194–5, 201

Rich, Colonel Nathaniel, 217, 218

Richelieu, Cardinal, 10, 14, 154

Rigby, Alexander, 101–2

Rinuccini, Giovanni Battista, 155, 163, 203, 204, 207

Ripon, Treaty of, 19

*Ripple Field*, 66

Robartes, John, 2nd Lord, 68, 98

Roche, Bartholemew de la, 35

Roche of Fermoy, Maurice, 8th Viscount, 209

Ross, Boetius MacEgan, Bishop of, 209

Rossiter, Colonel Edward, 136

Rostow, Captain Edmund, 101

Rosworm, Johann, 42, 52

*Roundway Down*, 55, 71–3, 79, 81, 85, 94, 112, 129

*Rowton Heath*, 151, 152

Rupert, Prince, 3, 35–6, 42, 43, 46, 49, 51, 53, 55, 56–7, 59, 61, 62, 65, 66, 67, 78, 79–80, 81, 82–3, 92–3, 95, 96, 98, 101–11, 112, 117, 119, 137, 140–1, 143–5, 149, 150–1, 154, 192, 219

Russell, John, 229

Ruthin, Colonel William, 68

Ruthven, Patrick *see* Forth

St Albans, 167, 168, 193

*St Fagans*, 181

Saffron Walden, 164, 165

Salusbury, Sir Thomas, 39

Sancroft, William, 239

Savile, Thomas, 2nd Lord, 40

Saxton, Christopher, 3

**Saye and Sele,** William Fiennes, Viscount, 32, 48, 193, 234

Scarborough, 74, 86, 147, 150, 153

Scotland, 2, 6, 15–19, 21–2, 28–9, 91, 123, 133–4, 158–9, 176–7, 191–2, 209–19, 221

Scott, Thomas, 180

Scrope, Colonel Adrian, 185, 201

*Seacroft Moor*, 75

Second Army Plot, 25

Selby, 92, 95

Self-Denying Ordinance, the, 132, 133, 162 *n*